Praise for *Parenting Mom & Dad*

". . . a broad-based, highly readable, and useful book, full of practical suggestions and specific information. Dr. Levy has emphasized the complex interplay of psychosocial and physical problems that may confront the caregiving family in crisis. His recommendations appropriately take into account a multiplicity of factors."

> —Kathleen C. Buckwalter, Ph.D., R.N., professor and associate director, Office of Nursing Research Development and Utilization, University of Iowa College of Nursing

". . . a compendium of clinical, psychological, financial, and legal information that is eminently readable. Dr. Levy's book will prove useful to layman and professional alike. The list of resources available to senior citizens and their families is worth the purchase price."

> —Barnett S. Meyers, M.D., associate professor of clinical psychiatry, Cornell University Medical School, and president-elect, American Association for Geriatric Psychiatry

"This is a book that should be within easy reach of everyone involved in the care and management of elderly persons. It is filled with practical information and concrete examples. . . . *Parenting Mom & Dad* is much more than a list of do's and don'ts, though. Each page attests not only to the author's knowledge of the field but also to the compassion and empathy he brings to the elderly and to the people who care for them."

> —Robert J. Campbell, M.D., director, Gracie Square Hospital, New York

Parenting
Mom & Dad

A Guide for the Grown-Up Children of Aging Parents

MICHAEL T. LEVY, M.D.

PRENTICE
HALL
PRESS

New York   London   Toronto   Sydney   Tokyo   Singapore

The ideas, procedures, and suggestions contained in this book are not intended to replace the services of a trained health professional. All matters regarding your health require medical supervision. You should consult your physician before adopting the procedures in this book. Any applications of the treatments set forth in this book are at the reader's discretion.

The cases and examples cited in this book are based on actual situations and real people. Names and identifying details have been changed to protect their privacy.

Prentice Hall Press
15 Columbus Circle
New York, New York 10023

Library of Congress Cataloging-in-Publication Data

Levy, Michael T.
    Parenting mom and dad / Michael T. Levy.
        p.   cm.
    Includes bibliographical references.
    ISBN 0-13-603101-3
        1. Aged—Care—United States.   2. Parents, Aged—Care—United
States.   3. Frail elderly—Care—United States.   4. Geriatric
psychiatry—United States.   I. Title.
HV1461.L467   1991
649.8—dc20   90-35807
                                                        CIP

Designed by Victoria Hartman

Manufactured in the U.S.A.

10 9 8 7 6 5 4 3 2 1

First Edition

For my wife and children,
Diane, Paul, and Lizzie

My parents,
Mildred and Sam

and
Rosie

Acknowledgments

If ever an author had to acknowledge a debt it is I—having learned most of what I know from those with whom I work. To those professionals who serve with me in "the front lines," caring for the elderly at home, in the hospital, at the nursing home, wherever the need may be, I offer my endless appreciation and admiration. Jan Adler, Robert Alperin, M.D., Loretta Anderson, Rita Appleman, Ilene Badain, Lorraine Bennett, Fanny Berger, George M. Berger, Mindy Braunstein, Judith Brickman, David Cohen, Maryann Czajkowski, Phyllis Diamond, Mark DiBuono, M.D., Gerald DiMaso, M.D., Steven Einhorn, Nancy Fink, Bonnie Joy Freda, Star Fuentes, Holly Gemme, Lynn Goldstein, Carol Greenberg, Judith Grimaldi, Judith Grossman, Jerry Harawitz, Howard Haskin, Mary Ellen Herbert, Margaret Hughes, Geraldine Hunt, Iraj Iraj, M.D., Ruth Irons, Esther Kane, Marisa Kantrowitz, Sarah Katz, Barbara Krinsky, Robert Kruger, Esq., Richard Krugley, M.D., Sharon Kurland, Rhonda Lehrer, Joanne Lovitz, Arnold L. Licht, M.D., Helga Lieberman, Marilyn Litwak, Marvin Lipkowitz, M.D., Gloria Marsh, Christine Masucci, Yakov Melamud, Ira Miller, Esq., Linda Miller, Chevonne Moore, Sol Mora, M.D., Ilene Rozell Orland, Sybil Paley, Geri Pena, Allen Perel, M.D., Rose Putman, Libera Rampulla, Richard Reetz, Sofia Reshansky, Edith Samuels, Fred Santo, Judi Sasnauskas, Tracy Schneider, Judith R. Schoenberger, Theodore J. Strange, M.D., Robin Strauss, Daniel L. Sussman, M.D., Nama Taub, Eleanor Tillmann, Diane

Walker, Dorothy Walsh, Shirley Weinreb, Freya Wiggler, Kathryn Wilday, Dianne Woitkowski, Elaine Zegun, Steven Zimmerman.

I single out for special thanks my friend and colleague Kent Shinbach, M.D., with whom I grew up in geriatrics, and who sparked my interest, showed the way, and has always been there with patient guidance.

Contents

Introduction

She had heard I was an expert and had come to ask for help. An intelligent, controlled woman, and a firm believer in efficient problem solving, Mrs. G. snapped open her briefcase, drew her notes out from an official-looking manila envelope sardonically labeled "Mother," and burst into tears.

When Mrs. G. had first taken her mother into her home after her father's death, it had seemed like a kind and reasonable idea. The children were young, Mr. G.'s erratic job history necessitated that she work, and the couple joked that mother would provide private day care service in return for room, board, and companionship. And it had worked at first, but that was ten years ago.

Things were no longer working. In fact, whatever the debt she owed to her mother, Mrs. G. felt as if she were going to be pulled apart. Mother had not aged gracefully; the now elderly woman's lively spiritedness and self-assuredness had hardened into an attitude of haughty superiority. She relentlessly patronized her son-in-law and disapproved of her adolescent grandchildren's behavior. She acted as if she were better and smarter than everyone else, but she fooled no one. For, despite her arrogant attitude, it was painfully obvious that her behavior was only a pathetic attempt to cover up her own forgetfulness and mental failings: The more forgetful she became, the more she insisted that she was right. Any attempt to correct or assist her was rejected. Her daughter saw her as a stubborn, selfish, demanding old woman, who insisted on respect she no longer deserved, and an unquestioning acceptance, even when she was entirely in the wrong. She had become a sad and pathetic tyrant, ferociously trying to cover up her increasing inadequacies.

While Mrs. G. could understand, if not quite forgive, her mother's behavior, the rest of the family was not so tolerant. Her two adolescent grandchildren had long ago outgrown their grandmother's earlier caretaking role, and were now either embarrassed or angered or both by her current behavior. They resented her rudeness toward their friends, of whom she always disapproved, and they never could be sure whether their missing phone messages were the result of Gran's memory lapses, hearing impairment, or judgmental decisions. Moreover, her superior attitude seemed almost bizarrely incongruous when coupled with the more unpleasant and increasingly obvious signs of her aging: Her walker, her occasional bouts of urinary incontinence, her unclean body odors were all too evident when their friends visited. Furthermore, they now had to be bribed into accompanying her on her ever more frequent visits to the doctor, during which time Gran would verbally abuse them for their lack of enthusiasm.

Visits to the doctor had become a regular necessity ever since mother had developed a mild case of diabetes. Although it could be easily controlled under normal circumstances, she had managed to make even this an ordeal by insisting on handling it entirely by herself. What she was doing with her medication and urine testing was never exactly clear. Her eyesight was so impaired that it was impossible for her to accurately manage the task. Gradually, everyone realized that her "testing" had become yet another ritual designed to underscore her supposed competence. This final charade was one that they all feared would get her into real trouble.

Her medical problems had placed considerable financial strain on the family's budget, with increased physicians' fees, transportation expenses to and from the office, and pharmacy bills, but mother had flatly refused to consider using the Medicaid benefits to which she was entitled. "I'm no charity case," she would snap,

"I took care of you. You take care of me! If your husband made more money. . . ." Mrs. G. marveled at how she could provoke so much guilt and anger in a single statement.

Mrs. G.'s always retiring and insecure husband was becoming more angry and withdrawn as his wife's attention was more and more directed at mediating between the children and the woman who only took notice of him in order to ridicule his lack of success. The couple's sex life was practically nonexistent. Mr. G. blamed this on the lack of privacy he felt because of mother's padding past their bedroom door every hour of the night on her way to the bathroom, while his wife listened, fearful of mother taking another one of her falls. Mother's presence seemed to be everywhere.

Mrs. G. had tried to get help before, but mother had rejected the idea of joining a senior center ("I don't like to be with old people, it depresses me"), or hiring a home attendant ("I'd just wind up taking care of her"). While her husband and children would settle for nothing less than placement in a nursing home, preferably as far away as possible, Mrs. G. was torn by feelings of guilt, indecision, and divided loyalties.

And just then, with family tensions mounting daily, her boss called her into his office and offered her the major promotion which she had sought for so long, provided that she was "free to travel." "Free to travel!" She was performing an uneasy daily balancing act between unwilling participants who demanded, craved, and pleaded for her constant attention. And what made it most difficult was that, from the moment the offer was made, she knew she would accept, and that a turning point had been reached. She knew that something had changed and that things would never be the same. What had been for ten years could be no more. Now she was here to ask me how she could move forward.

This overwhelmed woman who came seeking help is far from alone. She is one in an ever-growing population of adult children who are struggling to cope with aging parents while trying to maintain their own lives. Increased longevity of the population has brought a concomitant increase in the problems attendant upon advanced age, and the burden of care, quite naturally, has fallen upon adult children who must now shoulder unexpected responsibilities and make decisions and choices which may be extraordinarily confusing and painful.

The specific facts confirm the obvious. The ranks of the elderly are growing steadily and at a rapid pace. According to the 1981 U.S. Census, 25.6 million Americans, or 11 percent of the total population, were over age sixty-five, with the over seventy-five group being the fastest growing segment in our society. Every year, the number of people over age sixty-five increases by half a million, and by the year 2010, they will represent 15 percent of the total population. By the mid–twenty-first century, the elderly will comprise 25 percent of the population, and will require an even larger proportion of medical, social, financial, and emotional services resources. The implications for society as a whole are obvious; less obvious is that the direct impact of these statistics falls on responsible relatives. Already, between 7 and 8 million Americans are providing essential personal care to dependent elderly family members.

As these numbers and needs grow as never before in history, a new generation has been created; a generation of adult children caught between the responsibilities of caring for their aging parents and the concerns of raising their own children, to say nothing of attending to their own careers and lives. For many, this burden may seem unbearable, especially when the difficulties appear to be insurmountable and the answers elusive. In fifteen years as a psychiatrist and gerontologist, caring for the elderly, I have seen firsthand many such difficult situations, some of which seemed overwhelming and sometimes unsolvable. Gradually, I have learned that possibilities always exist, and that help is available that can throw light even on the darkest cases. My education in this area began with a request to do something almost unheard of in recent years. I was asked to make house visits to elderly patients in crisis. I must admit, it was with some trepidation that I agreed. It was a decision I never regretted. Being directly on the scene gave me the unique opportunity to witness firsthand the problems as they existed, the cast of characters in a patient's life, and the entire range of emotions, conflicts, and confusion at their very source. I have worked with these patients, their families, the networks of community social agencies that attempt to care for them, and, when home management is no longer possible, with hospitals and nursing homes. What I have learned is that there is a wide range of possibilities, often unsuspected by those overwhelmed, not only by the situation, but more by their own anxiety and distress.

My goal here is much the same as it has been over these past fifteen years: to help the reader understand the problems by taking all of the available information into account and to provide workable answers. As I have done with individual families so often before, I would like to be your guide on a difficult journey; one which may be confusing or even painful, but one which ultimately will be gratifying and intensely rewarding. I promise that light will be shed where there has been only darkness.

Along the way, we will look at the full range of problems connected with aging, starting with the most common and inescapable, continuing with those more complicated and conflicted areas which can create emotional distress, and concluding with the most serious and difficult to manage, all of which will be illustrated by case examples and discussion. Throughout, I will try to present an array of potential solutions which must be selected and individualized to the situation.

In addition to answering the questions that will enable you to assist your parents, I also want to help you help yourself. Very often, these two goals coincide, but if the burden of care becomes overwhelming, as it sometimes does, you must recognize your own needs, balance your other responsibilities, and accept your limitations. For any plan to be effective, it must suit you as well as your parents. I can offer any number of suggestions, but only you can decide what works for you and what you are capable of doing. Unnecessary and misguided guilt will only get in the way. There is no universally correct road to take, except to do what seems reasonable for your parents and realistic for you.

Let us start by seeing how Mrs. G., her mother, and her family resolve their crisis.

Part I

Understanding the Issues

·1·

Assessing Problems, Finding Answers

Mrs. G.'s situation is difficult and yet so typical in that it encompasses the wide and varied range of problems so frequently encountered in caring for an aging parent. In such crises, one seldom is dealing with a single, isolated problem to which there is a simple answer. More often, as in this case, one is confronted by a complicated interplay between a variety of emotional, physical, and social problems, all of which affect an aging person with real and unavoidable functional deficits. Unraveling these diverse difficulties can seem an almost insurmountable problem to a family in crisis, as it did for the overwhelmed daughter described earlier.

Even in this relatively brief example, it is easy to see how many different problems are involved, and how each exacerbates the other in a vicious circle, resulting in a sense of hopelessness and despair.

At the basis, we have the sad but very typical situation of an elderly woman who is beginning to fail and starting to show some of the most common and unavoidable characteristics of the normal aging process. Her diminishing memory and increasing physical frailty are silently attested to by the memory lapses, "missed" telephone messages, her walker, and bedside commode. Unfortunately, this particular woman's psychological makeup was such that she could not accept these deficits in herself. Instead, she vigorously denied what was obvious to everyone else and "turned the tables" by acting in a superior manner as if she were the one

3

who was totally intact and everyone else was to blame. Her "face-saving" attitude created a climate of anger and resentment which intensified the difficulties. Moreover, her psychological limitations were matched by those of her family who were singularly unable to see through her desperate attempts *to cover up.* Instead, they took her accusations at face value, perhaps because of their own self-doubts and insecurity, and responded with misguided anger of their own.

Further complicating the family's unfortunate psychological response to the normal aging process, were a variety of unpleasant, but not unexpected, medical problems of advancing age: diminished bladder control with occasional bouts of urinary incontinence and the development of maturity onset diabetes, a common but chronic medical problem of the elderly which required regular medical attention and incurred great expense as well as daily urine testing. While any of these rather mundane medical problems might have been easily remedied on their own, when coupled with the existing emotionally charged atmosphere, even these relatively simple matters seemed overwhelming.

More difficult still was, that as complex as this mix of problems was in itself, no one involved was capable of even beginning to sort it all out. Instead, we have a very confused but typical family, made up of distinct personalities, each member with his or her own needs, each pulling in a different direction, intensifying the general emotional distress and casting a cloud over any hope of a joint solution.

There are solutions, and they do not require any special stroke of genius or the judgment of a Solomon. Instead, solutions demand only that each and every complicating factor be noted, taken into account, and dealt with, individually and in relationship to the whole. Only in a careful, attentive way can answers be found that resolve underlying difficulties while satisfying the multiple needs of everyone involved.

Before exploring specific solutions to this family's situation, it might be helpful to see how professionals assess and cope with the full range of problems so commonly encountered in a geriatric crisis. We start by understanding and accepting the frequently hard realities of later life. At no other time in their life are people so likely to be beset by such diverse difficulties as in their final years, just when they are no longer in the best shape to deal with them alone. Unfortunately, the problems described in this case example are not only typical, but actually relatively minor in the scheme of things. Events that might understandably undermine a young person and even earn him considerable sympathy, such as a serious illness, a chronic disability, a major change in financial status, or the loss of a loved one, may all be sad but regular occurrences for an elderly person who is often given far less latitude in recovering from such assaults. Instead, one is far more likely to encounter the attitude that since such events are natural and expectable at an advanced age, they should somehow be accepted more easily; this idea could only have been devised by a very young person. Let's face it squarely: Later life can be a very difficult time and your parents may well need compassionate assistance from you.

Once this is understood, the next step in resolving a problem is to gather all of the pertinent data and see how the individual parts affect the whole, sometimes combining to create an overwhelming result. As already indicated, typical problems fall into several recognizable categories; this is well represented by the following diagram:

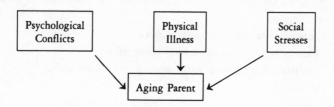

Each category is only a "headline," representing a variety of potential sources of difficulty. To help you recognize them and keep them in mind when assessing their contribution to a problem with your aged parent, I have listed some of the more general major trouble spots most frequently encountered in each of the categories. Naturally such a list is almost endless and must be carefully individualized according to your specific situation.

General Problems of Normal Aging

- Intellectual decline and memory impairment: slower reaction time, diminished absorption and retention of new information, decreased recent memory, slower mental processes and response
- Decreased physical strength and problems with mobility and ambulation
- Difficulty in performing the simple activities of daily living: dressing, washing, bathing, cooking, cleaning
- Sensory loss: diminished hearing and vision
- Changes in appearance and body image

Common Physical Problems

- Generalized physical frailty
- Arthritis
- Cataracts and other visual problems
- Nerve deafness
- Hypertension and cardiovascular disease with shortness of breath on exertion
- Diabetes mellitus (maturity onset)
- Constipation and other bowel complaints
- Diminished bladder control with stress incontinence
- Dentures
- Special diets (diabetic, low-sodium, low cholesterol)
- Doctors' visits, hospitalization, medication

Typical Social Problems

- Financial distress: diminished or fixed income, medical and drug bills, expenses for special care
- Forced retirement
- Housing changes necessitated by diminished capabilities
- Need for personal care assistance
- Diminished mobility requiring transportation and limiting independence and socialization
- Need for new social networks
- Family problems created by the stress of aging

Frequent Psychological Problems

- Loss of status: diminished self-esteem, sense of uselessness, loss of what once made one feel important
- Loss of loved ones as a consequence of death or geographic separation
- Isolation, especially when placed in an extended care facility
- Embarrassment over disability (intellectual and physical)
- Loss of independence
- Diminished sexuality
- Recognition of oneself as aged and the need to accept association with older age groups
- Fear of approaching death
- Pathological psychological reactions to all of the above: denial of deficits, personality changes, depression, anger, and paranoia

Once you gather the pertinent data concerning the diverse difficulties which may be affecting your parent and develop some insight into potential interactions between the problems, your next step should be to organize that information so that you can identify and familiarize yourself with all available options so that a workable solution can be achieved. A thorough examination of such options will occupy us throughout this book. For now let us turn our general technique for problem solving to the G family, so that you can see how it works in actual practice.

To assist this troubled family, I started with what is always a helpful first step: understanding and clarifying the basic situation. Such insight is essential to making a sensible decision and it affords an enormous sense of relief to family members so that one is no longer overwhelmed by the task ahead. In this case, the family had to see mother for what she was: a strong-willed, controlling woman who still prided herself on her intelligence and her ability to function independently, and who simply could not face the fact that these very assets, were fading. Rather than acknowledge, let alone accept, her failings, she used what remained of her waning powers to cover up, reacting with anger to those around her and involving them in her own unhappiness. For their part, her family needed to understand that if the elderly woman's attacks rang some internal bell of self-doubt, then they had best examine their own feelings of insecurity and deal with them personally, rather than taking the easy way out by blaming her alone for the entire situation. In short, in any crisis, the first step is to provide a realistic basic understanding of the situation, so that those affected can regain control of their emotions.

Once this is done, you can then begin to explore the specific individual issues involved, be they emotional, physical, social, or simply consequences of the normal aging process. I offered the G family a simple, straightforward, step-by-step approach to solving their problems:

Issues of Normal Aging

Problem	Solution
Memory Lapses	Accept mother's deficits with tolerance. Try not to "rub it in" by emphasizing or correcting her mistakes.
	Make simple changes to help her and yourself like using a telephone answering machine rather than relying on mother to take messages.

Physical Frailty

Create a safe physical environment at home without calling too much attention to it in a way that would embarrass her.

Check for hazards to avoid falls. Compassionately, but firmly, emphasize the need for mother to use her walker and bedside commode.

Psychological Issues

Problem	Solution

Mother's overbearing attitude, arrogance, and critical attacks

Try to understand mother's limitations and fears, her need to bolster her self-image. Learn to avoid arguing and instead try to respect whatever abilities remain intact. Divert her attention when she becomes abusive.

Mother's interference with implementing realistic plans (refusing Medicaid and home attendant services)

Involve your mother in making plans whenever possible, but do what is necessary even if she objects. For instance, applying for Medicaid does not require her permission nor does hiring a home attendant. While she may resist at first, perseverance will generally pay off. In this case, the family happened to choose an attendant who disapproved of the "younger generation" even more vigorously than the mother so that each could commiserate with the other. If chance opportunities like this should occur, take advantage of your good luck.

Physical Issues

Problem	Solution
Management of diabetes at home through daily blood and urine tests	Arrange for a visiting nurse service. This is provided and paid for by Medicare. Let a professional handle it. You don't have to be in the middle of every struggle.
Urinary incontinence with nocturia (nighttime urination)	Stabilizing your mother's diabetes will lower her blood and urine sugar. This in turn will decrease her need to urinate so frequently, making it more likely that she will sleep through the night.
Ambulation difficulties; assistance with washing, bathing and dressing; difficulty leaving her home alone	Arrange for supervision by hiring a home attendant once Medicaid approves (services paid for in full by Medicaid). Arrange for at-home physical therapy (covered by Medicare).

Social Issues

Problem	Solution
Financial strain: medical and drug bills	Find a physician who accepts full payment by Medicare, and a pharmacy that bills Medicaid directly.
Transportation to physician's office	Use a Medicaid ambulette.
Companionship	Arrange for a home attendant supplied by Medicaid who keeps your mother company and ensures her safety when you are not at home. Interview applicants carefully to find someone who is compatible. In this case, the home attendant began to accompany her to a local senior citizen center and to weekly physician's visits.

Mother's attacks on son-in-law, couple's sexual dysfunction	Don't blame your mother for personal problems that have little to do with her. Mrs. G. and her husband were advised to see a family counselor to help them identify the true sources of marital discord.

Hopefully this illustrates that when problems are disentangled and handled individually in a thoughtful and informed manner, that what has previously seemed overwhelming is no longer such a formidable problem. In retrospect, families often wonder what the "fuss" was all about. In this case, once the initial panic had been allayed by an understanding of the basic situation, individual problems could be identified and resolved, and a rewarding solution fell into place.

The family came to better understand mother's true distress about her aging and her reaction to it, so that they could accept it and begin to deal with her from a new perspective. Mrs. G. quickly applied for Medicaid despite mother's initial face-saving protests. This immediately solved some of the financial problems. Even more importantly, Medicaid allowed the family to hire a regular in-house attendant, further shifting the burden from the family. The home attendant provided the necessary physical and emotional support mother needed, and the elderly lady actually came to enjoy her company as well. Relieved of an unwanted burden since contact with mother was not so constant, the family eventually established a truce and could again even occasionally enjoy mother's sharp tongue and remaining wit. Mrs. G. and her husband were able to face their own marital difficulties, especially once Mr. G. owned up to his jealousy over his wife's recent career successes so that he was able to tolerate her good fortune more easily.

And Mrs. G. took her promotion and retrieved her life.

·2·

What's in Store?
Common Problems Your
Parents May Face

Even under the best of circumstances, later life can be hard, presenting your parents with unexpected problems which may be frightening and sometimes overwhelming. Commonplace as such difficulties may be, your parents may find them hard to resolve on their own, and find themselves in considerable distress if they try to hide or deny them. Your support and understanding may be vital in assisting them to overcome such obstacles so that they may continue to function in an independent and optimal manner. This may be an opportunity to reward them in kind for helping you over the rough spots in your growing up.

MEMORY LOSS

On the day that Alzheimer's disease made the cover of both weekly news magazines, my office was besieged by phone calls from people concerned about memory loss, all asking the same question: "How can I tell if I have it?"

"Senility" is the single greatest fear among the elderly. Far worse than physical illness, the idea of losing one's mind and becoming a vegetable to be cared for by others is a dreadful nightmare.

This fearful possibility is vigilantly watched for by the aged as they quietly check their own mental processes, and observe their spouse, friends, and relatives, secretly noting and evaluating every lapse of memory with mounting anxiety: "Is it coming?" Even if this concern does not become a daily preoccupation, it is hard to forget about, as the elderly see the evidence all around them. For the aged, this is not a distant threat; this is a daily reality.

The true likelihood of becoming senile is hard to determine accurately. Statistics mean nothing if you are the one who develops the problem, but they do give you a general idea. The latest evidence suggests that 10 percent of people over age sixty-five will eventually develop a significant degree of dementia, but surprisingly, less than 3 percent between the ages of sixty-five and seventy-nine are actually affected. The trouble really begins over age eighty, when more than 20 percent of people show some significant confusion and increases to almost 50 percent over age eighty-five. Still, even in this most advanced age group, many people live out their lives without any major deficits in their mental processes. While these statistics are obviously far from bleak, there are undeniable failings in thinking and memory that must be anticipated. And, when your parent is frightened by difficulty with recall ("it's just on the tip of my tongue" syndrome), it may be hard to differentiate such a normal lapse from a more serious problem.

Unfortunately some degree of memory loss in later life is inevitable. As we age, we simply are not as sharp as we were when we were younger. The reason is simple and inescapable. We are all born with a certain number of brain cells, and every day of our lives, more than one hundred thousand of these cells die. Unlike other body cells, which replenish themselves, nerve cells do not regenerate. Luckily, we start with a store of billions of brain cells so that the loss of many millions over a lifetime is no big deal, but it does make some difference accounting for memory problems and some degree of slowed thinking.

So, how can a frightened senior or his family tell the difference between normal aging and more serious memory loss which may be a beginning sign of dementia? This is a knotty question, but many carefully conducted studies have come up with a few useful distinctions to serve as generally accurate guidelines so that more extensive testing can be avoided.

To start with, it is important to have a basic definition of dementia (which is just the scientific term for "senility"). Dementia refers to a generalized and usually progressive decline in intellect, memory, orientation, and personality as a consequence of organic brain disease.

Next, you must always keep in mind that it is perfectly normal for older people to have some degree of memory loss. This is particularly true when it comes to recalling unimportant facts, especially about some recent experience (like a name, place, or a date). While a normal older person is quite likely to forget a minor detail he has just learned, the more impaired person will not only forget the specific name, place, or date, but the entire experience itself (for instance, Jane, who is aging normally, may have forgotten the name of the new lady at the senior center to whom she has just been introduced, while Sally, who has a beginning dementia, will not even recall that she has been introduced, and even deny it vigorously when she is reminded).

Furthermore, while a normal person may recall some forgotten detail at a later time, someone with dementia will not only never come up with the lost information but will soon even forget what it is that he had been trying to remember.

Finally, the normal aged person, particularly one who is concerned about memory loss, will be aware of his shortcomings and may find ways to compensate by making lists or notes to himself. The more genuinely confused person will often be surprisingly unaware of many of his deficits, or, even when he is, make up unconvincing explanations to cover up. Frequently, he may vehemently deny his obvious forgetting, even if it is apparent that everyone in the room is aware of his memory loss.

Gradually, as a person's memory deteriorates even further, loss of recent memory will become so severe that entire experiences will be forgotten as soon as they occur. Later, general information and remote memory (what happened a long time ago) will also deteriorate, and disorientation as to place and time will manifest. *None of these things will ever happen to a normal person.*

These good, simple, general rules are used by doctors themselves in making preliminary determinations of dementia. If you still have questions, the next step is for an experienced doctor to perform a detailed mental status examination to further investigate apparent memory loss.

A simplified form of the mental status exam was developed by R. L. Kahn who prepared ten questions:

1. Where are we now?
2. Where is this place located?
3. What is today's date?
4. What month is it?
5. What year is it?
6. How old are you?
7. What is your birthday?
8. What year were you born?
9. Who is the president?
10. Who was the president before him?

This simple test will provide more information than you might realize. If more than two questions cannot be answered, there is the strong likelihood of a serious brain disorder.

Still, such a simple test is only really a screening for memory loss and a full mental status examination performed by an experienced professional will be much more precise. This examination investigates:

Orientation: Person, place, and time.

Registration: A memory test to see if a person even registers what is said to him (Example: The doctor gives the patient the names of three unrelated objects and asks the person to repeat them to him).

Attention and calculation: The doctor starts with the number 100 and asks the patient to count backward by sevens. If this is too difficult, he uses threes, or asks the patient to spell a five-letter word backward.

Recall: The patient is required to recall the three objects he was asked to remember earlier in the interview, to see if the information is retained.

General information: Important historical events, names of famous people from the past.

The normal elderly person should be able to perform all of these tests with relative ease as long as he is concentrating and is not upset by the testing procedure. A patient with an early dementia will have some degree of difficulty with all of these questions, even if he seems superficially intact in social situations and is able to cover up.

Beyond mental status testing, there are a series of sophisticated neuropsychological tests which can be performed to pin down the degree and specific nature of impaired intellectual functioning and memory loss. Tests of brain function include the EEG (electroencephalogram) and the CAT scan (computerized axial tomography) which provide confirmatory evidence of diminished brain functioning. The EEG measures brain waves and can detect generalized and diffuse slowing of brain activity, which is a prominent finding in dementias of all sorts, as well as abnormalities in specific focal areas of the brain seen in strokes and other organic lesions. The CAT scan provides an actual picture of the brain. It will pick up shrinking of the brain which occurs in later stages of dementia. Most people do not realize that the EEG and CAT scan are not absolute diagnostic tests for dementia. Both may show perfectly normal results, even in cases of severe dementia. Only when they are positive, corroborating what has been observed by a clinician, can the diagnosis be definitively made.

What does all this mean to an elderly parent, fearful about memory loss, and how can a concerned family member intelligently reassure and advise him? To start with, you must help him understand that some memory loss sometimes called "benign senescent forgetfulness," is virtually inescapable in normal aging and will not result in a more serious condition. While annoying, this symptom must be accepted, faced up to, and dealt with intelligently so that it does not interfere more than necessary with daily life. Reassure your parent that he can make up for this natural failing because he has experienced life. We all become a little slower as we age, but we become wiser too.

As a concerned family member, you may be able to gently suggest a variety of extremely useful techniques to help your parent competently deal with memory loss by maximizing his remaining abilities.

When your parent becomes upset over some minor memory lapse, advise him to relax and not become excessively frustrated or panicky, convinced that every failure is an omen of impending senility. Panic itself will enormously exaggerate memory loss, making it momentarily impossible to recall. Often, once a person simply calms down, the forgotten item will spontaneously spring to mind.

When a problem does exist with recall, encourage your parent to try to focus more intently when he is first learning some new piece of information. If he can teach himself to concentrate initially, new information will be better registered and stored in his memory, maximizing his ability to recall it at a later time. A child can pick up data while listening to a Walkman with a television on, but an older person cannot, especially if he is distracted or simply uninterested, and must develop his own technique of intense concentrated focusing.

When elderly parents come to you, upset about being unable to remember necessary details of everyday life, advise them that while such difficulties must be taken seriously, they can be definitely overcome by finding ways to better organize themselves. Try to match your suggestions to suit your parent's personality. For instance, a normally relaxed person will never adhere to as rigid an organization plan as would someone who was normally compulsive anyway, but most will accept some changes in style to improve functioning.

There are lots of techniques for improving organization which will help avoid undue anxiety over memory lapses. For example, suggest that your parent make clearly written and understandable lists of important papers, financial documents, bank books, credit cards, and life and health insurance policies. For everyday concerns, recommend using shopping lists, keeping a calendar to keep track of appointments, writing down questions to ask a doctor before each visit, and keeping a list of all medications with their dosage and schedule. All lists should be kept in a designated safe place where they can be located easily. Papers, bank books, and valuables should be kept in a house safe or safety deposit box where they are accessible but protected. Important phone numbers should be posted by the phone, and emergency and frequently called numbers should be recorded on a phone with a memory device for automatic dialing. Explain to your parents that by keeping a special place for everything and sticking to it at all times, retrieving specific papers or items from that place will become a matter of habit. This way, items can be located when required without a daily anxiety-ridden search. Keys, wallet or purse, glasses, dentures, medication, financial and insurance papers, bank books, Medicare cards, bills, mail, jewelry—every item must have a place and the place should not be changed.

Sometimes more severe memory loss will result in forgetting to pay bills, lock the door, or, even in serious omissions, like forgetting to turn off the gas after cooking. Such lapses can often entirely be alleviated by setting up a series of routines which can be practiced, learned, and, if possible, checked by a spouse or a companion. If your parent cannot create his own routine, organize it for him and "walk him through it" until you are sure it can be followed automatically. Examples of routines include: Checking all locks and turning off appliances before leaving home. Some people find it useful to perform these routines in a set pattern, looking at each item to be checked and even speaking aloud the completed task. A final checklist at the door may be useful for exceedingly forgetful or anxious parents. After the house is satisfactorily inspected, instruct your parent to check his appointment book to make sure his schedule is set, as well as his pockets and purse to make sure he has what will be required on a day's outing (keys, glasses, wallet, umbrella, etc.). Have him check car doors and car lights regularly and if he is the driver, advise him to carry a spare key in his wallet. Arrange a specific date on which bills are to be paid. Have a specific and written schedule to take medication. Buy a weekly pill organizer (available in all pharmacies) so that the dosing schedule can be set up a week at a time. Children may find it best to assume this task themselves to improve accuracy.

If your parents want to be even more precise, here are some additional memory techniques. Some people find it easier to learn by hearing information, while others need to see the written word. Knowing what works best for your parent and taking advantage of it helps enormously.

If your parent learns best by seeing, it may be helpful for him to actually visualize what it is he wants to learn or to write it down so he can actually see it in front of him. If your parent learns by listening, he may need to say it out loud or have it repeated to him by another person. Another memory aid is to suggest that your parent make a personal mental connection between new information that he is trying to absorb and something he already knows well so that the link can be used later when he wants to retrieve it (for example, the lady he was just introduced to at the senior center has the same first name as his sister-in-law). Another old technique you may remember from school is to utilize mnemonics to memorize lists of unrelated items. This means that you take the first letter of each item that you want to recall and put them together into a new word (for instance, MADD Mothers Against Drunk Driving) so that the first letter will be a clue to each individual item. Make suggestions and encourage him to make up his own. It can actually be fun to do together, and intellectually stimulating as well.

There is no end to techniques. Find out what works for your parents, what fits their personality and degree of memory impairment, and is not childish or humiliating, and by all means, reassure them that by utilizing such aids they can remember all that is necessary if they don't panic. Remind them, as well, that you yourself, by age 40 or 50, frequently have to resort to similar devices.

PHYSICAL FRAILTY

It is a sad but all too common "joke" played upon the elderly that while some have severe memory problems and the physical health of a youngster, others are perfectly intact mentally but are encumbered by bodies that are failing them. Tragic as dementia is, how much more frustrating it is for a still vigorous mind to be trapped within a deteriorating body.

Physical frailty may be the consequence of a variety of ills that befall the elderly: heart disease, stroke, severe arthritis, anemia, a fracture, medication, or just the generalized weakness that frequently accompanies advanced age. The frail elderly will obviously require outside help, and their families will naturally be called upon to provide the necessary assistance, either personally or through hiring trained personnel. In either case, such assistance is most effectively provided if one understands the cardinal rule of personal care: Strike a balance between maintaining independence while insuring safety. To err on either side can be disastrous. If independent functioning is not permitted out of an exaggerated fear of injury, it will often lead to diminished self-esteem, regression to a childlike, helpless attitude, and to depression. If unrealistic independence is permitted, any number of dangerous situations may quickly develop.

With the understanding that such a balance must always be your goal, let us look at the major areas of personal care which will require assistance for a frail parent.

Creating a Safe Environment

Always remember the basic rule: The home environment must be made safe so that your parents may continue to function as independently as possible without injuring themselves in the process. To accomplish this, you may need to make some physical changes in the home.

Avoiding Falls. Debilitated parents are prone to falls because of generalized weakness, inattention to their environment, changes in blood pressure, and disturbances in balance. So common is this problem that it is now estimated that 20 percent of people over eighty will fall and fracture a hip at some time during their lives. A frail parent cannot be watched every second; therefore, the house must be made as secure as possible to avoid unnecessary injury.

Wall-to-wall carpeting will cushion falls to some extent, but it should not be so thick as to interfere with traction. Area or scatter rugs that turn up at corners or edges are particularly dangerous. Keep the floor clear of clutter and avoid exposed electrical wires and telephone cords.

Furniture should be placed close enough together to allow for physical support at all times in a planned path from one part of the home to another.

Beds should be low enough so that your parent can get in and out with relative ease. If necessary, obtain a hospital bed where height can be electrically adjusted to suit individual needs.

Your parent should be able to operate the bed himself, to allow him to make himself comfortable and to increase his sense of independence and ability to control his environment. Bedrails can be useful, especially if your parent is prone to nighttime confusion and does not always show good judgment in matters of safety; a situation that is not uncommon even in someone who is otherwise mentally intact. If a hospital bed is not available, high-back chairs placed at the bedside can be an effective, temporary solution.

Be sure your bathtub has nonskid mats or strips. Handrails also can be installed.

Night lights should always be used. If a parent does not like a light in his room, turn on a hall or bathroom light.

Sometimes structural changes in the house must be made. Bathrooms on the same floor are often essential to avoid having to climb stairs; wheelchair access may be necessary. Certain construction companies specialize in such renovation for the disabled and elderly.

Most important, involve your parents in their own care and patiently instruct them regarding situations requiring increased focused attention and possible danger: walking, bathing, using the stove or other appliances. Be sure to remind them that getting up at night is a particularly vulnerable time, and most falls occur at night. Tell them to get up slowly, to dangle their feet at the side of bed before rising, and to hold on to a secure object until they feel sure of themselves. Older people, particularly those taking medication, will have changes in blood pressure when they shift from a lying or sitting to a standing position, a situation which often results in falls.

For frail parents confined to bed for long periods, similar safety techniques can be used to help them function as independently as possible. All necessary objects should be within easy reach at the bedside: telephone, radio or TV with remote control, a bell to call for assistance, a water pitcher and glass, comb and brush, a mirror, tissues, books and magazines, a waste basket, urinal, bedpan or bedside commode, whatever is required in your parent's particular case. Medication, especially emergency medication like nitroglycerine, should obviously be immediately accessible.

The basic rule never varies. Whether ambulatory or bedridden, encourage your parents to operate on their *own* as much as is *safely* possible.

Assistance in the Activities of Daily Living

It is particularly difficult, even degrading and demeaning, for mentally intact parents to accept assistance in these basic activities, no matter how disabled they may be. In no other area is it more important to respect their emotional wishes to retain control and independence, something that can be successfully accomplished if the right attitude is struck. Your job is not to take care and do for them; your task is to instruct, advise, and coach them, so that they may again be self-reliant, using newly learned coping skills.

Dressing. Dressing may be difficult for a parent affected by severe arthritis, various neurologic disorders, or generalized weakness. The trick is to devise a wardrobe that can be easily gotten on and off without undue frustration and embarrassment.

Buttons are particularly difficult to manipulate and should be replaced by zippers or velcro fasteners whenever possible. Pants with elastic waistbands and jogging suits are easy to manipulate and comfortable, while slip-on shoes or slippers are the best choice for footwear. Sneakers or jogging shoes are favorites of the elderly because of the variety of foot ailments they are prone to, and are highly recommended because they provide good padding for their soles which thin with age, as well as providing traction and support. These too come with velcro strips for easy fastening.

Specific routines can be established by trial and error so that your parent can find the easiest method of dressing. Perhaps he needs to be encouraged to dress while sitting down, or not to bend forward precariously when putting on his shoes.

If incontinence is a problem, choose clothes that can be easily and quickly removed. Skirts or dresses for women with stress incontinence are better choices than pants outfits.

When an extremity is disabled, always put that arm or leg into a garment first, reversing the process when undressing; you will both find it easier.

If a parent has more complicated disabilities, occupational and physical therapy is available (paid for in full by Medicare) by professionals who can train you and your parents in regard to more complex dressing techniques.

In general though, no outside expert will be necessary. Play it by ear, be flexible, and find ways that work for you.

Bathing. Personal hygiene, particularly bathing, can be difficult to handle and may require special attention. If at all possible, allow your parents privacy and independence, but be on hand if needed, and never allow them to lock the bathroom door. This is something you must insist upon.

Washing is generally simple, as long as things are set up conveniently in the bathroom or by the bed. A chair by a washstand is always a good idea.

Bathing is more difficult, but can be safely accomplished with the use of certain aids. Support bars are easily installed, as are nonslip mats or strips. Often it is a good idea to install a removable handheld shower spray, so that a senior can sit and shower more comfortably. Special bathtub chairs are readily available for those who need them. Water temperature should be adjusted before bathing; if your parent suffers from any circulatory or neurologic diseases, he may not feel the temperature accurately and may get seriously burned if he is not monitored.

Getting into and out of a tub may be especially difficult and elderly parents who are at all uncertain of their ability must have personal support. One particularly safe method of assisting is to have your parent lock his wrists in front of him, stand behind him with your arms around him, and hold his locked forearms with your hands. In this way, you can more easily guide him into the tub.

Another practical hint to be kept in mind in regard to bathing is that elderly people tend to have dry and fragile skin, and should not take daily baths. Recommend that they use bath oils and apply moisturizers and lotions afterward.

Eating. Good nutrition is crucial for a debilitated parent's improvement. Poor intake results in rapid dehydration and malnutrition, and will immediately exaggerate any underlying disability.

If your aged parents live with you, encourage them to take their meals with the family. This makes them part of the family by involving them in the events of everyday life, while stimulating their thinking and providing emotional contact in a natural way. Home attendants may also be asked to eat at the same time, encouraging conversation and socialization.

For seniors who don't eat enough or have poor eating habits despite encouragement, commercially prepared supplements (e.g., Sustecal, Ensur) are readily available in any pharmacy. These have a high nutritional and caloric content, and are universally advisable except for those suffering from diabetes. Weight should be recorded weekly to make sure that your parent is getting enough food.

If there are special dietary restrictions, consult with your physician or dietician, and find creative ways to cook, providing tasty food which will encourage proper nutrition. If your parents must cut down their intake of salt and fatty foods, several herbs or flavorful spices can be substituted. Problems with dentures or difficulty in swallowing food can be overcome by pureeing food in a blender or food processor or with liquid supplements, like Jell-O, soup, ice cream, and milkshakes.

If your parent is confined to bed, take care that he is in a high sitting position when eating, propped up by pillows or a back rest, or use a hospital bed which can be easily adjusted. If you need to feed your parent, be sure to go slowly, allowing enough time for him to chew and swallow. Flexible straws are useful for liquid diets, and, as a last resort, large syringes can be used for feeding cereal and other pureed food.

Ambulation Techniques

One of the most important ways to maintain a disabled parent's well-being is to mobilize him through regular exercise and ambulation. It may seem easier to leave a parent in bed, especially when he objects vigorously to being moved, but to do so will quickly lead to increased disability, further weakness, bedsores with infection, and markedly diminished mental alertness. You must get him moving!

Again, the basic rule is to balance safety with mobility. If your parent is unsteady, a physical therapist can evaluate and suggest ambulation aids. If a cane is provided, make sure it is the correct height, which means the handle should be at the level of the hip joint and that it should have a rubber tip for traction. Walkers offer much more support and may be fitted with wheels for ease of use. If your parent uses a walker, make sure he knows how to use it properly. The proper procedure is to place it in front of him, plant it firmly on the ground or floor, walk into it, and then move it and resecure it, step by step. Carrying a walker in midair, as many seniors do, will lead to falls. While your parent is learning to use his cane or walker, you or someone else follow behind him as a "spotter," sometimes gently holding onto a pants' belt until he seems secure on his feet.

Psychological Attitudes Toward Frailty

It cannot be stated too often: The best approach to a physically debilitated parent is to maintain independence in functioning insofar as safety permits. The goal is to make your parent continue to feel useful and capable, and to maintain his self-esteem and sense of personal worth. To do otherwise leads to a state of psychological distress which may be further incapacitating and even irreversible. Often, shame and humiliation about one's disability may intensify the problem and result in a stubborn refusal to function. Be on guard in case such a situation develops and quickly respond to it. Failure to do so may result in a situation such as this:

> Up until her fall and hip fracture, Mrs. L. had been an active and social member of her local senior citizen's center. The fracture and subsequent hospitalization and surgery to replace her hip, had gone as easily as could be expected, and after 10 days she was out of bed, undergoing physical therapy, and walking with the assistance of a walker. Discharged from the hospital in excellent condition and with a hopeful prognosis, she was assigned a physical therapist who could visit her at home and encourage further advances in independent ambulation. It all seemed rather straightforward.
>
> That was eight months ago and she had not left her apartment in all that time. Her old friends were concerned, confused, and dismayed by her refusal to even allow visits; the senior center was frustrated by her turning down door-to-door transportation to accommodate her. She rejected all such suggestions with one excuse or another, and complained that "No one understood."
>
> When I visited her at her home, I received the same unsatisfactory explanations for her refusal to resume her previous life. It was not until I noticed the prominently displayed dance contest trophies, that I understood the true reason for her reclusiveness. Smiling ruefully, with a flash of her old vitality, she remarked, "You got it right away, sweetheart. No one is going to see me like this with this damn walker . . . I was a dancer!"

Psychological distress, with regression and withdrawal in the face of physical disability, can be a frail parent's worst enemy, and must be countered immediately by the alert family member. The longer it is allowed to exist, the more unlikely the possibility of reversal. Nothing is more important.

Make sure that whatever the disability, your parents continue to be involved in life: Include them in all family functions, keep them abreast of all news, consult with them, ask for their advice. Try to help them continue to pursue old interests, encourage new hobbies, at the very least ensure attention to TV, radio, and books. Invite friends in, have other relatives visit regularly and plan outings and events in which your parents are capable of participating.

Keeping them as active as possible, mentally and physically, will keep them in the best health, and often partially reverse disabilities which seemed permanent.

For Mrs. L., the solution could not have been simpler. Once her embarrassment was understood, a sympathetic friend was enlisted to be her "walker" by taking her arm as she entered and exited the Senior Center, positioning himself at her side during the day so that he could discreetly assist her whenever necessary. While everyone probably guessed what was going on, no one was cruel enough to mention it. Once the ice was broken, and she again felt accepted, she attended with her old vigor. And, with the daily walking practice on the arm of her friend, she was soon independent once again.

LONELINESS

Some years ago, I was asked to visit an elderly lady who had been frightening her neighbors by ringing their doorbells in the middle of the night, asking if anyone had seen her children. Although my services had been requested by the family, I was a bit surprised to find the patient at home alone when I came to call. When she greeted me at the door of her elegant rambling home, she seemed attractive and well-groomed and hardly looked like someone who would be roaming the streets at night. Eagerly inviting me in, she asked me to join her in the kitchen for lunch with her guest, Carol Bellamy, then president of the City Council in New York City. A bit confused myself, I followed her into the kitchen where I found my high-spirited hostess encouraging a not very receptive Carol Bellamy to eat some specially prepared cherry pie, "your favorite." The guest's reluctance to partake was easily explained by the fact that it was not Miss Bellamy, but a newspaper clipping, elaborately framed and sitting in a place of prominence on the kitchen table that my hostess was attempting to feed with growing impatience.

Throwing up her hands in dismay, the discouraged lady of the house decided that I might like a tour and took me around, room by room, obviously prolonging the visit as long as possible. The only room she missed was the bedroom, shutting the door with a nervous laugh because she didn't want to disturb Dan Rather, whose picture, I noticed, was on her night table.

Our tour ended with an elaborate introduction to each of her children and grandchildren, whose pictures, again, were on prominent display. At some point, as discreetly as possible, I ventured to ask her if the people to whom I had been introduced were really there in her house, or whether she was aware that it was only the photographs, and she looked sharply at me, then smiled and explained, "Oh, of course I know they are pictures, but if you look closely, very closely, you can make them out, hiding behind the picture . . . There! Didn't you see her smile and move her head for a moment?" She paused, looked around in some confusion, and said, almost to no one, but with desperation in her voice, "They are here with me. . . . They're my family and I need them . . . I can't bear to be alone."

While the loneliness felt by this isolated woman is particularly graphic, many elderly experience similar feelings of aloneness as their circle of significant people shrinks through death or relocation, just when they are most vulnerable because of their diminishing abilities to cope and care for themselves. I am regularly impressed with how frequently family members can leave an elderly parent alone, marginally able to cope and often terribly frightened, to make only periodic checks on their well-being, reassuring themselves with such banal excuses as "mother likes to be on her own."

Loneliness in older age has two components: the lack of emotional contact and support, and the fear of being unable to cope and even physically survive. Both can be overwhelming for some people, especially if they are unaccustomed to reaching out to others. Unattended, such lonely people will frequently become depressed or anxiety ridden, may start drinking, or may even become frankly psychotic as in the case of this woman who used photographs of famous people to replace the friends she so desperately craved.

Naturally, the best cure for loneliness is for an aged person who has lost old friends and family to make new friends, to place themselves in situations which are conducive to meeting others, such as senior citizen centers, and to be as flexible as possible in coping with the expected changes one encounters as one ages. Unfortunately, many people seem unable to do this, a fact that they may either openly admit, or about which they may make endless excuses ("I'm not ready. I'm a loner"). When the impact of loneliness is recognized, those interested in the well-being of an isolated parent must forcefully intervene to at least make an attempt to alter the distressing isolation. One of the easiest activities to arrange is participation at a senior citizen center. These centers can be found in most areas, providing many programs which allow for as much or as little social contact with others as desired. Many centers will arrange transportation if this is a realistic problem, so that even the disabled can be encouraged to attend. Family members may be called upon to initiate the original contact and to be there during the first visit, until your parent is comfortable and established, much like taking a child to school for the first time. Skilled personnel will often be there to take over eventually, introduce the senior citizen, and ease his integration into the group. Many centers offer day trips which give your parent something to look forward to, and summer camp programs are common as well.

Volunteer jobs, foster grandparent programs, organizational work, and church activities, to name a few, are all possibilities which provide social contact as well as a feeling of productivity.

If a parent is truly homebound, loneliness can be a more difficult, but still not an irremediable situation. Agencies can provide home attendants, shoppers, physical therapists, or just friendly visitors who will make regular calls. Homebound elderly can be encouraged to take up hobbies, adopt pets, watch TV, become involved in religious or political projects, and to maintain telephone contact with friends and relatives.

The decision for a parent to live with you is, of course, the touchiest problem of all and depends on the personalities involved, and a realistic appraisal of the situation. More often than one might expect, such an arrangement can work out if both sides are aware of the potential difficulties and have the capacity for an open exchange of feelings and joint problem-solving. Financial pressures may actually be minimized by such an arrangement; for example, if the elderly person is capable of providing childcare and other services for his working adult children. In some situations, people can live together and come in and out of each others' lives in mutually helpful ways. Loneliness and lack of productivity can obviously be greatly alleviated by this living situation if it works. I do not have to list the many reasons that such an arrangement might not work, and everyone must decide for himself, without attempting to enforce an impossible situation.

If joint living is ruled out and none of the previous possibilities are effective in penetrating the isolation then communal living of one sort or another is often a positive alternative. The well elderly can obviously consider relocating to areas of the country with significant populations of elderly folks, a situation which allows for the maximum potential in making new friends and establishing better support systems. Also, there are now more and more apartment complexes that cater to the needs of senior citizens. These facilities often provide one meal each day, and allow for both independence and contact to be self-regulated by the senior. Additionally, for more frail elderly, there is a wide variety of adult homes in which social contact can be promoted, as well as necessary care provided. (A more comprehensive discussion of these possibilities is found in chapter 4, in the section, "When Home Is No Longer Safe.")

I had an opportunity to revisit the "lady of the photographs" about two years later. At the time, I had suggested a home attendant to keep her company, a situation which had not worked out, and she was now living in a nursing home. When I saw her, she was involved in an animated discussion with some other elderly women at lunch, and seemed content. The administrator told me that she had made a very easy adjustment and recently had been elected "floor representative to the governing council" which seemed a nice extension of her political interests. I asked how often her family came to visit, and the administrator smiled and said, "Oh, they are lovely, intelligent people, but they are so busy . . ."

RETIREMENT

Freud recognized the essential need for work by suggesting that what life comes down to is "love and work." Work fulfills many basic needs: a sense of productivity, a structured way in which to fill time, a bolster of self-esteem, an involvement in an activity which energizes the personality. It may provide an exciting interest and involvement, or it may be a wearisome burden, but in either case, it forms an important foundation in everyone's life. It is not surprising then that retirement is something which ought to be planned for as thoughtfully as possible, to avoid difficulties for which one might otherwise be unprepared.

In most instances, retirement is relatively free of conflict and many people are perfectly happy to be relieved of a job they have found unpleasant and unrewarding for many years. Often they feel that their responsibilities to society and family have been fulfilled satisfactorily, allowing them to live out the rest of their lives, enjoying themselves without guilt or anxiety, free from a lingering sense of responsibility. Others have an even more positive outlook and look forward to retirement as a real opportunity to cease doing

MEN/JOB
WOMEN/HOME-KIDS

FEME!

ALCOHOL

what they have had to do and do what they want to do. Successful second careers have grown out of just such an attitude, as well as fulfilling hobbies and special interests previously ignored or undiscovered. Still others enjoy their work and plan for semiretirement, working at their old jobs at reduced levels, permitting a compromise of leisure and work which serves their special needs.

While any of these possibilities seems a sensible and reasonable solution, there are many people who do not find retirement so simple or positive a matter, and who find themselves lost as soon as they reach what they may have longed for previously. While men in particular may be totally identified with their work, developing no interests or even friends outside of it, some women have seen themselves entirely as housewives and mothers and are similarly lost and without an identity when their children have left home. If not prepared for the reality of retirement, such people may find themselves bored, anxious, and depressed. Alcohol may offer a way to get through the day for some, while others focus on their bodily ills to an alarming degree, becoming hypochondriacs. Unstructured time seems endless, and they are totally unprepared to change or find new involvements or interests. For many of these people, work has been their life, and without it they simply do not know what to do.

If you notice your parent at such loose ends, the best solution to this confused paralysis may be a frank discussion in which positive options suited to their particular personalities and needs are suggested. Often such conversations may require a bit of pressure, as the longer a parent avoids action, the more frightening any action may seem. It is often difficult to "think things out" in a vacuum, and new interests may have to be "tried out" to experience them, before they can be seen as worthy of pursuing or rejecting. If your parent is unsure of or timid about initiating a new interest, it may be helpful to have a spouse or friend, who is in a similar situation accompany him.

Failing this, short-term counseling can be especially helpful in this area. A counselor can help determine the reasons for your parent's underlying indecision. By reassuring your parent, whose self-esteem is now shaky, and relieving his doubts about his self-worth and ability to be useful, this temporary paralysis can be alleviated. It is important to remind the older person that he no longer needs to fulfill anyone else's expectation, and that at this time of his life he should try to do whatever he likes, or thinks he may like, and that an involvement in a hobby, sport, volunteer job or political activity may be as valuable a way to spend time as a new career.

A parent who appears to be unable to cope with retirement should not be ignored indefinitely with the idea that it takes time to find oneself. While this is true, and anyone is certainly entitled to an extended period of time to relax and decide on his future course, if anxiety, bewilderment, and depression develop, no time should be lost in seeing this as a legitimate problem, and seeking appropriate assistance.

BEREAVEMENT AND WIDOWHOOD

> The elderly man sat with his relatives, "sitting shiva," the week-long period of mourning specified by Jewish tradition. He had spent a long and happy life with his wife and was inconsolable at her loss. His relatives tried in vain to comfort him, pointing out that he had his children, his friends and interests and that, painful as it was, he would get over his wife's death and make a new life in time. He smiled ruefully at them and said, "I know I will, but she won't."

The loss of a spouse, expected as it may be in later life, is obviously one of the hardest events with which to deal. The fact that it is unavoidable, if one lives long enough, does nothing to dispel the pain and grief, and the idea that it should be expected and accepted by an elderly person is only a rationalization to spare a younger person his own emotional distress. In fact, the death of a spouse is not only an extraordinarily difficult event for anyone, it is often particularly hard for an elderly person who may have limited coping mechanisms and less chance of finding another relationship in order to alleviate his distress.

Normal mourning, individual as it must be, tends to follow a rather standard and recognizable progression. It takes time; it must be permitted; it is natural. Distressing as mourning may be for others to witness, it would be of greater concern if no mourning took place.

A bereaved person passes through several stages in the mourning process. At first there is numbness and shock, a form of psychological denial of the death. It takes time to take it in. Sometimes a person can go through funeral arrangements and burial without showing any evidence of grief, but they may be going through these experiences in a sort of trance, with magical hopes that the spouse will somehow return. After this initial brief phase, the period of true mourning sets in, with distress and grief both prominent and undisguised. This period is marked by sadness and depression, tearfulness, sleep disturbance, disinterest in eating, and mainly by a preoccupation with the deceased. The work of the mourning process is the gradual giving up of the deceased and it can only be accomplished slowly, by remembering and remembering again, recalling the person, their past together, the happy and sad times, their wishes and regrets. Gradually, as each memory is mulled over and over often with tearful remembrance, the death can be accepted and the deceased remembered with feelings that are no longer overwhelming. This normal process of mourning naturally will take a variable period of time, but generally the worst should be over in about three months. No decision or value judgment should be made about the individual nature of the mourning process, even if the survivor's reaction becomes more exaggerated—including irritability, anger, guilt, temporary inability to function, nightmares, or excessive physical concerns. Even hallucinatory experiences, in which one briefly experiences the presence of the deceased, may occasionally be present. All of this may be part of a normal working-through of mourning, with understandable distress about both the loss and about one's new vulnerability. Giving up the deceased is a slow and natural process as is the gradual reorientation of the living toward a new and different life.

In time, the period of intense mourning is replaced by a less acute period, which may last for a year or longer, and is characterized by similar concerns, but with decreased intensity. Commonly there may be guilty preoccupations about not doing enough, not saying goodbye, leaving issues unresolved and unspoken, not being there at the moment of death, and these should be expected. Reassurance by relatives and friends is probably useless, as the person has some need to put himself through a period of pain as a price for his continued survival.

There may be anger, too, frequently directed at other family members or doctors who "failed" the deceased. While this anger may have some basis in reality, frequently it may represent displaced guilt over one's own feeling of not having done enough. Your surviving parent may fear his own death and become obsessively concerned about his own physical illness. Sometimes he may imitate the deceased, taking on character traits as a way to "hold onto" the loved one by becoming a living representation. All of this is natural and common, and will diminish with time.

Occasionally, however, normal mourning may give way to a more disturbing process, an extended or pathological grief reaction which is indistinguishable from a severe major depression, and cannot be left unattended.

At first it is hard for anyone, even an experienced psychiatrist, to differentiate between what is normal and acceptable and what is darker and more ominous. It takes time and careful observation to detect more disturbing signs and symptoms of illness replacing mourning. Gradually, if the mourning period continues without any letup for an extended period (more than a year), one must question what is going on, especially if the symptoms of grief seem to be intensifying rather than disappearing, and if your parent is becoming more withdrawn, isolated, and self-absorbed. Anger, withdrawal, total preoccupation with death, inability to function, a sleep or appetite disturbance with weight loss, guilty rumination, and thoughts of suicide are all hallmarks of a pathological process. Such a situation cannot be ignored or neglected. You must get immediate psychiatric attention for your parent, with appropriate treatment through psychotherapy and, frequently, antidepressant medication. Untreated, such a reaction may become chronic, as in this dramatic vignette I witnessed during a home visit:

> I was startled when the front door opened into total darkness. The elderly woman inside saw my confusion and reassured me that she was prepared for my visit. "Don't worry, I have a bulb. I checked it yesterday and it works." I followed her uncertainly as she fumbled at a bureau drawer, carefully extracting a light bulb which she awkwardly screwed into a table lamp. It flickered on, 25 watts, the allotted light.
>
> "I live in the dark since my daughter committed suicide," she explained. "It makes it easier. I don't really know why."
>
> "How long has it been?"
>
> "Fifteen years."

Such pathological grief reactions seem to result from either of two psychological events. First, not everyone who loses a spouse or child, sad as that event might be, necessarily had a good relationship with the lost person. While it may seem paradoxical at first, it is easier to mourn and accept the death of a loved one, than to deal with someone about whom the person had mixed feelings. The problem is that it is often difficult for some people to allow themselves to feel anger and dislike for someone so recently dead. A refusal to mull over and resolve the angry, even hateful, ideas about the deceased, thwarts the normal mourning process. The result is unresolvable guilt which cannot be mastered because the person will not allow himself to think about it. Such a situation can be treated with psychotherapy, allowing the distressed person to accept the full range of feelings toward the spouse and thereby gradually accept the death with all of its personal meanings.

The other possibility which creates a prolonged and pathological grief reaction concerns a surviving spouse's feeling that he is unable to live on his own. In such cases, the death of a spouse is perceived psychologically as an abandonment and the dead person is hated and blamed for leaving the survivor to face life alone. Again, this may not be a permissible idea for the survivor, and such feelings may be suppressed so that they cannot be dealt with consciously.

Again, psychological intervention can be helpful, not only in allowing the person to recognize the depth of his true feelings but in helping the survivor to see that he can go on.

Once the process of mourning a dead spouse has been accomplished, the survivor has next to deal with widowhood. This new situation presents its own challenges which may be difficult to overcome.

For the first time since early life, your parent is alone. A lifelong pattern of mutual interdependence has been broken and he must continue without relying on someone whose presence and assistance had been taken for granted. Friends and family members are notoriously unsupportive during this period, frequently withdrawing out of awkwardness and anxiety about being in a similar position themselves some day. Having just lost a spouse, the widow may now find herself a social leper, having lost her social position as well. Men are even more likely to find it difficult to cope, finding themselves required to work and manage a home for the first time. Not infrequently, men have relied on their wives to establish social connections and activities, and may find themselves entirely cut off from social contact. In fact, widowed men die more quickly than women and have far greater adjustment problems. Particularly unhelpful is the common reassurance that death is a natural event of later life to be accepted, an idea that, true though it may be, deprives an elderly person of the feelings to which a grieving younger person would feel entirely entitled.

If widowhood is proving to be a stumbling block, don't leave your parent to his own devices, hoping that he will work it out on his own. He may be afraid or ashamed to ask for the help he so sorely needs. Involving him more actively in the life of your family may help, as will introducing him to new social opportunities through widow support groups or senior centers, but if such pragmatic suggestions fail, don't be afraid to advise psychological counseling. An experienced therapist can become a sort of confidante, providing a supportive relationship which replaces, however inadequately, a measure of the lost marriage. Once such a trusting bond has been established, the therapist can offer an opportunity for your troubled parent to honestly and openly explore the sources of his difficulty in accepting his loss and going on. Without worrying about the judgment of others, he will be free to discuss his innermost feelings about his deceased spouse, which may run the gamut from undiminished devotion to acknowledged relief from the burdens of caring for someone during a long illness. He will be able to talk about his anxiety about being on his own, concerns about his ability to cope, guilt-ridden interests in beginning a new romantic involvement, sexual concerns, anger and resentment about his situation, envy of others, or whatever is really on his mind, in a nonjudgmental atmosphere which allows for expression, acceptance, and potential resolution. At the same time, concrete techniques for improved independent coping can be suggested. Therapists who work regularly with the aged generally are knowledgeable about financial concerns, can offer specific possibilities for renewed socialization geared to your parent's special needs, and even make recommendations for new living accommodations. They can help your parent cope with details that previously were handled by their deceased spouse and offer alternative ways of managing. Most important, a therapist may basically need to give your surviving parent permission to go on living, a simple but common concern, which may take skill to get across and time to accept.

SEXUAL PROBLEMS

A very elderly man entered a nursing home carrying two heavy valises for which he refused assistance, explaining that they were "private." His private belongings turned out to be samples of his carefully selected pornography collection, which he arranged on a wall of his room, altering his graphic displays periodically. The staff was divided about the acceptability of his collection, especially such an ostentatious exhibition, and a compromise was reached where he agreed to draw a curtain partially around his bed, to block the view from the crowd of interested female residents who seemed to make his doorway a popular area of congregation.

Among the many misconceptions about the aged, no area is more laden with mythology than that of the sexual interest and activity of this population. The consensus of the young seems to be that the elderly are too old and uninterested, unable to perform even if they wanted to, and that if they do, it is humorous or "dirty." Unfortunate misconceptions all, but even more so when these wrong-minded ideas are picked up by the aged themselves and accepted out of guilt and anxiety.

The fact is that those who want to maintain sexual functioning are able to do so almost indefinitely as long as they are in reasonably good health. The real reasons for discontinuing sexual activity, sadly a not uncommon situation in later life, are almost always psychological, exaggerated by society's disapproval and misunderstanding.

While sexual activity is a natural need, driven by powerful physiologic forces, it can be derailed surprisingly easily when people become anxious about their ability to perform. Masters and Johnson recognized that even in young people, one sexual failure, as a result of excessive drinking, for instance, can lead to a lifetime of impotence, so unsure are some men about their prowess and testing it again. Once anxiety about performance sets in, it can be difficult to overcome and too often people will withdraw from the whole arena, to avoid repeated blows to their self-esteem.

Such a situation, common enough among younger generations, is even more prevalent in the elderly. This may stem in part from misunderstanding about natural physiological changes. As men age, it will generally take longer for them to get an erection, and even longer still to ejaculate. Women will find that it takes longer for vaginal lubrication to occur and may experience some pain with intercourse because of a lack of lubrication or the gradual thinning of the vaginal wall. While both of these are expected changes and can be dealt with and overcome, if one is unprepared, it may be enough to induce performance anxiety, cause one to question one's virility or femininity, and create a climate where avoidance is easier.

While increased performance anxiety and avoidance is generally the most pervasive sexual difficulty, other issues may be at work. Elderly people are sometimes frightened about physical concerns, especially cardiovascular illness, and may be afraid that they will die of exertion during intercourse. While numerous studies have actually been done in an effort to document this possibility with rather clear evidence that it is very rare, such studies have not made their way into general awareness, and this fear persists. Cardiologists should prepare their patients to dispel this concern, but frequently even physicians are anxious about discussing sex with elderly patients.

Psychological attitudes about surgery can also interfere with sexual functioning. Following colostomies, ileostomies, and mastectomies, for example, patients may doubt their sexual appeal and their partners may harbor their own anxieties and discomforts. Doubts about personal appearance and desirability clearly become exaggerated with age and such partly disfiguring procedures may tip the balance toward sexual avoidance, further exaggerating a person's self-doubt and insecurity. Even after hysterectomies, where there is no obvious physical change, these fears may produce similar consequences.

Sometimes sexual problems may have deeper roots. A person who may have always been guilty or at least uncomfortable with sex uses age as an excuse to finally stop having sex. While this may actually be comforting for the conflicted individual, it may disturb or enrage a spouse who finds his or her sexual outlet closed and is chided as abnormal for continued interest. Marital discord is a common consequence of sexual avoidance, and may also be the cause.

It should not be forgotten that, especially in the elderly, sexual uninterest may also be a symptom of a more serious depression. If other symptoms of depression coexist, such as diminished functioning, lack of interest, sleep or appetite disturbance, treatment of the underlying illness will often resolve the sexual symptom.

While psychological causes account for the majority of cases of sexual dysfunction in the elderly, there are some real physiological difficulties which must be understood so that they can be investigated if problems occur.

In men, two illnesses may present variable degrees of impotence. Diabetics with vascular insufficiency may be unable to effect an erection in 7 to 50 percent of cases (depending on the study), although even in these, treatment resulting in better diabetic control often reverses the difficulty. It is only in men with severe diabetic neuropathy (damage to the nervous system) that this can be an unresolvable symptom. Prostate surgery also can lead to impotence; this consequence, however, is greatly exaggerated by the patient's fear, poor preparation by physicians, and misinformation which can lead to psychological impotence after surgery. In reality, at least 70 percent of men have full potency after a TURP (transurethral prostatectomy), the most common form of prostate surgery. The only consequence, for which men should be prepared, is that they will develop retrograde ejaculation, which means that they will deposit their semen into their bladder, rather than ejaculating it externally. Physical sensation will remain intact, and this usually is not a devastating difficulty for the partner.

As women age, there is thinning of the vaginal wall with diminished lubricating capacity, a normal condition, though, if severe, can lead to "senile vaginitis" so that intercourse becomes painful and there are frequent urinary tract infections. If this develops, hormonal therapy may be recommended, and gynecologists are all well-versed in its administration. Another solution is for both partners to understand that lubrication takes more time as you get older and either to prolong foreplay until lubrication occurs, or use a lubricant like K-Y jelly, available in any pharmacy.

The only other common physical difficulty that can affect sexual performance is medication. Blood pressure medication, propranol (Inderal) in particular, and many psychotropic drugs (antidepressants and major tranquilizers) can interfere with potency in men and sexual interest in women.

While for some elderly couples these physical problems may cause very real interference with sexual functioning, remember that the vast majority of elderly men and women should be able to maintain their sexual capacity to an advanced age. If your parents do not understand this, they may never agree to consider seeking treatment, leading to continued sexual avoidance at the very least and, frequently, to depression, anxiety, irritability, anger, and marital distress. Alcoholism and other substance abuse are common consequences as well.

 Of all issues, sexual problems are probably the least likely ones to be confided by a parent to an adult child. Nevertheless, if a passing reference is made, even as a "joke" or in regard to a "friend," you may be suprised to find that discreet questioning results in more information than you may have been prepared for. In fact, this may be a harder area for you to discuss than for your parent. If so, try not to show it and listen to whatever extent you can comfortably take. If your parent does need help, by all means help him to get it.

Psychological treatment for sexual dysfunction, once the need is recognized, is essentially the same as for a younger patient and can be highly successful. Sex therapy operates along a behavioral model which basically involves a gradual relearning of sexual activity in stages, in a nonthreatening situation with one's spouse, so that the anxiety is gradually diminished, allowing the affected partner to perform once again. In studies of elderly patients, a 50-percent success rate has been found, even in cases where couples have abstained for twenty to thirty years. Sex counselors, psychotherapists, and urologists are all good resources to which your parent may be referred.

Many of these cases can be averted in the first place with greater awareness, education, and a realistic attitude, in yourself as well as your parent. In sex, as in all other areas, the aged are individuals with common human needs.

FEAR OF DEATH AND DYING

One of the most common dreads of the elderly is the fear of dying alone. Unfortunately, that is too frequently just what happens, not so much because of any physical isolation, but because they are emotionally cut off by loved ones, who are afraid to discuss the inevitability of dying. The person is left alone with his fears, his sorrow, his need to talk.

The strange idea of protecting your dying parent from the fact of his approaching death is misguided, hardly ever "works," and generally results in what has been called a "mutual pretense" in which both parent and family act as if nothing is wrong. To avoid discussing what is foremost on everyone's mind is particularly painful for a dying parent, who must not only face his death alone, but must hide his feelings from those around him, just when he has the greatest need to show them.

There is no universal rule as to how to approach a dying parent. Everyone is different, with different attitudes and different needs. While many individuals find it comforting to be able to talk frankly with those who love them, others prefer a more limited approach, and a few really do seem to avoid taking in any information about their condition. In my experience, the most compassionate approach is to follow your parent's lead, promote an atmosphere of honesty and openness, and then allow him to ask the questions. When he asks, he should be answered. When he stops, no further information or discussion is required. In this manner, it is not really difficult to walk the line between being there emotionally for your parent, whatever his need, and not badgering him with more than he can bear to hear.

The psychological process of dying has been well explained by Elisabeth Kübler-Ross in her extensive writings, in which she describes five stages of dying. Again, while everyone is different, it is good to be aware of the typical psychological process involved so that your parent can be helped through each stage by caring family members. Frightening though death may be to all of us, it is another life event and we respond to it in characteristic and understandable psychological ways. The five stages include:

- *Denial.* The initial refusal to accept the inevitable. In our own unconscious we never really believe our own mortality and we secretly believe that we will live forever.
- *Anger.* Once some degree of acknowledgment is present, we will rage at the unfairness of our fate, even be angry at those

closest to us for continuing to live once we are gone. Families must accept this hostility and respond with compassion.

- *Bargaining.* Frequently we will try to strike a deal with God, belying our intellectual grasp of the situation. "If I do good things, I'll live after all, or at least live longer."
- *Depression.* When the first three stages fail, as they must, and patients are no longer able to avoid the realization of their fate, depression will set in.
- *Acceptance.* Finally, there will be a calmer, quieter awareness of approaching death, and withdrawal from others.

While these stages serve as important guidelines, permitting us to understand better what a dying parent is going through, they should not be thought of too literally as if a person neatly moves from one stage to another in an orderly progression. More realistically, the stages will overlap and swing back and forth between acceptance and denial and everything in between. Compassionate awareness and sensitivity offer the best possibility to be in touch with your parent so that true comfort can be provided to the end.

One practical note. . . . When death is inevitable and imminent, it is sometimes useful to consider a hospice. This program provides overall care for patients and their families and permits a parent to die with dignity and as free of pain as possible. A discussion of this option is included in chapter 4 (page 81).

·3·

When Your Parents Require Assistance: Taking Care of Basic Needs

During the course of my consultation with the G family, Mrs. G.'s mother herself came to see me, with her daughter in tow. She took immediate control of the situation in her usual fashion, and, with a no-nonsense approach, pointed accusingly at her daughter and got right to the heart of the matter:

> "She's been trying to run my life since she got that big promotion. Such a big shot. You'd think that she was the mother and I was the child. She always wanted to be the boss. Now she thinks she'll get her way."
>
> Her daughter replied, "She doesn't remember. She needs help but won't accept it. She must be protected." I ventured, "Let's see if we can work this out together."
>
> Mrs. G.'s mother snorted, Mrs. G. shrugged wearily, and we sat down to try and sort things out.

As in the case of the G family, there may come a time in their life when aging parents require help from their adult children, in any of a variety of areas: in arranging for medical care, in seeking out and securing community resources to assist them, in financial planning, and, most difficult of all, in deciding when a controlled living environment may be necessary. On occasion, that time may be obvious, as in the case of some sudden major incapacitating illness, but more often it is not: It is gradual and ill defined; the need may exist in some areas and not in others; it is unclear as to how much help is needed, exactly what is required, and what a parent will accept and what she will resent. The dilemma is tricky and requires sensitivity and discretion. Despite the inherent difficulties, however, it is essential, unavoidable, and must be faced if you are to responsibly plan for future care and provide protection from the often unexpected crises of advanced life.

Given the very real difficulties involved in knowing when to "step in," you and your parents may be at a loss. Without a plan in mind, you might avoid the issue entirely until an emergency develops, or take over prematurely without regard for your parent's feelings and need to retain independence and self-esteem. If handled properly, however, a joint and realistic effort between yourself and your parent may not only lead to optimal planning but deepen your relationship, resulting in a renewed closeness and understanding that neither of you anticipated. To avoid the most frequent pitfalls, I suggest the following flexible guidelines as an approach to providing assistance as it is needed.

GUIDELINES

If at all possible, it is always best to handle all issues in an open, honest, and direct manner. Involve your parents at every step, explain the issues satisfactorily and exhaustively, and get their agreement before you reach any final decisions. If this can be successfully achieved, it provides a sense of continued independence and control, maintains self-esteem, and avoids suspicion and accusations of self-motivation. Remember, whatever their limitations, parents are *not* children and must be treated with respect by listening to them, involving them, and taking their opinions into account.

If you are still unclear about whether or not help is needed, let your parents be the guide while you discreetly observe their ability to negotiate whatever obstacles may be confronting them. Give them space, allow them their self-determination, but don't hesitate to step in when the situation requires it. If they ask for your help, never deny their request out of your anxiety about their dependence and failing abilities. Without question, listen to them and provide the assistance they need.

In reaching decisions, even when parents are most disabled, always take their desires into account even if only in a limited way. People must have some satisfaction in order to survive. It is always possible to provide it, in thoughtful and creative ways.

Always thoroughly investigate and research alternative answers to problems. Present choices to your parents and guide them to realistic but satisfactory solutions. Give them time to understand, consider, and reconsider. It may take a while, but if they come to accept an idea as their own, the result will be worth the effort.

When you encounter resistance, listen carefully to the objection. Often such resistance is concerned not so much with the issue itself, but with the way it is presented or with some underlying psychological conflict. For instance, when Mrs. G.'s mother objected to a home attendant, she was objecting more to the open recognition of her failing abilities than to the realistic need for physical assistance. In her case, an attendant could only be accepted if the attendant would allow the elderly woman to "boss her around" so that she could maintain the "superior" position that was so important to her.

If the true underlying problem can be identified, it can often be resolved in a way that is acceptable to a resistant parent who will then accept the help on his own terms.

Always allow parents to retain independence whenever and wherever they are still capable. In fact, maximize those areas, and even continue to accept help and advice from them whenever possible. Finally if all attempts to work things out have failed, consult an "expert" to assist, referee, and provide direction. A knowledgeable third party brings a sense of fairness, impartiality, and objectivity, and allows for mutual respect and the recognition of a parent's continuing ability to be involved in decision making. Often, a solution which is objectionable when presented by an adult child, will be rather easily accepted when explained by a physician, social worker, or other professional.

These are the basic guidelines for tactful assistance. Let's now begin to examine the major areas most often requiring support and intervention.

FINANCIAL PLANNING

In protecting your parents' interests and insuring their well-being, nothing is more basic than arranging for their continuing financial security. If this foundation is not established, your efforts in all other areas will be rendered worthless by the realistic anxiety so often engendered by poor financial planning.

Money is a very hot issue at any stage of life, and never a more delicate issue than when a parent must consider relinquishing some degree of control over his own. Despite fears and objections, protection must be secured in this vital area in which aging parents are most vulnerable.

The trick to financial assistance is to give your parents a sense of control for as long as is realistically possible by keeping in tune with their diminishing capacities, and stepping in when required.

Let us begin with the simplest and gradually proceed to more complex financial maneuvers which may only be necessary if further physical or mental incapacity develops or emergencies arise.

Establishing an Organized File of Personal and Financial Information

While such a file would seem a sensible idea for responsible people at any stage of life, most people are rather lax about it. While the young may be able to get away with it, the more frequent unexpected turns of later life must be anticipated with a greater degree of organization.

A central file will be of enormous practical assistance in emergency situations of either a medical or financial nature; for ongoing financial planning; and even in making provisions after death. This information should be kept in a safe place and you *must* always have access to it as needed. If you find that any documents are missing, they must be obtained and included in the file in advance of any unforeseen emergency.

This information should include the following: Social Security numbers, insurance coverage with plan numbers (Medicare, co-insurance policies, Medicaid, disability insurance, homeowner or car insurance, etc.), financial records (bank books, brokerage accounts, treasury bills, mutual funds, property, tax records, etc.), life insurance documents, names, addresses, and phone numbers of financial advisers (attorneys, banks, stockbrokers, insurance agents, etc.), important personal papers which may be required for securing financial assistance in the future (birth certificates, marriage certificate, death certificate of a spouse, divorce papers, naturalization papers if foreign born, funeral arrangements, and will).

Making a Budget

Very often parents will require assistance in budgeting limited financial resources, especially when adjusting to any change in a financial situation. Older people on fixed incomes are obviously vulnerable to economic changes or unexpected expenses, and may become desperate if they feel that they have insufficient funds to provide for their needs. Recent widows may be particularly overwhelmed if they have been accustomed to letting their husbands handle financial matters, and may need guidance in becoming self-sufficient.

You can best help by working out a sensible budget with your parents. Show them that a realistic solution can always be found by working out the details for them. If their financial situation is not workable, better to face facts than to deny it, and assist them in securing the financial assistance to which they may be entitled.

One common area of difficulty is the typical fear of "spending the principal." So frequently, no matter what their need, parents will object to spending anything over the interest they accrue, understandably seeing any further spending resulting in gradually diminishing future income. In addition to the reality of the situation, there is an even greater psychological anxiety inherent: spending the principal, no matter to how limited a degree, means that at some point in the distant future, funds will run out entirely, confirming the reality of eventually becoming totally dependent. Furthermore, holding on to the "principal" can become an unconscious way of maintaining one secret, but universal, fantasy, that they will live forever. When parents have some insight into the roots of this dilemma, they may ease up a bit and permit a more realistic financial approach.

Simplifying Financial Dealings

There are several ways that you can help your parents keep track of their finances: Arrange for the direct deposit of monthly Social Security checks, pension funds, annuities, and so on into a bank or brokerage account. This lessens their anxiety about the danger of checks being lost or stolen in the mail or the possibility that your parent might misplace the checks. If your parents cannot manage even this simplified approach, Social Security checks can be sent directly to responsible children if a licensed physician fills out a representative payee form.

If at all possible, keep the funds in one place, accessible in times of need, both to your parents and to a designated family member. It is very difficult to track multiple bank accounts, mutual funds, and other assets, especially when the need for emergency money is pressing. If the funds are at all significant, consider transferring all accounts and deposits into an insured account in a bank or reputable brokerage firm where it is easily monitored by one monthly statement. Make sure that the money is wisely invested, neither used for reckless speculation nor forgotten in savings accounts at minimal interest rates.

Set up a routine for paying regular bills. If your parents are capable, they can manage independently, but should be monitored. If their ability is questionable, you can provide monthly personal assistance or secure the now easily obtainable services provided by local banks.

Always have easy access to funds for emergency situations.

Suggest a joint checking account or having both names put on bank and brokerage accounts. If your parents balk at this, make sure that they at least permit some access to a more limited financial account which will tide you over in emergencies until more comprehensive legal maneuvers can be accomplished.

Maximizing Income

Elderly parents may be hesitant about any sort of financial manipulation which they fear may jeopardize their savings. While their natural desire for security is certainly understandable, you may be able to show them simple ways to stretch their income without sacrificing safety in any way.

For instance, if your parents have placed their entire savings in a pass book account, as is so often the case, or even in low-yield CDs or Treasury Bonds, suggest a money market mutual fund or even investing a portion of their assets in safe blue-chip stocks or mutual funds. Even a small percentage increase may give them sorely needed dollars.

For parents who are house-rich, cash-poor, a number of possibilities exist by which home equity can be converted into monthly income. They may consider moving into a less expensive smaller home and banking the difference, taking advantage of the one-time tax exemption of up to $125,000 of their capital gain. Or, if they do not want to move, they may be willing to sell their home to you and lease it back. Such an arrangement affords them a new source of income from the interest on the purchase price, allows them to remain in their home, and provides you with both a potential tax advantage and an investment in terms of appreciation. One new development, still in its infancy, and available only in some states, is a reverse-mortgage. This reversal of the usual mortgage arrangement works so that the bank pays your parent a fixed monthly income, deferring repayment of interest and principal until the house is no longer needed and can be sold, repaying the debt.

Another possibility is a split-interest purchase, an arrangement by which you and your parents buy an asset together (usually a bond) and agree that they will receive the income during their lifetime while you retain the asset.

All of these maneuvers accomplish the same thing: maximizing their monthly income by taking full (and legal) advantage of existing assets. To be sure that the right choices are being made, always consult a reputable financial adviser, who is knowledgeable about such arrangements.

LEGAL DECISIONS

When mental or physical incapacity is more evident and begins to interfere with effective financial management, more complicated legal steps must be taken.

Parents with significant degrees of confusion are particularly vulnerable to financial mismanagement and victimization, and will need to be protected, sometimes against their own wishes. There are a variety of options to choose from, and although they may vary a bit from state to state they are substantially the same. Again, it is always best to start with the easiest measures and only go to more complicated legal maneuvers when they are necessary.

Here, one suggestion already outlined will come into play. Utilize your established financial file or create a file and comprehensive inventory of all assets and liabilities. Then consult a knowledgeable attorney. Chose someone who is skilled, not only in financial and tax matters but also in dealing with the particular problems of the incapacitated aged.

Power of Attorney

The simplest situation is when an elderly person requires someone else to handle his financial affairs because of increasing infirmity. If your parent is agreeable, still competent mentally, and trusts someone in the family, power of attorney is the best legal instrument. A general power of attorney allows a parent to sign a document which simply permits a designated party to handle the management of his financial affairs, including real estate. In the past, under common law tradition, a power of attorney signed when a person was competent to do so was automatically revoked when that person became incompetent, at the very time it was meant to be used in the first place. As a result, most states have now adopted the concept of a "durable power of attorney." This means that a power of attorney, properly written originally, will be valid and remain effective if your parent becomes mentally incapacitated. Families must make sure that their attorney knows how to protect them via the proper wording of this document.

Often a general power of attorney is not sufficient. Most banks have their own power of attorney forms and will not recognize a general power of attorney. One must obtain separate forms from each bank account and safety deposit box and file them with each bank. Stock brokerage accounts are handled in the same manner.

Again, while there is no difficulty with this sort of procedure if your parents are willing, people frequently are reluctant to grant such broad powers to another person, and elderly people in particular are especially fearful about theft, fraud, and loss of control. After all, they are trying their best to hold onto their capabilities, and it is difficult for them to let go. Even with the most minimal degree of confusion or paranoia, these concerns become more prominent and your parents may understandably feel that they are being taken advantage of. Generally, despite this concern, you can convince them if your attorney explains everything carefully and in detail. Make sure they understand that they can always revoke the power of attorney and have complete control in choosing the person to whom the power of attorney is granted. Further doubts can be diminished by placing the power of attorney in escrow with the attorney for use only when the need arises, and by having the attorney explain that your parent may continue to hold onto his own bank books, making abuse unlikely. Retention of the bank books themselves may be the most important issue, giving the feeling of continued control and financial security. It is also possible to create a special power of attorney called a "springing" power of attorney which becomes effective only after mental incapacity.

Trust Arrangements

More complicated, but even more useful for financial planning and tax consideration, is a capital trust. Here your parent must be not only competent but attuned to such financial matters. Again, suspicions and fears can be alleviated by careful and precise explanation, often best handled by the attorney rather than a family member.

The trust best suited for the management of financial affairs for a senior citizen is the "inter vivos trust," sometimes called a "living trust."

This procedure creates a document that names one or more persons or a bank as trustees to administer the trust, which contains specific instructions as to how the income and assets of the trust are to be managed and distributed, naturally according to the wishes of the senior citizen. Your parent then signs the document, transferring his property into the trust. While his money is now in the trust rather than personally held, he is fully protected by law because the trustees are bound by the legal document to comply with the grantor's instructions written in the original trust document.

While this may sound like a lot of legal mumbo jumbo, it provides a variety of advantages:

- The trust is more efficient and reliable than a power of attorney because it is more widely accepted and recognized by banks, stock brokers, etc.
- The trust document can provide for distribution of your parent's assets at death, taking the place of a will.
- Tax savings can be achieved (see your attorney for specifics).
- Revision is generally unnecessary, saving future legal difficulties and expenses.
- Trust assets are protected from the family members who are trustees, even better than with a power of attorney.
- Finally, and probably most significantly, trusts can be created in a way so that your parent, who technically no longer has any personal assets, may be entitled to government benefits, particularly Medicaid, since the trust retains the assets. This is

a complicated transaction, but attorneys can manage it and the government still accepts it.

Until this "loophole" is plugged, you may wish to take advantage of it to protect your parents and your inheritance. Such a trust is known as a "Medicaid Qualifying Trust" (or an Irrevocable Medicaid Trust). It must be set up in a letter-perfect form by an attorney who knows exactly how to proceed in the matter. Clearly, it must meet specified criteria, the most important being that, from the day it goes into effect, only the interest can be used, never the principal; this rule makes it advantageous mainly for the well to do. There are countless variations on this idea, well known to tax laywers skilled at finding advantageous solutions to personal finance problems. If you are interested in pursuing this strategy, you can consult Armond Burdish's book *Avoiding the Medicaid Trap* (Henry Holt) or obtain the name of an experienced attorney in your area by writing to the National Academy of Elder Law Attorneys, 1730 E. River Road, Suite 107, Tucson, AZ 85718.

Your parent may want to establish a trust without giving up control at the present time. In such a case, a "standby trust" can be created, but not funded. Here your parent executes a durable power of attorney which contains a clause through which his assets are transferred to the trust in the event of his incapacity and inability to manage his affairs. If such a situation arises, the assets automatically are assigned to the trust.

All of this naturally can get quite complicated. In the simplest terms, if your parent is willing and still competent, a variety of legal maneuvers exist which can financially protect everyone in the family, minimizing tax consequences and even allowing for advantages in terms of government entitlement programs.

The problem arises, naturally, when you are unable to work with your parent despite your best and most diplomatic efforts, even with the assistance of an experienced attorney. When mental illness or senility interfere with a joint cooperative effort, the more complex legal measures that follow must be undertaken to protect the financial situation.

Conservatorship or Guardianship

Again, the criteria for such measures vary from state to state, but follow a similar pattern. Generally speaking, a legal proceeding of one sort or another is held in which a parent's capacity to manage his finances is determined, and some procedure is established to manage his revenues in the future which is acceptable to the court. Sometimes the proceeding takes over the entire management of an elderly parent (in which case your parent would be declared incompetent) and a "committee" or "guardian" is appointed; sometimes the proceeding is restricted to the future management of financial matters alone.

Although variations exist, the usual procedure is similar. Once legal action is taken to judge a parent's competence, those bringing the action need to have a doctor examine his, prepare papers, and testify at a court hearing as to his competence. Other evidence will be heard from family members, involved agencies, nursing home administrators or social workers, and other individuals. In addition to this, the court generally appoints a temporary guardian to make an independent investigation into the situation, to avoid any potential for abuse. All of this is presented in a court hearing where a judge decides on the validity of the action. If it is granted, there is some legal vehicle established (a conservatorship, a guardianship, or whatever) which will manage the senior's finances, but is accountable to the court for review. The manager of the finances may be a family member, an attorney, a bank, or a social agency and, generally, a small fee is paid for the ongoing management.

While such a hearing is certainly more complicated than the procedures described earlier (power of attorney, trust), it is also not particularly difficult or stressful. Financial mismanagement will be far more expensive and potentially disruptive than such a procedure which generally can be accomplished expeditiously. If a parent is confused or psychotic, her presence at the court proceeding can usually be avoided, although she will be informed of the proceeding and examined by the temporary guardian, to protect her rights.

Wills

It goes without saying that you and your parents should be protected by an up-to-date will, periodically revised, and drafted by an attorney who specializes in estate planning in order to minimize tax liability and avoid unnecessary complications. Failure to make a will, usually out of anxiety about a not too distant death, may result in increased estate taxes and legal fees, unneeded court hearings, the appointment of an outside executor, a delay in dividing assets, and the possibility of family disagreement over distribution. All are unnecessary and avoidable complications.

Should you suspect that your parents are having some difficulty making appropriate arrangements, and you are embarrassed to bring it up directly, it sometimes helps to raise the issue in terms of what you are doing to write your own will and what you are doing to protect your children. Or, ask if they have made sure that their will is in accordance with recent reforms in tax law and whether they have provided properly for each other should one die first. Any such approach will open the door to a realistic discussion and allow you to assist them, preventing headaches later on.

Sometimes parents will express a wish to draft a "right-to-die" clause into their will to avoid prolongation of life by "heroic" life-support systems, a decision respected by statutes in many states. If so, a living will should be signed and witnessed, and discussed with your personal physician, who should retain a copy for his files.

One other special situation bears mention. If one parent suffers from a chronic health problem so that you are maneuvering to arrange Medicaid (an issue that will be dealt with more fully in the next section on health insurance), make sure that the will takes this into account. For instance, if you are divesting an ill parent of all assets so that he qualifies for Medicaid assistance by transferring them to the healthy one, all of your work will be in vain if the healthy parent dies first leaving the estate to the one who is ill. Such a situation can easily be avoided with the aid of an informed attorney.

In financial planning, as in all areas of care, there is always an answer that can be modified to fit each and every problem. While conflicts involving money can be especially difficult, they are so common, and taken so seriously, that courts have spelled out procedures to follow. By being properly informed through the assistance of a competent attorney, early and successful resolution of an obvious problem usually can be assured.

HEALTH INSURANCE

Medical illness and chronic disability are perhaps your parents' greatest potential financial liabilities. A lifetime of careful saving for the future can be quickly wiped out, leaving them virtually destitute and dependent on you for even marginal financial viability. If such a possibility is anticipated rather than ignored, sensible protective measures can be taken in advance to protect them and yourself from such an eventuality. While this may seem obvious, it is always impressive for me to see how frequently people will deny the possibility of future infirmity as long as they remain in good health. If your parents have a tendency toward this sort of short-sighted denial, you must step in to protect them, particularly because realistic health insurance planning can avert many unforeseeable crises.

Medicare

The basic insurance policy for all senior citizens entitled to Social Security benefits is naturally Medicare. While there is a good deal of talk about the gaps in the system, it affords your parents excellent basic coverage and protection, exceeding most policies available to the younger population. Even without supplementary policies, it may very likely be better than your own. Still, given the likelihood of illness at this stage of life, it needs to be and you and your parent will want everything in place when the time comes.

The coverage provided by Medicare is somewhat confusing and is regularly modified, but the essentials can be easily explained. Medicare is a comprehensive federal health care insurance program, established under Title XVIII of the Social Security Act and consists of two parts:

Hospital Insurance, Part A. This portion is free and pays most hospital expenses for up to 60 days per spell of illness (that is, each new hospital admission), excluding the first day which must be paid for privately or by a supplemental coinsurance policy. Basically, this means that every time a person requires hospitalization, he is fully covered after the first day, provided that the entire hospitalization is not in excess of 60 days. This includes the room rate, the nursing care, all laboratory tests, x-rays, special procedures, operation costs, blood transfusions, rehabilitation, medication in-hospital, etc. In essence, the coverage is comprehensive while your parent is in the hospital. Unfortunately, the moment he leaves the hospital, he is on his own. Medicare does not cover outpatient medication, extended nursing home or convalescent care, nursing care at home (except for a very limited time following hospitalization and arranged by a doctor and home care agency), eyeglasses, hearing aids, preventive services, or any sort of chronic custodial care.

Medical Insurance, Part B. This portion is voluntary, costs a modest monthly amount which is automatically deducted from Social Security checks of those who participate, and pays 80 percent of physician fees and hospital outpatient services, after a yearly $75 deductible, provided that your physician "accepts assignment" which means that he will accept the amount specified by Medicare as 80 percent of his entire fee. Many physicians regularly accept assignment, and others will do so if your financial situation merits it. If your parent's physician does not accept assignment, however, find out what his fee is in advance, and what Medicare will allow, so that you will know the extent of your financial liability. There is no need for surprises.

It should be pointed out that Part B is just as vital to have as Part A. Unfortunately, occasionally seniors foolishly reject Part B because of the small fee involved, a situation which allows them a hospital bed, but no one to take care of them in it. Both Parts A and B are obviously essential. Check your parent's Medicare card itself, the red, white, and blue one, to see that he is enrolled in both.

"Medigap" Plans

While Medicare, Parts A and B, jointly provide fairly comprehensive coverage, there are decided gaps in protection which can be substantially reduced through a variety of supplemental insurance programs which are widely available and provide payment for such noncovered fees as deductible expenses, extended hospital stays beyond the 60-day covered period, and the missing 20 percent of the physician's fee. Such programs are offered by Blue Cross and Blue Shield, a variety of major medical plans, AARP (American Association of Retired Persons), and others. Most of these policies provide similar coverage, so that it is almost never necessary to purchase more than one comprehensive plan. Beware of aggressive insurance salesmen. So abusive have been the sales of multiple policies that Congress is now looking into tightening federal restrictions. If you're confused about advising your parent, a helpful booklet, *A Guide to Medicare and Health Insurance for Older People*, is available from L.T.C. Incorporated, Bellevue, WA 98033 (206) 827-5889.

Health Maintenance Organizations (HMOs)

An alternative strategy which circumvents the entire Medicare system is to enroll in an HMO. Participation in such programs generally means that your parent must surrender his Medicare coverage (although he can change his mind later and be reinstated), pay a set monthly fee, and have all of his medical needs provided for by physicians and hospitals participating in this prepaid program. Such HMO programs have significant advantages in that they often provide not only those services prescribed by Medicare but additional coverage for dental work, eyeglasses, hearing aids, foot care, some nursing care at home, and brief respite programs in nursing homes.

Sounds good? Well, it can be, but there are distinct disadvantages as well. First, your parent can no longer choose whatever physician or hospital he wants as he could under Medicare, but will now be restricted to participating physicians and hospitals. Second, HMOs are cost effective, which means that such organizations receive a certain set amount of money annually to provide medical services to each participant. As a result, there is a built-in financial incentive to keep costs down, by limiting unnecessary medical care. The inherent danger in this incentive is that they may be overly restrictive in providing health care, since they make more money the less service they provide. On the one hand, when participating in the Medicare system, there is the opposite danger of private physicians and hospitals overutilizing services (that is, subjecting your parent to more care than is really necessary, in order to build up their fees). Naturally, neither system is supposed to work that way, but when financial incentives are there, that is exactly what may happen.

What is the answer? As in most complex situations, there is no single correct answer. You and your parent have to make up your own minds by investigating your local HMOs, comparing these programs with other local facilities, and being aware of the potential pitfalls in each. My personal choice would be to favor individual Medicare insurance in large urban centers where medical facilities and physicians are abundant enough to permit wide options for care, but might choose an HMO with a good track record in any area where medical care is less widely available, or when the extra covered programs are particularly attractive because of a parent's own special needs. But I would not let a parent trade a Medicare card for a free pair of eyeglasses.

It is a decision—"You pays your money and you takes your chance." But investigate carefully, and do it with full knowledge beforehand.

Medicare Catastrophic Care Act of 1988 (MCCA)

Originally conceived as the final word on health care insurance for the elderly, the government insurance policy designed to fill every gap and provide for any contingency, the Medicare Catastrophic Care Act of 1988 was ushered in with great fanfare, and was about as controversial as apple pie and motherhood. Within a year, it was dead, killed by the very people it was designed to protect. What happened?

Without doubt, the original plan offered substantial benefits in the form of extended hospital coverage, a "ceiling" on physician's fees, partial payment for prescription drugs, and even some assistance with short-term rehabilitative nursing care. Had it been implemented, it would have provided financial relief for many ill elderly in need, particularly those who could not afford private "Medigap" policies. And that was the root of the problem. Any plan that provided for so much would, of necessity, cost a great deal. In this case, the method of financing the measure also doomed it.

What happened was that in an unusually progressive spirit, Congress took the innovative step of paying for MCCA by taxing the ones who would benefit from it, instead of sharing the cost among the general population. Not only were the elderly to shoulder the entire cost, but the more affluent would pick up most of the tab by supplementing a $4 premium that everyone paid with a sliding surcharge of up to $800 per person per year. Since the more affluent elderly already had private "Medigap" policies in place which covered substantial portions of the proposed plan, those who had the least to gain in additional benefits had the most to pay. Organizing rapidly and effectively, they forced a quick repeal. And, given the unpredictable expense that such a plan would have entailed, the government was relieved of an unwanted burden. Many doubt that Congress will be quick to reintroduce alternative legislation.

I bring up the repeal of MCCA not so much as a history lesson, but because it illustrates an important issue which must be kept in mind when arranging for your parent's health care. Flawed as the plan was and controversial as its selective taxation provision, it provided an effective safety net worth far more in a crisis than the $800 maximum annual expense, a basic fact virtually ignored by the elderly. What incensed them was that they had to pay for it themselves and the elderly are notoriously reluctant to pay anything at all for health care costs. While many people have the idea that medical care should ideally be free, Seniors tend to have the even more intense feeling that they are entitled to it. This often unshakable conviction, coupled with an almost universal fear of spending their remaining assets, can result in a potentially hazardous but not unusual situation if they refuse to pay for care that is vital (especially common in neglecting to hire home attendants, private duty nurses, even arranging transportation to a physician's office or filling costly prescriptions—all noncovered medical expenses).

Should such a situation arise with your parent, recognize the fact that you may have to step in quickly. Always attempt to discuss the need rationally, remind him that this is the rainy day for which he has been saving, and reassure him that you will provide assistance should savings diminish. If reasoning fails, you may have to consider making legal arrangements so that you have emergency access to funds (through power of attorney, a conservatorship, or other system) or simply pay for such expenses yourself even if substantial assets exist. Don't allow a parent to jeopardize his health by getting into a stubborn power struggle. It is pointless and dangerous, and no one will win. Intransigent seniors may bring everything down on their own heads as some feel they did with the repeal of the Medicare Catastrophic Care Act.

One final word: While all catastrophic medical care coverage has been repealed, two little known financial provisions of the bill have been retained by both the House and Senate and are of particular interest. One is "Medicaid Buy-In," which means that if your parent's income and resources are below a certain level (approximately $500 per month with less than $4000 in savings), he will be eligible to have his Medicare premium paid for in full by Medicaid, a significant savings in such a borderline financial situation. The second, and more significant provision, is "Anti-Spousal Impoverishment" (transfer of assets), a proposal designed to protect the finances of the at-home spouse should the other require chronic nursing home care, a subject that will be discussed at length later in this chapter.

Providing for Long-Term Care

Even without Medicare Catastrophic Care Insurance, your parents are afforded excellent protection from the cost of an acute medical illness provided that they have Medicare, parts A and B, along with some supplemental health insurance policy or belong to an HMO. These plans will pay the lion's share of hospital expenses and physicians fees, and you really need not be terribly concerned about unanticipated costs. Unfortunately, what no existing insurance plan can do is to protect them from the incredible expenses of a chronic disabling illness requiring very extended hospital stays, prolonged home care with nursing attendants, or chronic custodial care in a nursing home.

While private insurance companies are now actively grappling with the problem of covering such long-term care, none provide what many seem to advertise: full or even substantial coverage for nursing home care. What many do offer is reimbursement for selected special services like nurses or attendants in the home, or for home health visits by professionals. Other policies provide a specified, but very limited, dollar per day allotment for nursing home care (up to $60 per day as a rule) which offsets a portion of the cost. Still other plans will pay out a fixed amount should the policyholder come down with a prespecified illness. One new creative possibility offered by the Golden Financial Group in New York is a special annuity plan designed to provide for a tax-free increased level of annuity payments should your parent become physically or mentally disabled (Golden Financial Group, 909 Third Avenue, New York, NY 10022). No doubt others will come up with alternative interesting possibilities. But, no matter how innovative the concept, before purchasing any such long-term care plan, read the fine print carefully and know exactly what you are buying. Remember only something as large as a government could realistically fully underwrite nursing home care, and even the government has shied away from doing so, fearful of the unpredictable expense involved as we live longer and require more extended care. Despite the obvious limitations, if you want to consider such a policy, write for the Consumer's Guide to Long-

Term Care Insurance from the Health Insurance Association of America, 1025 Connecticut Avenue NW, Washington DC 20036.

The present facts of paying for chronic care are really rather simple even if they seem unfair to many. When faced with long-term disability requiring chronic care, if no provision has already been made to transfer assets or safeguard them in a trust arrangement, your parent must pay for the required care himself until his funds are essentially exhausted, at which time he is eligible for assistance through Medicaid.

As discussed earlier in this chapter, there are legal maneuvers which can be undertaken to transfer assets so that your parents become eligible for Medicaid without spending all of their savings. Understandably, this cannot be done at the last minute when the need is immediate. Generally, 30 months must elapse between the disposition of assets and Medicaid eligibility. That is why intelligent financial planning with an eye to the uncertain future can be essential.

However, if such an arrangement has not been made in advance, and personal funds are still available, they simply must be used to pay for uncovered medical and nursing home expenses. Such fees will vary widely depending on the state in which your parent lives and his health care requirements, but can certainly run to more than $50,000 per year for skilled nursing home care, excluding such additional expenses as physicians' fees, private duty nursing, and so on.

Obviously, since few will have sufficient funds to maintain themselves indefinitely, your parents may eventually require Medicaid assistance.

Medicaid

Medicaid is a health care program established under Title XIX of the Social Security Act, funded by a combination of federal and state monies, locally administered with differing eligibility requirements and differing covered services, and available to those with very limited financial resources. While generally thought of as a form of welfare for the poor, and unfairly stigmatized in the eyes of many, it is an unavoidable option for many elderly parents who require chronic medical care.

Medicaid is an enormously useful plan which will provide for many of the essential services neglected by all of the current insurance programs. Such services include nursing care in the home, regulated by government rules and agencies; transportation to and from hospitals, clinics and physicians' offices; all deductible fees to hospitals and often to physicians; coverage for extended or repeated hospital stays after Medicare benefits are exhausted; medication; eyeglasses; hearing aids; dental services; and podiatry; among others. And, most significant of all, for chronic nursing home care of a custodial nature.

Acceptance into the Medicaid program varies from state to state, and involves an examination of both assets and regular income by a state agency. Your local eligibility requirements are easily determined by contacting the local Medicaid office or an agency specializing in senior care. The financial investigation requires the presentation of various specified documents (birth certificate, proof of citizenship, death certificate of a spouse, rent receipts, telephone bills, etc.) as well as proof of your parent's financial status through savings and checking accounts, brokerage accounts, life insurance policies, etc., which will be scrutinized for the 30-month period prior to the application. Accounts not presented for review may be traced by Social Security numbers.

The rules governing Medicaid eligibility are straightforward, but vary significantly from one state to another and are always being revised. There are three typical situations, each with a rule of thumb: (1) If you have a single parent with limited savings (generally under $5000) and marginal monthly income, apply immediately since you are almost certainly eligible. (2) If you have a single parent with significant savings, you must "spend down" the assets to the Medicaid level, carefully documenting the reasons for the withdrawal of funds, or simply transfer excess funds and wait for 30 months to apply. (3) If you have two living parents, only one of which is in need of Medicaid assistance to pay for nursing home care while the other needs to retain assets and income in order to live in the community, a remaining provision of the Medicare Catastrophic Care Act, known as Anti-Spousal Impoverishment or Transfer of Assets, provides protection never permitted before. Under this new statute, each state can now decide what amount the couple can keep in savings (anywhere from $12,000 to $60,000) as well as what level of monthly income they may receive and still be eligible for Medicaid benefits. New York State, for instance, allows the most generous allotment ($60,000 in savings and $1500 per month in income) and other states are currently making decisions as to permissible amounts. Also, the family house is exempt, allowing the healthy (at-home) spouse to remain in the home without fear of eviction. All of this is brand new, varies enormously from state to state, and may not be finally determined in your area. Check with an experienced attorney, an agency dealing with senior citizens or the local Medicaid office, who can advise you as to local requirements. Don't make this decision on your own. To do so may be far more costly than any consultation fee.

There is one additional new Medicaid allowance, which may be enormously helpful in certain situations. In several states, an elderly parent requiring care in the home may be able to simply give away his assets and immediately qualify for something known as "Community Medicaid." This special program allows for the hiring of a home attendant, paid for in full by Medicaid, without the customary 30-month waiting period following the transfer of assets. Community Medicaid does not pay for nursing home care, which still requires the standard 30-month waiting period.

While Medicaid rules may sound complicated and confusing, they can be dealt with if you are not overwhelmed by the paperwork. It will be more than worth the effort in the end. If your parent requires care for a chronic disability, or even may require it in the future, find out if he qualifies and apply. Even if there is only the possibility of eligibility, do not hesitate to apply. Processing such applications takes time, and prolonged waiting to apply can leave you in an emergency situation without options. Furthermore, even if not eligible for full Medicaid because of income or savings slightly above the acceptable level, a senior may still be eligible for Supplemental Medicaid which provides benefits once a prescribed sum per month is spent for medical care.

Other Benefit Programs

In addition to the major assistance programs already described, there are a number of other benefit plans that may further "fill the gaps" in providing optimal care. Such programs vary so greatly from state to state that it is impossible to summarize them, but I include as a local example descriptions of options available in New York City. Check with your local senior citizen agency specializing in entitlement programs for the elderly for comparable programs in your area.

Supplemental Social Security (SSI). A federal program designed to assist those with low income and limited assets by providing monthly cash benefits for food, clothing, and shelter. The allotment varies according to income, and whether the recipient lives alone, with others, in another's household, or in a residential care facility. Apply to Social Security (800) 234-5772.

Food Stamps. Monthly coupons for the purchase of food in stores, for home-delivered meals, and even some restaurants. Amount depends on income and household size. All SSI recipients are automatically eligible. In an emergency, ask for "Expedited Food Stamps."

Home Energy Assistance Program (HEAP). Cash or credit to vendors to assist in the payment of heating and utilities bills. Available to low-income homeowners or renters. Emergency benefits available for repair of heating equipment, help with fuel bills and even temporary relocation.

IT 214—Circuit Breaker. Tax credit or cash to homeowners and renters who spend unusually high amounts of income on rent or property taxes.

Senior Citizen Rent Increase Exemption (SCRIE). Provides relief from obligations to absorb rent increases by reducing real estate taxes for the landlord. Applicants should live in rent-stabilized, rent-controlled apartments, hotel rooms, or Mitchell-Lama housing where the rent is more than a third their income. Contact your local Rent Administration Office.

Section 8 Housing Assistance Payments (HAP). A federal program which assists with rent payments in apartments or home. Under the provisions of this plan, the elderly need not pay more than 30 percent of their income for rent. Housing and Urban Development (HUD) will pay the difference.

Real Estate Tax Exemption for Senior Citizens. Based on income, this program can reduce property taxes on a sliding scale by up to 50 percent.

Emergency Assistance for Adults (EAA). A New York State program designed to meet the emergency needs of those eligible or receiving SSI benefits. Assists with specific "hardship situations" such as lost or stolen SSI checks; prevents eviction or shutting off utilities; provides funds for food. Contact local office of the Human Resource Administration (HRA).

Elderly Pharmaceutical Insurance Coverage (EPIC). A New York State plan which assists in the cost of prescription drugs for an annual premium. AARP has a similar private program which reduces drug expenses.

Protective Services for Adults (PSA). A program designed to protect those unable to manage their own lives safely by offering individual case management and supervision.

SECURING OPTIMAL MEDICAL CARE

Choosing a Physician

Since the elderly are naturally the major consumers of health care, like any intelligent consumer, you and your parents should be as well informed as possible so that optimal choices can be made. Since Medicare combined with any standard supplemental policy is basically an excellent insurance plan providing comprehensive coverage with no scarcity of physicians who will accept it as reimbursement, seniors are in a position to pick and choose, and should do so wisely. Foremost in personal health care planning is the choice of a primary physician, but you may be at something of a loss as to how to make that decision. Earlier in life, unless one has developed some significant or chronic illness, there is generally no pressing need for regular medical care, so that your parents may find themselves unprepared, without a comfortable established patient-physician relationship, just when such care may be required.

Generally, people will choose a physician by a referral from a satisfied friend or relative. While this method can be perfectly successful, it is too much of a hit-and-miss approach to a decision that may be of vital importance in the near future. Here are some strategies to increase the likelihood that you and your parents will make a satisfactory choice:

- Contact a large university, medical center, teaching hospital, or local medical society to request a referral, especially if your parents are in a new area. You are certain to get someone who is well qualified and well connected.
- Check to make sure that the prospective physician is well trained, certainly board certified in his area of specialty. Diplomas are likely to be displayed in the office, and there are directories of medical specialists with their credentials available in local libraries.
- Be sure that the physician has admitting privileges to a good local hospital which is well respected in the community. Future hospitalizations must be provided for, and your parents will need good care, not only by the primary physician, but by a facility that has high standards, good nursing care, and a well-trained house staff.
- If at all possible, select a physician who has specific training in geriatrics, so that you know in advance that he will be both knowledgeable and interested in treating the elderly.

There is now subspecialty certification in geriatric medicine, which is a definite plus. Mt. Sinai Hospital of New York has a national listing of local physicians specializing in geriatric care. For information write The Ritter Department of Geriatrics and Adult Development, Box 1070, Mt. Sinai Medical Center, One Gustave Levy Place, New York, NY

10029. Include a $5.00 check payable to the Department of Geriatrics.
- Consider the prospective physician's personal qualities. "Bedside manner" does not replace medical competence, but given equivalent training, I would rather have someone taking care of me who I liked.

On the first meeting, tell your parent to make sure that the doctor listens fully and is easy to talk to; seems careful and thorough in taking a history and evaluating the problem; seems to have a good grasp of the medical situation, and seems interested in your parent's life, his needs, and his personality; and will return phone calls and is generally accessible, especially in emergencies. In order for your parent and you to trust a doctor's judgment, you both need to feel comfortable in the relationship. If your parent expresses any doubt, go with him to make your own assessment.

None of these criteria should be particularly difficult to fulfill, and I strongly suggest that you not skimp on any of them. They are basic requirements for a good patient-doctor relationship, and it is very likely that at some point you and your parents will need a physician-friend whom you can trust in difficult times.

Medication and Your Parent:
Avoiding Unnecessary Complications and Side Effects

"I cure more patients by stopping their medication than I do by starting them," an experienced clinician is fond of saying. While somewhat overstated, such observations are supported by new studies attributing 10 to 15 percent of geriatric hospitalizations to adverse reactions to medication.

Despite these potential liabilities, medications can hardly be avoided in the elderly, especially since proper use prolongs life and effectively maintains patients who are suffering from a wide range of chronic illnesses. Because of the widespread administration of drugs (it is now estimated that 85 percent of the elderly use medication regularly, with more than 60 percent taking at least one drug daily and 25 percent using three or more), it is obviously advisable for concerned families to have a working knowledge of the basic rules in order to avoid confusion about side effects, drug interactions, and excessive use.

Why are the elderly more prone to adverse drug effects? The basic principle to keep in mind is that as a person ages, drugs remain in their body longer and tend to build up gradually in the system. As a result of this unpredictable elevated blood level, there is a danger of toxic effects.

There are seveeal reasons for this excessive medication buildup. To start with, in the elderly, both liver and kidney functions tend to be somewhat diminished, so drug excretion is slowed down.

Since the elderly have a much higher percentage of body fat than do younger people, fat-soluble medications which are absorbed and retained in the body's fatty tissues are retained longer resulting in accumulation and potential long-lasting delayed effects. Older people have less blood volume, so water-soluble drugs may become more concentrated in the blood stream. Due to diminished cardiac function (poor circulation), drugs get distributed more slowly and their effects are less predictable.

Also, the elderly have less serum albumin, which is necessary for binding drugs in the blood stream. Unbound drugs may cause increased toxicity. Finally, and perhaps most important, because the brain itself is often compromised as a result of diminishing brain cells, it will be far more sensitive to the levels of medication in the system. The all too frequent result is oversedation, confusion, and unstable blood pressure.

While all of this may sound complicated, the end result is evident. The combination of gradual medication buildup over time with an increased sensitivity to its effects, can often result in toxicity and dangerous side effects if these biological principles are not understood and taken into account.

While drug buildup is the most common difficulty, occasionally there is the opposite problem of poor absorption of medication into the system. This may occur when changes in the stomach lining and increased acidity, both common consequences of advanced age, slow absorption so that the patient never gets the medication in his system in the first place.

Besides unpredictable blood levels, other potential problems, specific to the elderly, have to be taken into account.

Elderly patients are likely to be taking more than one medication at one time and this can cause problems. One drug may simply cancel out the benefits of another or exaggerate the action of another so that a toxic result occurs (for example, alcohol enhances the effects of tranquilizers). Also, a drug administered to treat one health problem may adversely affect another (for example, some antidepressants aggravate glaucoma, while antihypertensives can cause depression). Older patients are far more likely to suffer from multiple health problems, all of which must be taken into account with each new prescription.

Poor patient compliance is very common in the elderly. In fact, they are notorious in this regard. They may misunderstand initial instructions; forget to take drugs on a regular schedule (easy to do with multiple daily doses); stop taking medication when they develop a transient side effect, when they feel better, or simply when the bottle is empty; or simply never bother filling a prescription because of the expense involved.

To avoid what are often completely unnecessary hazards, you should make sure that the following steps are always followed:

1. Be certain that the prescribing physician takes a complete and careful history, so that he is aware of all health problems and all medications taken, past and present, as well as all known allergies and adverse reactions. If there is any doubt of your parents' ability to give adequate information, accompany them to the evaluation and prepare a concise list of pertinent details.

2. A complete medical evaluation should be done prior to starting a new medication. Assessment should include a physical examination, blood pressure readings both sitting and standing, EKG (electrocardiogram), CBC (complete blood count), urinalysis, and a blood test for body chemistries and total protein with albumin and globulin ratios.

3. A proper diagnosis must be made. Medication should not be

prescribed haphazardly. Avoid physicians who say "Let's see if this helps" or who dispense samples given to them by drug salesmen.

4. You must understand the reason for the medication. The proper instructions for administration, and the potential side effects. Do not be afraid to ask questions or to call to clarify any areas of confusion.

5. Once you understand the instructions, follow them to the letter of the law. Noncompliance will obviously interfere with treatment and may be dangerous as well, especially if covered up. The dosing schedule must be understood and is best written down if there is any doubt. If your parent has difficulty swallowing pills or if there is any question of compliance, liquid medication can often be prescribed, which can be mixed in food or liquids to facilitate compliance. If any side effects develop, the treating physician must be immediately informed so that appropriate changes can be made.

6. Be sure your parent knows when medication should be taken: with meals, before sleep, and if alcohol should be avoided.

7. Never allow your parent to self-medicate or take a pill from a friend or relative because "it worked for them."

8. Follow-up is important. All elderly patients on medication must be checked regularly, particularly in the early stages when the proper dosage is still being established. Phone contact is important but not sufficient. Even if your parents are being chronically maintained on medication, regular checkups are essential to proper care.

9. Be aware that, whenever possible, multiple medications should be avoided.. Not infrequently, patients are found to be receiving more than one drug of the same type, creating unnecessary side effects and interactions.

10. Never be afraid to request a second opinion, especially if symptoms persist or there are any questions as to side effects or the medication's efficacy.

Finally, if you want more specific information, several recently published books are quite useful: *Worst Pills, Best Pills: The Older*

Adult's Guide to Avoid Drug-Induced Death or Illness (Public Citizen Health Research Group, 1988); *Prescription Drugs: An Indispensable Guide for People Over 50*, by Brian S. Katcher (Atheneum, 1988); *Drugs and the Elderly: Clinical, Social and Policy Perspectives*, by Dr. Helene L. Lipton and Dr. Philip R. Lee (Stanford University Press, 1988).

The reason for pointing out and stressing the potential dangers of medication is not to alarm you or your parents, or to suggest that medication is excessively hazardous or should be avoided. I do want to emphasize that the combination of educated awareness in the consumer with a personal physician whom you trust and who is knowledgeable, concerned, conscientious, and accessible, makes proper usage both safe and desirable. Advances in medication have not only prolonged life, but greatly improved its quality for many elderly people.

·4·

Looking at the Home Environment: When It's Time for a Change

As your parents age, you must anticipate that they will deteriorate mentally and physically and naturally may be less able to function independently. In order to flexibly meet their growing needs for assistance, it may be necessary to modify their living situations to some extent to protect them while providing the best quality of life possible.

Despite your good intentions, any intrusion into another person's lifestyle is likely to be resisted, no matter how glaringly necessary, so that it is always important to keep in mind the basic rule: You are not trying to take over their lives. Just the opposite. You are facilitating their independence by offering them realistic assistance so that they can *continue* to be in control of their lives for as long as possible.

Of course, parents have different personalities and differing reactions. When they are aware of their own limitations, they may be eager to accept suggestions and assistance. When they are not, or when they deny their increasing difficulties, as did Mrs. G.'s mother, it may take some discreet negotiating on your part to convince them to accept a realistic plan of action. Whatever their attitude, whenever feasible, they must be included in all discussions and decision making. You must find out what they want, see what they will accept, follow their lead, back off if a sensitive nerve is struck, but, at the same time, have a variety of realistic alternative plans in mind which you can modify in accordance with their wishes and needs.

If conflict does arise, a proper balance must be found between respect for their desires and a compassionate, yet firm guiding hand, so that a safe resolution can be achieved. If need be, a professional consultant or community agency, knowledgeable in such areas, may be called in to suggest and mediate alternatives.

Frequently, parents struggling to live on their own, yet floundering because of deficits, may be in more emotional distress than they or you realize. Often the best results can be achieved by making relatively minor adjustments which permit them to feel comfortable and secure so that they can function more effectively. Such changes in their environment are extremely varied and run the gamut from the most minimal assistance in their own home to total care in a long-term facility. It is a good idea to have a working knowledge of the almost endless options so that you can keep pace with your parents' ever changing needs.

MAKING HOME A BETTER PLACE

If your parents agree, it is always better for them to stay in their own home for as long as possible. Unnecessary changes are likely to be confusing and disorienting, and will subject them to unnecessary stress. If they are having difficulty caring for themselves, however, you may want to look into three areas which may provide substantial benefits: Creating a safe home environment, using community resources, and providing personal care in the home.

Creating a Safe Home Environment

If your parents are becoming physically frail or confused to any significant degree, their own home can become unmanageable or even dangerous if not modified to accommodate their changing needs. Every situation is different, and you must look at your own as carefully and objectively as possible so that solutions can be found. To help you anticipate potential difficulties before real problems arise, I suggest that you take a thoughtful look at the specific suggestions made in chapter 2 in the sections on "Memory Loss" and "Physical Frailty." Using those general ideas as a foundation, assess your parents' home and their ability to function within it, and come up with a potential list of modifications. Then, go over it with them. They may want to add or delete items that you wouldn't have thought of yourself. After all, they know best what areas present difficulties for them. In your discussion and final decisions, always remember that you are trying to balance safety with continued independence. A successful solution should prolong their ability to take care of themselves without endangering them.

Using Community Resources

Once you have secured a safe home environment which your parents can negotiate independently, they may still require assistance to maximize their ability to function and permit them a better quality of life, assistance that you cannot personally render. You'll find an impressive array of home assistance is currently available through community agencies, which administer both private and public programs.

So that you can make your own plans depending on your parents' particular needs, I offer a comprehensive list of possibilities. Payment for community programs naturally depends on your parents' resources, either out-of-pocket or through government assistance entitlement plans where they are eligible.

A community referral agency will help you get your bearings. It will provide you with basic information as to community resources, housing, entitlement programs, legal services, health care, health insurance, taxes, understanding various government forms, or even provide emergency crisis counseling. Furthermore, such an agency will refer you to appropriate specialized resources in situations where you require special assistance.

If you are not aware of any local community organization with such a service, your local state agency on aging (see Appendix A) can provide the needed information. There are a number of other organizations specifically designed to make such recommendations (see Appendix B).

In addition to such central resource agencies, you may want to obtain a regional resource directory which outlines local resources as well as giving special discounts to seniors (which parents find particularly attractive). Southwestern Bell publishes *The Silver Pages* (available by calling (800) 252-6060), and there are numerous such publications available locally.

Once you have an idea of what you need and how to go about getting it, here is a list of options that may be open to you:

- *Meals-on-Wheels.* This program may have different names in different areas, but generally consists of one hot meal delivered daily to your parents' door. Such a simply arranged device can keep your parent's diet nutritionally sound and enable them to stay in their own home.

- *Shopping and House-Cleaning Assistance.* In situations where daily care is not essential, but parents are no longer completely independent, weekly or twice weekly assistance with grocery shopping and cleaning is helpful in maintaining them at home with only minimal assistance. Local stores may also provide free or low-cost delivery services to seniors.

- *"Friendly Visitors."* These are local agencies, set up to visit the homebound elderly and provide regular contact in order to lessen isolation and loneliness, while also periodically assessing their condition and potential need for further assistance. Sometimes daily phone calls are arranged as well.

- *Escort Services.* Agencies may provide a personal attendant to escort parents to medical appointments, shopping, banking, and other errands.

- *Transportation Services.* Qualified seniors will be eligible for transportation through Medicaid to doctors' offices, hospitals and clinics. Many senior centers and church groups will also provide a free van to transport seniors to daily activities.

- *Senior Centers.* Senior centers are among the most important services available and provide daily programs which include low-cost hot lunches, social activities, guest speakers, outings, and other events. Such programs encourage socialization for lonely parents, and provide mental stimulation to keep them active and involved. Centers also arrange day trips and offer summer camp programs. Furthermore, they are well connected to agencies providing more extensive services should the need arise.

- *Continuing Education.* Programs especially designed for seniors are now offered at local colleges, libraries, and community centers. There are even home study programs available which can be explored by obtaining *A Guide to Independent Study Through Correspondence Instruction,* National University Continuing Education Association, Peterson's Book Order Department, P.O. Box 2123, Princeton, NJ 08540.

- *Volunteer Programs.* Seniors can enlist in a variety of volunteer programs. This can provide an enormous boost to a parent's self-esteem through productive activity. Programs exist at local hospitals, foundling homes, and charitable organizations. If your parent is interested, but unable to find a program, you can research possibilities through ACTIONS, a federal agency which oversees a variety of local programs. These include RSVP (Retired Senior Volunteer Program), FGP (Foster Grandparents Program), and SCP (Senior Companion Program).

  FGP and SCP are designed for marginal income seniors and actually provide a small stipend for a 20-hour work week, while RSVP is open to all and will assist volunteer placement in hospitals, schools, libraries, courts, daycare centers, boy scout and girl scout organizations, and other community service organizations. Free transportation and meals are generally provided.

  There is even a more sophisticated volunteer organization for retired executives called SCORE (Service Corps of Retired Executives) or ACE (Active Corps of Engineers) which counsel local businessmen.

- *Legal Services.* Community organizations will assist or refer seniors for help with IRS or other tax difficulties, tenant-landlord disputes, bills, government benefit programs, litigation, and crime victim programs. Legal aid organizations often have special advocacy programs for the elderly, as do local bar organizations and law schools.

- *Information About "Government Papers."* This is an important category. Senior citizens, especially those receiving government assistance of any kind, are often besieged by mail which is increasingly hard to decipher and frightening to many. I have seen several instances of major psychological decompensation precipitated by such confusing mail, which can put an elderly person into a tailspin believing that they are about to lose essential services on which they depend. Local community agencies are expert at explaining these matters and at solving difficulties as they arise.

- *Mental Health Services.* Local agencies, generally districted according to your parent's address, provide counseling for patients with psychiatric disorders, those in crisis, or simply when emotional distress is overwhelming. They can be located by calling your local hospital, through the Yellow Pages, or through a local social agency.

- *Services for the Handicapped.* Organizations that serve the blind are often particularly well organized to provide audio tapes and records of books and newspapers as well as other specialized services suited to your parent's needs. Other agencies specializing in the care of particular disabilities can be investigated.

- *Cancer Care.* These organizations are well known and are expert at dealing with the needs of terminally ill cancer patients, as well as the stress such situations place on their families.

- *Hospice.* A program designed to provide comprehensive care for terminally ill patients and their families during the last months of life. It is an alternative to a traditional medical approach in that it avoids life support systems and other heroic measures, and focuses on permitting a patient to die with dignity, free from pain, at home or in as comfortable surroundings as possible. The hospice program uses a multidisciplinary team of doctors, nurses, social workers, counselors, and clergy so that all of the needs of the dying patient and his family can be met.

Hospice programs are now well recognized and accepted, are paid for by Medicare and many other private insurance companies as long as the local program is certified, the physician and hospice director agree that death is inevitable within six months, and the patient signs a statement choosing hospice over traditional treatment (naturally the decision can be reversed at any time).

For specific information about local hospice organizations, contact your local hospital, any of the social service agencies in your community, or: The National Hospice Organization, 1901 North Fort Meyer Dr., Suite 901, Arlington, VA 22209 (703)243-5900. Also the *Consumer Guide to Hospice Care* is available from National Consumers League, 815 15th Street NW, Suite 516, Washington, DC 20005, (202)639-8140.

• *Day Hospitals.* There is a growing availability of day hospital programs for patients with a variety of medical problems, run by local hospitals, nursing homes, government agencies, and religious organizations. Such programs are particularly well suited to Alzheimer's patients, because increased stimulation through reality orientation, therapeutic activities, and socialization groups allow respite for overburdened families of these patients.

• *Self-Help Groups.* Don't leave yourself out of the picture. If you are feeling overwhelmed by the burden of responsibility, seek out any one of a growing number of support groups for adult children. These tend to be organized around specific problems like Alzheimer's disease, heart disease, or cancer. Such groups allow for sharing of information and provide needed emotional support. If you are unable to locate a local organization, contact *Children of Aging Parents*, 2761 Trenton Rd., Levittown, PA 19056, which keeps track of more than 200 support groups throughout the country.

•*Hire a Case Manager.* If you are unable to personally supervise your parents, you can still provide the help required by hiring a private geriatric care manager. These professionals can arrange and oversee comprehensive home care, whatever your parents' needs, and keep you regularly informed. You can locate an experienced worker through the National Association of Private Geriatric Care Managers, 1315 Talbott Tower, Dayton, OH 45402 (513) 222-2621.

Personal Care in the Home

However helpful community resources may be in mobilizing seniors, there may come a time when regular daily personal assistance is required if your parent is to be maintained at home. Home attendants can be extraordinarily useful, providing assistance with activities of daily living (grooming, washing, bathing, preparing meals, feeding, and ambulation), as well as performing cleaning services, shopping, and doing other household chores.

Selecting the appropriate person can be difficult, but it is worth putting in some hard thought and effort in advance since the right choice can save you endless difficulties in the long run. In making this decision, I can advise some basic guidelines:

Assess your parent's particular needs and determine what services will be required. Make no secret of what will be expected of a prospective employee. The trick to proper care is to strike a balance between protection and care on the one hand, and mobilization and fostering continued independence on the other. Obviously you want someone who will do what has to be done, but you do not want an excessively mothering caretaker who will infantilize your parent, a situation that will quickly lead to regression.

Choose someone whose personality suits your parent, not necessarily someone who is compatible with you. If your parent wants privacy and limited contact, do not be averse to hiring a more retiring person. On the other hand, avoid someone who'll ignore socialization altogether and foster further isolation.

The single most important attribute for a home attendant is reliability. No matter what other qualities he or she may possess, an attendant who does not show up regularly is of little value to this situation. Check this carefully through personal references. Pay no attention to what the person says or if you "get a good feeling." The only way to be sure is a prior work record. Often a particularly good sign is when a prospective attendant has a back-up person. Sometimes families of home attendants will "spell" each other.

Include your parents in the decision process and selection. They need not be present at every interview, but any final selection must meet with their approval. Such an agreement is important because allowing a stranger into the home is frequently enormously traumatic for an elderly person, no matter how desperate the need may be. Occasionally families may need to work with counselors to implement home care, especially when the suggestion is met with vigorous and unrealistic resistance. Such resistance can often be overcome when dealt with by a firm and united family. If family pressure is sustained and cohesive, your parent will generally come around and accept what simply has become an unavoidable reality. Such common early resistance is easy to understand since people are frequently unwilling to accept their own increasingly limited capabilities and would literally rather die than acknowledge their diminished ability to take care of themselves.

Home attendant arrangements should be modified to meet your parent's individual needs. Almost any arrangement can be worked out (be it three times per week, half a day, full day, split 12-hour shifts, or sleep-in). These possibilities all depend on what your parent needs and what he is willing to accept. Try to respect his desires within reasonable bounds, but overrule what is unrealistic.

Payment for these services is through your parent's savings if available (as you recall, Medicare does not not pay for home attendants except for a brief period following hospitalization, two weeks at most). Every regional area has agencies that specialize in providing home attendants, and they will interview, train, and provide replacements if attendants prove unreliable. Agencies can be useful in the selection process, but in the end, your personal choice is what counts. Do not rely on someone else's judgments.

You probably know your parents best. Agencies are relatively costly but are reliable as a rule. If expense is a priority, it is often cheaper to hire someone privately through advertisements in local newspapers or notices on church, synagogue, and community center bulletin boards. If the family is lucky enough to hire somebody through these channels, the fee is often half of what an agency fee would be, but be prepared for emergency replacements. Naturally agencies can always be called upon for temporary replacement personnel. For parents who do not have private funds, expenses for home attendant care can be paid for by public assistance through the Medicaid program. In such situations, the local designated government agency providing such services will evaluate the patient and decide on how many hours are necessary for home maintenance. This is highly variable, and is generally on the lean side.

When you have selected a home attendant, *be nice* to the home attendant, especially if your parent is not receptive to what he may see as an intrusion. Treat her with respect, be gracious and understanding and offer her emotional support in caring for your parent. Side with her when it is appropriate, but don't be afraid to discreetly point out what is required. Again strike a proper balance between understanding support and realistic expectations.

If your parents have an ongoing medical problem and you need to supplement the number of hours provided by your home attendant, you may also call upon visiting nurse services that provide in-home care. A wide range of ailments can be excellently managed at home, avoiding unnecessary and exhausting doctor's visits. Medicare covers visiting nurse services in full.

Home visits by physical and occupational therapists are now covered by Medicare too. Such services are essential for victims of stroke, amputees, and others in need who, with the help of these specialists, can continue to make progress with ambulation and independent functioning after they have left the acute hospital care setting.

Finally, more extensive home care programs are available, and these are likely to expand with recent increased government interest in maintaining seniors in the home environment. Such programs may provide a comprehensive range of services including social workers, nurses, physical therapists, and physicians who will assess patients at home. Many medical centers now provide this assistance for qualified patients, achieving a "nursing home without walls," sometimes with 24-hour attendant services as well as medical supervision at home.

WHEN HOME IS NO LONGER SAFE: WHERE CAN MOM AND DAD GO?

Even with the aid of extensive community resources and home attendant services, there may come a time when a change in the living environment can no longer be avoided: when your parents are too physically frail or mentally confused and require special care; too lonely and isolated, or frightened and depressed; or when, for a variety of reasons, alternatives just make more sense. As with other decisions, such a change should not be viewed in a negative way. It may very likely afford relief from emotional distress, while providing better care, companionship, and an all-around improved quality of life.

When alternative housing plans are being considered, your highest priority is to find a new situation that best suits your parents' needs. A change in living environment is always an enormous stress, and you want to be careful to select an appropriate new situation. Select a place which can best accommodate your parents' level of functioning. If you aim too high and expect too much of them, your parents are likely to be overwhelmed and nothing will be gained. If you aim low, they will quickly regress and sink to the level of those around them. In making your selection, I would make the following general suggestions:

• **Plan ahead.** Anticipate your parents' needs and become informed as to alternatives. Many options have long waiting lists and may have to be ruled out simply because you have delayed. If a future change is being considered seriously, don't wait, get in line early by putting your name on a variety of waiting lists. You can always cancel.

- Consult your parents about their wishes and allow them as much control as possible. Listen to them. Don't be surprised if they are more interested than you might expect in alternatives and have been waiting for you to help them.
- Take your parents to visit a variety of alternative living arrangements so that they can experience the situation firsthand. Such visits can go a long way in reducing exaggerated fears as well as providing a realistic basis for decision making.

In making the appropriate choice, a wide range of possibilities exists. They may not all be available depending on your locality, but check with state units on aging or social service agencies in your area for guidance (Appendices A and B). The following is a comprehensive review of the usual options, starting with choices which offer minimal assistance and progressing to those which provide maximum care.

Simplified Living Arrangements

Occasionally elderly parents feel overwhelmed because they are unable to deal with an excessively complex and unwieldy living arrangement, either because their home is too large or expensive to maintain, because it is too far from shopping areas and other essential services, because they require a car which they no longer feel comfortable driving, because they are too far from family and have no support network on which to rely. Such common situations, left uncorrected, can frequently cause extreme stress and lead to emotional and physical ills. In this case, solutions are relatively simple and only require locating a manageable home space, in realistic proximity to necessary facilities and with a supportive structure to assist them. If such an alternative is being considered, make certain that your parents are truly capable of functioning on their own. An unrealistic move is very stressful and frustrating, and even more so if it accomplishes nothing.

Retirement or Adult Communities

Such communities are becoming increasingly popular as the general population ages. Residents need to be entirely independent and generally do not require their adult children to be involved in this decision. Sometimes, however, isolated parents with little to occupy them and diminishing social networks need some encouragement to try out such living arrangements which often involve moving to another part of the country. Short-term rentals are often possible as a way to "try out" the experience before a commitment is made.

Adult communities are composed of a complex of condominium apartments or individual houses and often provide special services particularly attractive to seniors: good security, so that parents are no longer targets for crime; some assistance with home maintenance through community handymen and gardeners; convenience to shopping, banks, pharmacies, and doctors, sometimes with regularly scheduled transportation provided by community vans; opportunities for socializing with peers through community centers, social events, recreational facilities, club houses, and other activities—this may be a particular advantage for those who are recently widowed; support from peers when adult children are too busy, so that they can help each other with transportation, doctor's visits, crises, notifying family members when problems arise. If financially viable, residents can maintain their old homes so that they can have the best of both worlds, wintering in an adult community when weather conditions prohibit staying in their home community, while maintaining a home base for visits close to family and old friends.

Such communities are increasingly popular and exist nationwide, although some states like Florida and Arizona, as well as California, New Jersey, and Texas, have focused on their development so that they have become something of a statewide industry.

Congregate Housing, Senior Citizen Apartments, or Enriched Housing

These are alternative names for an important and useful concept in housing for the well elderly still capable of independent functioning. Seniors live on their own in an apartment with a kitchen. They have a choice of at least one communal meal. There is a social worker on the premises, a building manager to oversee and assist, sometimes housekeeping services, good maintenance services, access to medical care, senior citizen centers which may even be attached to the housing complex, group activities, and organized trips. Although elderly residents must be self-sufficient, able to make their own meals, and able to ambulate independently, they welcome the general structure and supportive services offered by these communities. Set up as condominiums or as rentals, they are frequently federally subsidized for those who meet financial requirements.

Such facilities are increasingly popular and often have long waiting lists (months or even years) before acceptance.

Continuous Care Communities (Life Care Facility)

These communities are a new concept in dealing with the problems of aging. They offer the entire range of potential living arrangements and are designed to take people from independent living to limited supportive care to skilled nursing, as the need arises. Generally residents must be in relatively good health on admission and able to function independently, but they are guaranteed appropriate care should they deteriorate. It is a sort of housing insurance policy, and the closest thing available to prepaid nursing home care. These facilities are not cheap and require both a large entry fee as well as a substantial monthly maintenance charge. Prices vary widely from area to area and from community to community.

Some seniors avoid such situations, resenting the idea of signing up for life when they are still well; others find them comforting and protective, knowing that they will be cared for no matter what happens.

Shared Group Homes

Some seniors who are still self-sufficient, yet no longer entirely comfortable living independently, will choose to live in a shared group home with 5 to 15 other elderly adults. Such communal living enables older people to take care of themselves as long as possible. Like an extended family, each person helps the others depending on their individual abilities. In this way, your parent can continue to be relatively independent, bolstering his pride and self-esteem, while living in a family setting that's safe, affordable, supportive, and social. The drawbacks are all those you might imagine in a situation where strangers are attempting to live together.

These homes are run by both nonprofit and for-profit organizations, but are relatively inexpensive and a good choice for those who find it attractive.

Roommates

A related alternative to shared group homes for parents who require some assistance or companionship is to find a roommate or to locate a room in someone else's home. Agencies now exist to match up senior roommates, to coordinate homeowners with available spare rooms with senior renters (home-sharing), to find separate apartments in homes (accessory apartments) or private cottages on a homeowner's property (ECHO, Elder Cottage Housing Opportunity). Write for ECHO Housing Fact Sheet, 1909 K Street, N.W., Washington, D.C., 20049 (AARP, 1983).

Moving In with You

As the initial case history of Mrs. G. and her mother suggested, one of the most complex and potentially problematic arrangements is taking an elderly parent into your home. Many criteria should be considered in this choice: personality issues, yours and your parents and how you interact; how your growing children and their needs fit into the overall picture; financial issues; health care; day-to-day household management; possibilities for parents' continued outside socialization; and so on. All such potential trouble spots should be appraised and openly discussed. The ease of the discussion process itself may be a good way to gauge the likelihood of the new living arrangement's success. If the issues are too "touchy" to discuss openly, consider another alternative. Such an arrangement will almost necessarily involve areas of conflict, and there must be a mechanism for dialogue, compromise, and decision making.

Obvious advantages exist for both sides. Parents are capable of providing increased financial resources, free child care, limited housekeeping, cooking, taking telephone messages, and other other small chores, while retaining all of their entitlement insurance benefits so that you will not be burdened by the cost of their care. In return, they should expect support when required, and companionship, while having the opportunity to be useful as part of an extended family working alliance.

Placement in a Long-Term Institutional Setting

Of all living alternatives, placement in a facility is without doubt the most sensitive, often provoking guilt through self-accusations of ingratitude, lack of devotion, and abandonment. I think that this decision is a particularly difficult one to make for several reasons: It is permanent; it openly acknowledges that you are no longer capable of caring for your parent yourself as they did for you; it removes any pretense of independence, and it foreshadows the death of the parent, precipitating the acknowledgment of mortality long before the actual death occurs. Some families recognize their own limitations and the extent of their capacity, realizing that when things reach a certain point, they can no longer cope. Others will unfortunately be tied by guilt and loyalty far beyond the point where such devotion makes any sense. Each person must decide for himself and understand that there are no perfect choices.

While long-term institutionalization is a painful issue, it is frequently essential to appropriate care for a debilitated parent. A child who says, "I'd never put my mother in a nursing home, no matter what!" is as ill-informed and inflexible as the one who arranges placement at the first sign of trouble. This is not a matter of absolutes. This is a decision, obviously more difficult than most, which should be made extremely carefully, with a full investigation of the alternative options, and with the focus clearly being that of providing the best care for the patient. And, if it is, it should be implemented like any other treatment. To do otherwise is simply not in the best interest of your parent.

When, then, should placement in a nursing facility be considered? I would consider the following factors as most compelling in making this decision:

- Your parent needs supervision 24 hours a day.
- Your parent needs supervision in the normal activities of daily living. That is, they can no longer dress, wash, bathe, or feed themselves without personal direction and assistance.
- Intense loneliness and the wish for contact with others which cannot be provided in a home setting has become overwhelming.
- Proper medical supervision, whether the medical problem be psychiatric or physical, cannot be provided at home. Your parent may need chronic monitoring of a medical condition, daily evaluation by physicians and nurses, regular administration of complex medical regimens, and periodic reassessments of his symptoms to modify treatment approaches.
- Parents with particular needs for specialized nursing supervision: parents confined to bed; those who need to be moved to avoid bedsores or who need dressing and treatment of bedsores; those with catheters who need catheter care; insulin-dependent diabetics who require daily injections and blood monitoring of diabetes; a parent who requires specialized physical therapy following stroke, accident, or other trauma. The list is lengthy, but includes any area of specialized care that cannot be provided for at home without a full staff of professionals around the clock.
- A home situation which simply does not work, despite everyone's best efforts, where your parent is deteriorating, life is untenable for everyone, and untold emotional damage is being done to all concerned.

- When your parent is so confused that he no longer knows where he is or recognizes those around him, and requires a massive effort for home maintenance beyond the abilities of his family caretakers.

If any of these situations exist, nursing home placement may not only be the only alternative, it may actually be a superior alternative. Placement in a nursing facility does not mean "putting your parent away," or at least it shouldn't. Family involvement remains essential for proper care, from the first step of choosing the facility, to maintaining an ongoing relationship with the staff, to regularly visiting your parent and involving him in family matters, festivities, and celebrations.

If institutionalization is being contemplated, a word to the wise: The application and placement procedures may be arduous and confusing. To avoid unnecessary confusion, it is often possible to retain the services of a professional experienced in placement procedures. Call upon a social worker, physician, or an attorney who specializes in this area. Financial considerations have already been explored in chapter 3 in the section on "Financial Planning."

Nursing institutions are generally geared to the patient's level of functioning and requirement for care. Every state uses a different system and you should become acquainted with yours. Generally there is some form of scoring system by which the patient's capacity to function is measured, so that the correct level of care can be arrived at prior to placement in a facility. These evaluations are generally filled out by qualified doctors or nurses and are used by the facility when they review your application.

In choosing the proper setting, the family must visit the institution and interview and, in turn, be interviewed by the staff. One should never be intimidated! All involved family members should look around, check the dining room and the recreation areas; talk with the staff; observe how patients are treated; inspect for cleanliness; inquire about the grounds, visiting hours, day trips, and so on. You should check with other families who have parents there, or, when available, use a local rating guide which often exists about the quality of care at the institution being considered. Local doctors can be consulted for recommendations. Additional information can be requested from state agencies responsible for supervising nursing home care (see Appendix C). Families must be thorough, but should never be obnoxious or excessively demanding. After all, the best care can hardly be rendered if the staff is angry or afraid. Basically, family members must strike a balance between investigating the facility and "selling" your parent and yourself to the institution. If your parent is institutionalized, from then on you and the nursing home are in it together, and a working alliance must be struck if optimum care is to be rendered.

Once a parent is placed in an institution at the appropriate level of care, you will certainly continue to be involved and hopefully gear your visits to what is best for your parent and what makes sense to you. Spending entire days with someone who no longer recognizes you is senseless. You must gradually find what is right for you and your parent. If one parent is institutionalized and the other remains at home, allow the at-home parent to work out visiting arrangements on his own. Don't interfere unless a bad situation develops. The institution will often be very helpful during this separation period, and assist in weaning the spouse from the feelings of being obliged to visit as often as possible.

Nursing homes have had a bad press. Are they really so bad? Does one need to be so careful? My experience is quite the contrary. Nursing homes are certainly among the most regulated industries in the United States. They are monitored constantly by state inspecting agencies and have to render a high level of care to exacting standards in order to stay in existence. The unexpected truth is that many patients actually do far better in facilities where they can function with the proper care, be surrounded by others, be involved in therapeutic activities and physical therapy, than they had previously done at home. What for many is the ultimate fear can sometimes be a vast improvement in the quality of life for a parent.

While individual states have significantly different arrangements for providing long-term care, there are generally three levels of custodial care offered.

Homes for Adults, Senior Citizen Hotels, "Old-Age Homes"

These are for the most functionally independent aged who are ambulatory, capable of finding the dining room and recreational areas, and who do not need daily medical and nursing assistance. They are by far the least expensive because they offer the least professional staff and supervision. They do provide a room (shared or private); full housekeeping services; communal meals; supervision of medication if required; easy access to physicians, nurses, laboratory tests, X rays, physical and occupational therapists (while such professionals are not on the premises daily, they can be called in immediately whenever the need arises and are often available in scheduled on-site medical clinics); therapeutic activities; socialization opportunities (group trips and entertainment); supervision. Administrators and social workers keep a careful eye on residents and notify families immediately should problems arise.

Health Care Centers, Health-Related Facilities

This middle range of supervision is not always available. Patients admitted to such facilities must have substantial illness requiring medical care, but generally must be either ambulatory or self-mobile in a wheelchair, and mentally alert enough to find their way about with only minimal guidance.

Such institutions have all of the services provided by the adult homes plus LPNs and supervising RNs are on duty at all times and physicians are on the premises daily to provide ongoing health care.

A medical chart is maintained on every resident. Staff carefully supervise and record all medication and are authorized to give injections and perform surgical dressings. Personnel includes physical therapists, occupational therapists, and activity therapists. These facilities will provide access to hospital admission should the need arise. Finally, residents can expect some assistance with activities of daily living.

Skilled Nursing Homes

Nursing homes are for the most incapacitated elderly, who require extensive care. They offer all the services already listed plus full care of nonambulatory bed or chairfast patients. All activities of daily living are attended to, including toileting and feeding as needed. The ratio of medical staff per patient is higher and this staff is trained to provide intravenous and oxygen therapies, maintenance of urinary catheters as well as treatment of bedsores.

There are daily visits by a physician, if required, to supervise care and adjust medication regimens.

By presenting the full range of alternatives, I hope I have made the point that your options are far from limited. A working knowledge of the available possibilities should allow you to assist your parent to whatever degree is required and in as flexible a manner as you like. At every point, you and your parent have a variety of choices which can be modified again as the situation continues to change.

Always take your parents needs and wishes into account, including what may be their very reasonable desire not to overburden you with their care. If this is their wish, let them be parents still and allow them to continue to take care of you in this way.

Part II

Caring for Parents with Psychiatric Illness

·5·

When Your Parent Suffers from Mental Illness: Facing Facts

U p until her husband's unexpected and sudden death, eighty-one-year-old Sarah G. had been a busy "organization lady," active in a number of charitable societies to which she dedicated her not inconsiderable energies. Never content to sit still, and disdainful of those who did, she was continuously energetic, some even said driven. No one expected her to ever stop or even slow down, but her husband's unexpected death abruptly changed all of that.

At first, everyone agreed that she was brave, making the funeral arrangements in her usual style, even writing personal notes thanking friends for their condolences. Suddenly, to everyone's surprise, that formidable presence seemed to almost evaporate overnight. She gave up her clubs and committees, irritably claiming that "she had worked hard enough for others," seemed preoccupied, self-absorbed, and unusually distant. Friends began to notice that she appeared vague, even forgetful at times, certainly uninterested in them, and they felt hurt and confused. Her daughter, with whom she was very close, was aware of the change, but thought it reasonable given the circumstances: "They were married for forty-five years. She will adjust . . . give her time. She'll soon be her old self." But she didn't adjust. In fact, she became more and more distant, distracted, not even particularly concerned with her grandchildren on whom she had doted.

Withdrawing more and more, she neglected her usually fastidious appearance, picked at her food, and slept fitfully. When she took to her bed, feeling too weak to get through an entire day, friends became alarmed and suggested that she consult a doctor, perhaps even a psychiatrist. She impatiently shooed them away, and her daughter shielded her from their good intentions. No one gave much credence to the idea that she would soon be back to her old self, but they now conceded that she was old and not too much could be expected.

When she began to stay in bed all day, stopped eating for all practical purposes and lost more than thirty pounds, her neighbor demanded that a psychiatrist be called in, but again her daughter resisted: "There's never been mental illness in our family."

When she became confused, mixing up day and night, and called out loud for her husband, her daughter said: "She loved him so. She can't go on without him. Perhaps it's better this way."

And finally, when she developed phlebitis and a blood clot from her leg traveled to her lung as a consequence of her remaining in bed for months, she was brought to the hospital. Silent and staring blankly into space, her withdrawal now complete, an underlying emotional problem was suspected. A psychiatrist was called but immediately dismissed by her outraged family, incensed by the unrequested intrusion. After all, this was a serious medical situation. No time for any psychiatric mumbo jumbo.

Two months later she died of "natural causes," her reputation intact. Of a treatable illness. Of depression.

For whatever reason, perhaps out of some universal private fear, no society has ever been really comfortable with mental illness. Despite widespread public education and information campaigns, psychiatric disturbance is still regularly ignored, misunderstood, and covered up. When it occurs, as it often does in an elderly parent, it is even more likely to be hidden or dismissed by embarrassed and frightened families.

Unfortunately, all too often a family's reluctance to face such difficult issues regarding their parents is reinforced by misinformed professionals who uninterestedly mislabel treatable psychiatric disorders as "old age" or "senility." As a result, the true prevalence of psychiatric illness in the elderly is difficult to ascertain. Numerous field studies have come up with widely differing statistics. While some indicate numbers as low as 2 percent, most studies approximate that 20 to 25 percent of the aged are in need of some psychiatric health services. The institutionalized elderly have been found to require psychiatric intervention in even greater numbers, so that 40 percent of nursing home residents are seen by a psychiatrist at some time during their stay. Despite the large number of older patients in need, studies of outpatient psychiatric hospital clinics reveal that only 2 percent of patients served were over age sixty-five, while community mental health centers, private psychiatrists and day hospitals each estimate that only 4 percent of their patients are elderly. Such statistics confirm the obvious. The need is tremendous; the attention limited.

What then accounts for this personal and public avoidance of so common and pressing a problem? In studies of public attitudes, it has been found that people generally avoid subjects that make them uncomfortable. Denial may not be the healthiest attitude, but it works, at least temporarily. Don't think about it and you won't catch it. Ignore it, and it will go away by itself. Illogical as it is, this psychological mechanism is not only common, but bolstered by a variety of other ideas and feelings that support the general avoidance of psychiatric help for the elderly. There seems to be a consensus that aging and mental illness are not only unpleasant, but frightening, overwhelming, disgusting, embarrassing, uninteresting, and hopeless in any case. If this is not enough, another idea in common circulation is that since resources are limited so that not everyone can be helped, it is therefore more valuable to treat younger patients who have a long life in front of them. False stereotypes of old age confuse the issue and create a myth of general hopelessness about any intervention in this age group. Common notions about the aged are that old people are all alike—sick, boring, nasty, self-absorbed; that they will all become senile eventually and enter a second childhood; that they are incapable of change; that they are all depressed because they are obsessed with thoughts about physical illness and death; and they will all wind up in a nursing home in the end. This faulty thinking is not only demeaning to the elderly, but demoralizing to those who care for them. It causes concerned families to become frustrated and even to give up, while it encourages government agencies to abandon social programs, a measure for which they are already primed in these days of budget deficits and cost consciousness.

Psychiatric illness in the aged is a true medical and social problem which is responsive to treatment when it is diagnosed and understood correctly. Like all real problems, avoiding it does not make it go away; it only brews quietly, until it explodes. Then it is called an emergency, by which time solutions may be limited, too late, and unnecessarily expensive in human and financial terms.

When an elderly parent falls ill of a mental disorder, it may be confusing and overwhelming for him, his family, and those who may be caring for him. Too often, people mix up normal aging, senility, and pure psychiatric illness, and are unable to tell the difference. Because it is so confusing, people may simply decide that the aging person is failing, give up on any potential treatment, and doom any positive intervention.

THE FIRST STEP: A GOOD PSYCHIATRIC ASSESSMENT

In order to understand any problem, it is obviously necessary to perform a complete and comprehensive assessment. A good psychiatric assessment is basically a method of looking at a problem by taking everything into account, organizing that information so that a decision can be made about what is wrong, and, finally, arriving at potential solutions and treatment methods.

The process of assessing psychiatric illness in the elderly tends to be more complex than making a similar diagnosis in a younger patient, for exactly the same reason that assessing any problem in the geriatric population is more difficult. As in the case of Mrs. G. and her mother, described in some detail in the Introduction, any fully comprehensive geriatric assessment seldom involves a single problem, but generally requires the unraveling of a complex interplay between physical, social, and emotional problems, all of which are affecting an aging person. A complete psychiatric assessment is no different and, if anything, depends even more heavily on keeping these interacting factors in mind. If this is not done, and the situation only partially understood, endless time and energy may be expended in the wrong direction.

For instance, not infrequently, a purely medical problem may masquerade as a psychiatric illness. The sudden onset of confusion and paranoia, for example, can be the result of a wide range of physical disorders which temporarily cloud thinking, of a newly prescribed medication with unexpected side effects, or simply of a change in environment which can be enormously disorienting for an elderly person. Such acute confusion will resolve only if the underlying cause is identified and reversed without any psychiatric intervention.

Even more frequently, psychiatric illness may appear to be a medical disorder. I have seen countless patients and their families make endless rounds of general practitioners with referrals to specialists for expensive and sophisticated testing procedures in a search for illnesses which are entirely psychological in origin. Depression, in particular, may present itself as vague abdominal complaints, complicated by the inability to eat and then with weight loss. Such symptoms commonly lead to an extensive series of GI tests, with upper and lower GI series, colonoscopies and endoscopies, all of which prove to be negative and eventually lead to the discreet suggestion, "Perhaps you should consider seeing a psychiatrist." Gastroenterologists are far from alone in assessing psychiatrically ill patients. Neurologists see endless patients with headaches, tingling, and weakness; orthopedists treat psychogenic back pain; radiologists do countless studies for which no medical diagnosis can ever be made; and every specialist in medicine is well aware that a large percentage of their practices are filled with patients seeking relief of physical symptoms, for which there are no physical bases.

Purely social problems can also be misinterpreted as psychiatric illness. An isolated, lonely aged person will frequently feel depressed, but no amount of psychotherapy or sophisticated psychotropic medication will alleviate his pain unless his situation is changed. In such a case, arranging for a home attendant to provide daily companionship, will be a far greater benefit than the latest antidepressant medication. Similarly, providing transportation to the nearest senior citizen center so that a previously homebound senior gets out and becomes involved with other people, obviously offers more help than talking to a patient about how he feels about his isolation.

Intolerable family situations, hidden out of embarrassment, may also be at the root of what appears to be an individual mental problem. Mrs. W.'s history provides a clearcut example:

> Mrs. W., a dignified elderly lady, was brought to see me because of a chronic profound depression. Years of psychotherapy, medication, hospitalization, and even electricshock treatment, had provided only brief periods of relief, with rapid return of her severe depressive symptoms. Self-contained and proud, she had simply never admitted to anyone the real reason for her unhappiness. Years before she had lent her favorite son a good deal of money, money which represented a substantial portion of her savings, and which he had invested badly. A successful physician himself, he was easily able to honor his responsibility by paying her the same interest rate that she would have received if the money was still in the bank, and he did so without difficulty. What he never understood, and what she could not bring herself to say, was that she was no longer in control of her own money and she now felt like an aged pensioner, waiting for her monthly stipend, instead of being the proud, independent, and rather controlling dowager that she had been before. No medication could ever relieve her outrage at her diminished social position and her fury at her son.

Sometimes the situation is reversed. What initially appears to be a social or environmental problem may actually be psychiatric in origin.

A penniless elderly gentleman in his mid-eighties was about
to be evicted from his apartment for nonpayment of rent.
Protective Services for Adults, a city agency, had been called
in to protect this unfortunate man from a nasty and unfeeling
landlord, widely known as a slumlord, who was busily preparing for court proceedings. The man in question was a sad but
resigned man who likened his present experience to his previous ordeals at the hands of the Nazis who had taken his
possessions once before and killed his wife and family. In
discussing with me what he felt to be his realistic plight, he
spoke with great passion about his landlord's links to an
unspecified "German organization," and how surveillance de-
tectors had been placed in his walls to broadcast his thoughts
to a central intelligence office. Taking me into his confidence,
he showed me a secret fund which was to be used for "emergency escape," $34,000 in cash hidden throughout his dirty,
fourth-floor walkup apartment.

What had seemed at first to be an everyday landlord-tenant
dispute, with disregard for the rights of the elderly, was actually a
simple case of a severe paranoid disorder, treatable with medication, and with sufficient funds available for his continued
maintenance.

In general, situations are usually not as "neat" as those described
above. More often, what is found in the course of a complete
psychiatric assessment is a combination of factors, all of which
must be evaluated and weighed, so that an intelligent decision can
be made and the best treatment plan arrived at. Such a treatment
plan will necessarily involve the recognition and resolution, if
possible, of each and every contributing factor involved. A scenario
more common than the cases described might be that of an elderly
parent who has become depressed, who lives alone and has limited
financial resources, whose spouse has died, and whose friends have
moved away, who has some degree of memory loss and periods of
disorientation, and whose atherosclerotic heart disease, for which
he takes multiple medications, is supervised in a uninterested
fashion in a busy city hospital by a resident who changes every six

months. This is the more typical situation: a complex combination of psychiatric (depression), medical (atherosclerotic heart disease with multiple medications), and social problems (alone, and in financial distress), all of which affect an aging person (memory loss and disorientation) who is increasingly unable to cope. Difficult and even overwhelming as it may seem, when each and every factor is taken into account and evaluated, progress can be made in making the patient more comfortable, and improving the quality of his life. If it is handled sloppily or, more frequently, neglected altogether, the patient will deteriorate and become overwhelmed by the increasing burden of his difficulties in all areas, over which he has less and less control.

What constitutes a complete psychiatric assessment of an elderly parent? It starts with a careful history, one that takes all areas of concern into account. Especially in the case of an elderly parent who may not be capable of giving all details, the history requires consultation with available family members and caretakers (home attendants, social workers, other physicians, even neighbors). If possible, the optimum situation would be to conduct such an initial assessment in the patient's home, where viewing the entire living situation can provide a more complete picture.

The history must include an investigation into the patient's presenting problem (what the symptoms are, how long they have lasted, precipitating factors when understood); his previous psychiatric and medical history; prior hospitalizations; medications taken currently and in the past (whether with success or not); present living arrangements; social and financial situation; his interests and activities; details of his daily functioning; his ability to perform the usual activities of daily life; all done with an objective and appraising attitude as to what is said and what is left unsaid.

Such an evaluation should be carried out by an experienced investigator who provides an empathetic ear in a private confidential atmosphere. All interviews should best be conducted when your parent is not tired or frightened, with proper attention given to hearing deficits and communication difficulties, or other physical impairments that may interfere with a fair evaluation. Almost always, you must apprise your parent of the nature of the interview, and never keep him in the dark out of some fear of embarrassing or angering him. Further consultation with family members or outside caretakers can provide additional information and frequently suggest additional areas for exploration, as well as potential solutions to problems which may have been overlooked.

Once the history is taken, a mental status examination is performed. This is the psychiatric equivalent of an internist's physical examination. Such an examination is not mysterious, but is simply a sophisticated way of observing and evaluating the patient's mental state so that it can be correlated with the history, to confirm or negate information acquired, by comparing it first hand with the patient himself.

An experienced observer will note the following:

* *General appearance and behavior.* Does he look his age? Is the person neat and cared for, or unkempt? What is his activity level? Is it normal, overactive, or slowed down? Can he walk unassisted, or does he require assistance?
* *Thought organization.* Can he get his ideas across in an organized way? Or is he disorganized, rambling, or incoherent?
* *Thought content.* Is it normal or are there delusional ideas, paranoia, hallucinations? Is he suicidal, homicidal? Is he sexually preoccupied?
* *Affect.* What is his emotional expression? Depressed, euphoric, appropriate or inappropriate to the situation?
* *Sensorium.* Is he oriented? Is his intellectual functioning appropriate for his age? Is his memory, recent and remote, intact or impaired? How is his attention span and ability to concentrate?
* *Insight and judgment.* Is the patient aware of his situation? Does he have realistic ideas about assistance and solutions?

The above questions are only examples of what an observer is attempting to determine during a mental status exam. Obviously, one keeps an open mind and pursues any question until an answer is established with some degree of certainty.

Whenever a psychiatric evaluation of an elderly parent is made, a comprehensive physical examination must also be done. This is not optional and cannot be put off until a more convenient time. Failure to arrange a full physical examination with appropriate lab tests is inexcusable and may result in overlooking an easily reversible medical condition.

Such an exam should not be difficult to arrange and can be successfully performed by a private physician, hopefully one with an interest in geriatric medicine, or at an outpatient clinic of a good local hospital. A complete physical exam will involve a full medical history, present and past, reports from previous treating physicians and, again, evaluation of medications taken as well as dosages. A complete physical should be performed including neurological, rectal, and pelvic examinations. Full laboratory testing should be done, particularly if any element of confusion is present, and a diagnosis of dementia is being entertained. Appropriate laboratory examinations include:

- CBC (complete blood count)
- Blood chemistries (blood-urea nitrogen [BUN], electrolytes: sodium, potassium, chloride, carbon dioxide, phosphorus, calcium, magnesium)
- Liver function tests
- Thyroid function tests (T3, T4)
- Fasting blood sugar levels
- Cholesterol and triglycerides levels
- Vitamin levels (B_{12} and folate)
- Serology (venereal disease testing)
- Basic x-ray examinations (chest x-ray; when appropriate skull films)
- Urinalysis
- Electrocardiogram
- Stool guaiac (testing for occult blood in stool)
- Special neurologic testing: CAT scan (computerized axial tomography, serial pictures of the brain by a combination of x-rays and computer techniques which give a picture of the

brain), EEG (electroencephalogram to measure the electrical activity of the brain, showing evidence of focal or diffuse lesions)
- Sensory examinations (visual exam, audiology testing)

A comprehensive and intelligent psychiatric assessment can only be considered complete when all of the discussed evaluations have been completed. Only then can all of the potentially relevant data be extracted, compared, and utilized in determining all areas of difficulty, so that a reasonable solution can be achieved. While this may seem unnecessarily cumbersome and time consuming, it can actually be carried out in a relatively short span of time with very little demand placed on your parent. It is a question only of finding the right place, where the staff and facilities are capable of obtaining, investigating, and organizing the information.

·6·

Depression

A DEPRESSED PARENT: MRS. K.

When I first met Mrs. K., she was being carried, unceremoniously, into my office by her son, a no-nonsense dentist, who had clearly had more than enough of his mother's refusal to accept psychiatric help. Her husband, confused and overwhelmed by his wife's deterioration, trailed along behind, meekly and apologetically.

As her son detailed her illness, Mrs. K. stared ahead, her face set in a blank, frozen, dejected scowl, only occasionally displaying a flicker of interest in the proceedings. Her apathetic withdrawal stood in stark contrast to her usual personality which kinder people would describe as strong willed, while others would more honestly characterize as so domineering as to completely control her passive and frightened husband, whose small contracting business she ran with fierce determination.

Despite her reputation for toughness, she had long suffered from unaccountable periods of feeling "blue," as had her mother before her, but none of these had ever remotely prepared her family for her present state. Six months before, her husband had injured himself on the job and, uncharacteristically, had unilaterally announced his retirement. His wife did not take him seriously at first, expecting that she would get him back to work after a legitimate period of recuperation. For the first time, however, despite a valiant attempt to restore her previously unchallenged authority, she failed. He was adamant. He was retiring and they would move to Florida.

At first, although she seemed a bit preoccupied, Mrs. K. continued as if nothing of substance had changed, attending to household duties with the same single-minded dedication and drive that had characterized her business activities in the past. But her activities didn't seem to involve her in the same way, and within a month or two she began to lose interest and slow down.

At first her family was a bit relieved at what seemed to be relaxation of her usual critical and driving presence; then they became disquieted because she "seemed different, no longer herself." She slowed her pace even further, finding it somehow difficult to keep up, and lost interest in things. When she started to take daily afternoon naps, everyone began to become alarmed. Not only her family noticed the difference. She was unusually abrupt with friends, discouraged their phone calls, and declined social invitations. She soon abandoned any pretense of cooking or cleaning.

"Resting" became a way of life, and the more she rested, the less energy she seemed to have. Her husband persuaded her to visit her internist, a request with which she reluctantly and disinterestedly complied. A full battery of tests revealed nothing and she was referred for a psychiatric consultation which she scornfully refused.

She began to brood, blaming herself for past wrongs and even for the very willfulness she had cheerfully enjoyed before. She no longer ate regularly and began to lose weight. Her husband feared cancer, but their son pointed out that she was "eating like a bird" and not likely to sustain herself. She woke early after a fitful sleep, pacing the floor at 3 A.M., and was unable to return to bed. She no longer dressed and grew careless about her personal hygiene. When her grandchildren visited, she all but ignored them. They became frightened as she retreated further into her own world.

Her face became expressionless except for a worried look, and she no longer responded in more than monosyllables.

While Mrs. K.'s deterioration was particularly drastic and dramatic, it is hardly an unusual story. In fact, depression has been called "the common cold" of geriatric psychiatry. It is by far the most frequently encountered psychiatric illness in older people, and affects a sizable portion of the population, disrupting the lives of patients and their families if not detected and promptly treated. Fortunately, despite its prevalence, depression is also the most treatable and reversible of serious psychiatric disorders.

WHY IS DEPRESSION SO COMMON IN THE ELDERLY?

The likelihood that an elderly parent will become seriously depressed in later life increases directly with longevity. Even more impressive and ominous is that the incidence of suicide increases in a similar pattern. There is no question about it. The longer you live, the greater the risk of depression and suicide. While researchers have not yet demonstrated why this is the case, both those who have a purely psychological approach, and those who offer a biochemical theory, have substantial data to back up the markedly increased incidence of depression with advancing age.

Complex psychological theories for depression have been expounded since Freud, but basically boil down to two basic ideas: Either depression is a reaction to the loss of an important love relationship, or a consequence of diminished self-esteem. It is easy to realize that the aged are especially vulnerable to both of these issues. At no time in one's life is a person so likely to be struck, and repeatedly so, by the loss of people close to oneself: a spouse, relatives, friends. Death is a regular part of life. It cannot be denied or put off in quite the same way that it can when one is young and death seems very far away. Loss and loneliness are facts of life that are simply inescapable.

While loss may be an almost unavoidable event, difficulties in maintaining one's self-esteem may also present a serious problem. Everyone needs something about which to feel important and special, and the elderly may often lose whatever sustained their egos throughout much of their adult life: workers who retire from responsible positions, parents whose children no longer need them, athletes who were proud of their bodies, those who were vain about their looks and sexual attractiveness, and especially those whose bodies are ravaged by chronic and debilitating illness who can no longer even pride themselves on their independence and ability to function physically. All of these changes, and many more, may precipitate an intolerable loss of self-esteem. Some find new answers, developing new ways of maintaining their self-respect, remaining vigorous, self-assured, and productive. Others are not flexible enough to change, and find themselves feeling useless, outmoded, weak, and worthless. One might suspect that Mrs. K.'s self-esteem was particularly tied to her ability to dominate and control those around her. When she was thwarted, her ego plummeted, making her susceptible to depression.

Psychologically speaking, advancing age is a difficult villain to confront, and those who find themselves overwhelmed may be particularly prone to depression precipitated by their inability to cope.

While psychological stress may lead to depression, there is also substantial evidence that biochemical changes that occur in the brain in later life may also make the elderly individual more vulnerable to depression. The suggestion has been made that, as the central nervous system ages, the supply of certain brain chemicals (specifically, tyrosine-hydroxylase and tryptophan-hydroxylase, resulting in diminished monoamines), which are responsible for the regulation of mood, decreases. In a general way, these chemicals are involved in the transmission of brain impulses, and when they are diminished, the brain literally slows down. This produces the general slowing down which manifests as depression, with the lack of energy, apathy, and loss of interest in life seen so classically in the case of Mrs. K.

A third, and far from uncommon precipitant of depression in the elderly, is the use of medication which may inadvertently trigger a depressive reaction as an unsuspected side effect. A variety of drugs are notorious offenders in this regard, including antihypertensives (Aldomet and reserpine in particular), antiparkinsonian medications, steroids (which may also produce psychosis), hormones, antitubercular drugs, potassium-depleting diuretics, and, most frequently, the chronic abuse of minor tranquilizers such as Valium and sleeping pills. Similarly, such untreated medical illnesses as hypothyroidism may also be accompanied by severe depressive symptoms.

In conclusion, therefore, it is probably safe to say that the elderly are particularly prone to developing depressive episodes through a combination of psychological, social, genetic, and biochemical factors. Most likely, not one, but a combination of these interrelating factors produces the end state of depression as we often see it.

WHAT IS DEPRESSION?

Depression is one of the most misused and misunderstood terms in psychiatric jargon.

Unfortunately, "depression" has been carelessly used by professionals as well as the lay public in several different ways, and it is important to know the proper distinctions if you are to understand what they are talking about.

Depression is commonly used to describe the normal human emotion of intense sadness. There is nothing pathological about feeling depressed from time to time; indeed, it would be far more disturbing to find someone who was always happy.

Depression is also used to describe a longer lasting reaction to an unhappy event. Such a depression is relatively shortlived, and if the person resolves his sorrow, it is naturally perfectly reasonable. Mourning is an example of this, a normal, self-limited event, certainly common to the elderly. Sometimes, however, what begins as a normal reaction to a tragic event may go in an extended fashion and seems to take on a life of its own, so that the initial precipitating event may no longer seem appropriate to the exaggerated and prolonged reaction. Such a situation is termed a reactive depression and suggests some unconscious overreaction to the original event which may not be obvious to an outside observer or even to the patient himself. Such depression may respond very nicely to psychotherapy where the true underlying cause is understood and revealed.

Depression also may be used to describe the mood of a person with a very common personality type; that is, a chronically depressed person, someone who is never happy, who cannot be pleased, who always looks on the dark side of everything, and whose entire life seems to exist under the cloud of unhappiness.

Finally, depression can refer to a serious illness, like Mrs. K.'s, a tormenting, devastating illness that takes over a person's life, interferes massively with its functioning, and at its worst can be life-threatening by increasing the risk of suicide. This form of depression has been called many things: endogenous depression, clinical depression, primary affective disorder (an attempt to take even the word depression out of the diagnosis so as not to confuse it with the more benign emotional states described before), unipolar depression, bipolar depression (if there are manic or "up" periods as well as "down" periods), and, most recently, as major depression. Whatever the name, we are talking about a real illness with physiological components. It can be readily treated, but it has a tendency to relapse, requiring further treatment in the future. And it does run in families.

How, then, are we to separate this form of major depression from the less serious, depressive states? Sometimes this is not evident at the start, and people may dismiss the early symptoms by attributing them to "old age" or "normal slowing down." While such early lack of recognition is understandable, once the full-blown picture develops, it should not be hard to make the diagnosis. A major depression, like any other medical illness, has a natural history. That is, it looks the same in different patients, and follows an expected course which can be clearly and repeatedly identified.

The most important symptom of depression is not necessarily the intensity of the sadness associated with it. In fact, some people with severe depression do not even feel "depressed" at all. The most constant symptom is actually a marked change in a person's ability to function, accompanied by an intense lack of energy, or a lack of interest in functioning at all. A depressed person may describe it differently: "I just don't feel like myself any more." Or, "I don't care." "I can't get out of bed in the morning." "It's not important anyway." But these are all just variations on the same theme. These people feel devoid of energy and interest. What is more, they feel that they will never be better and that the situation is hopeless.

This basic symptom, sometimes called anergy (no energy), is almost always accompanied by a group of other important symptoms. One doesn't have to have them all to have a major depression, but it is unlikely that they will be totally absent. Commonly, there will be a sleep disturbance generally characterized by awakening early in the morning, sometimes being unable to sleep past 3 or 4 A.M. Frequently a depressed person develops what is known as a diurnal variation of mood, a fancy term which means that a patient will feel worse in the morning and gradually improve as the day goes on so that they may feel almost normal by evening, only to awaken to the same depressed state the next morning. Often there is a marked decrease in appetite, or even a total disinterest in eating at all, called anorexia. Anorexics may lose great amounts of weight, 10, 20, even 70 pounds, as a result of this condition, and often come to psychiatrists only after going through months of unneeded medical workups.

Other symptoms are also common: Preoccupation with physical illness is frequent, especially in the elderly, sometimes overshadowing all other symptoms; development of constipation; great difficulty in concentrating, to the point where she may be unable to even read the newspaper or watch television no matter how hard she tries; a general loss of interest in any activity; a refusal to attend to former activities and responsibilities; actual physical slowing down (psychomotor retardation); a complete lack of interest in sex; guilty ruminations and self-reproaches about real and imagined failings.

As the illness progresses, which it almost invariably does if left untreated, the person may neglect his own personal hygiene and refuse to wash or bathe, or change his clothes, withdrawing more and more from social contact. He may become childlike, reverting to an earlier stage of life. Feelings of extreme hopelessness and a common conviction that things will never get any better become so prevalant that he can no longer be reassured.

The depressed person may become frankly psychotic, losing touch with reality. Delusions may develop, commonly an exaggeration of the earlier episodes of guilty brooding. He may believe that he has committed some terrible crime for which he is about to be punished, that he is to be taken away by the police, that people are repelled by him, even that he has a foul odor which others can detect. All of these add to a self-image of being no good, of being bad, of needing to be punished. At times, they will lose all connection to the world and become entirely withdrawn, mute, totally self-absorbed, and fail to respond to any external stimuli.

Some may see no way out except suicide, and many do succumb to this morbid solution. In fact, 7 to 15 percent of depressed patients do eventually commit suicide. The most treatable of all psychiatric illness is also potentially the most lethal.

In order to treat a depression, the diagnosis must be made as early as possible. Occasionally this may not be easy to do. If the full picture just described develops, the diagnosis makes itself. Unfortunately, not only may the symptoms be less overt at first, they may even be entirely masked.

MASKED DEPRESSION

Masked depressions are particularly common in the elderly, and frequently present themselves in two basic ways which may go unnoticed if they are not understood. The first is as physical illness. Patients may simply feel physically ill without other symptoms of depression. They may have a series of unrelated physical ailments, a common syndrome, or one particular physical symptom which turns out to have no physiologic base and persists despite the best efforts of some well-meaning physicians to treat it. The patient may focus on bowel movements, urination, breathing problems, chest pain, arthritis, or whatever, in endless combinations and variations. It is typical for such patients to go from doctor to doctor, undergoing complicated, expensive, and even dangerous tests, none of which ever demonstrates any organic basis. Despite this, they commonly persist in pursuing medical evaluations, never wanting to consider an underlying psychiatric disorder. Even more unfortunate, many physicians will also persist in repeated testings, unaware of the depression which is responsible—or even afraid to suggest such an idea to their patient.

Another form of masked depression is, pseudodementia, an increasingly recognized phenomenon found specifically in the elderly in which depressive illness presents itself as a dementia for which there is no organic basis. Such patients may initially be indistinguishable from those with a true dementia, showing the same intellectual deterioration and memory loss, but if scrutinized more carefully, will show some important differences.

Pseudodementia presents with sudden onset and rapid progression. The person is aware of deficits and is upset and open about them. He exhibits other symptoms of depression such as sleeplessness, loss of appetite, and weight loss. Usually, he has a history of previous depressions.

True dementia, on the other hand, has a slow, insidious onset and progression. In this case, the person is unaware of deficits and tries to cover up. There are no symptoms of depression and no history of previous depression.

It is vitally important that this distinction be made early, because pseudodementia will respond to treatment just like any other depression, while a true dementia may be irreversible. Failure to make the diagnosis will often result in the relegation of a parent to the "hopeless" category of senility, so that he is given up for lost and eventually may be placed in a nursing facility where the depression deepens to the point that it is truly irreversible. It is sometimes estimated that up to 20 percent of nursing home residents may be suffering from an undiagnosed pseudodementia.

Your awareness of this information may be vital in protecting your parent.

TREATMENT OPTIONS FOR YOUR DEPRESSED PARENT

The treatment of major depression is one of the most advanced, well-understood, and sophisticated areas in all of psychiatry. As in all geriatric psychiatric illness, intelligent and comprehensive treatment must be subtly geared to take all of the aggravating variables into consideration.

If there are social issues involved, for instance, loneliness and isolation, these must be corrected by whatever means before any treatment will be ultimately successful. (Any of the suggestions noted in chapter 4 in the section on "Using Community Resources," can be effective.) If there are real and substantial physical problems, naturally they must be attended to. If there are family issues, you should attempt to remedy them.

However, while these interrelated factors must be taken into account and reversed if possible, once a major depression is in full force it tends to take on a life of its own, and will no longer be resolved even if the precipitating issues have been corrected.

Unfortunately, for these serious depressions, psychotherapy or "talking therapy" of any type is not particularly effective, and people can waste a good deal of time, becoming frustrated in the effort, and further convinced that they will never be better. That is not to say that psychotherapy has no place in the treatment of depression. For the milder reactive depressions, for instance, in which the illness is obviously related to some real life event with which the patient cannot cope, psychotherapy can be quite effective by making the patient aware of his underlying reaction. Furthermore, once a major depression is under control, psychotherapy can be tremendously useful in discovering underlying psychological stress in a patient's life which, when understood, may help to avoid precipitating future episodes.

However, the truth is that the treatment of a major depression can only really be successfully handled medically, usually with antidepressant drugs.

These medications have been around for a long time and their actions are reasonably well understood. They are effective in about 70 percent of cases and are generally safe if administered with caution by an experienced psychiatrist or other physician. Despite the variations in the drugs, they all work to produce a similar effect in the brain. That is, they enable the neurochemical transmitters in the brain to transmit brain impulses more effectively and thereby speed up the brain and reverse the general slowing down seen in depression.

There are many drugs utilized in the treatment of depression but they fall into several groups, characterized by their basic chemical structure:

Tricyclic Antidepressants

Tricyclic antidepressants are the most commonly used because they are generally the most effective agents in the treatment of depression. These include such commonly prescribed medications as amitriptyline (Elavil), imipramine (Tofranil), nortriptyline (Aventyl or Pamelor), desipramine (Norpramin), and protriptyline (Vivactil).

One difficulty with these drugs, which makes for many complaints and misunderstanding by patients, is that they do not act immediately as do some minor tranquilizers which afford some relief from anxiety in an hour. Generally, they may take two to three weeks to relieve the depressive symptoms, because it takes time for them to enter the brain and build up to a sufficient therapeutic level. This lag time is particularly annoying for the distressed patient who has "nothing but side effects" during this initial period, which he must "wait out" before the desired effect is achieved. Refusal to comply, or taking an insufficient or irregular dosage is an understandably common problem. Unfortunately, these drugs simply do not work unless taken properly, which means following the doctor's advice exactly

for a period of several weeks. You may need to vigorously supervise your parent's compliance in outpatient situations.

All of the drugs mentioned are good, effective medications, and
none is more effective than another. In reality, antidepressant
drugs are selected according to side effects, attempting to eliminate those that present specific difficulties for the elderly patient.
For this reason, the two original antidepressants, the so-called
secondary amines (amitriptyline or Elavil; and imipramine or Tofranil)
are used less often because of a higher incidence of side effects,
while the newer tertiary amines (nortriptyline or Aventyl and
Pamelor; desipramine or Norpramin; and protriptyline or Vivactil)
are more easily tolerated by the geriatric age group. In treating
healthy younger geriatric patients, there is generally no special
problem with side effects and patients can be medicated in much
the same manner as younger patients. Older patients, particularly
those with compromised cardiovascular function, must be monitored with caution. Starting doses should be lower, increases in
dosage more gradual, and the final therapeutic dose generally
lower. (Some psychiatrists say that a third to half the dosage
used with younger patients is sufficient, while others utilize a
full dose without difficulty in many patients who require a higher
level.)

Careful selection may reduce side effects, but side effects are
reversible in any case by discontinuing the medication. All of
these drugs are generally safe if monitored with caution by an
experienced physician, but since side effects are of major concern to elderly patients, you should be aware of the following major
ones:

- *Dry mouth.* One of the most benign but irritating side effects
  is a dry mouth. This results from the medication blocking the
  autonomic nervous system, which enervates the salivary glands
  that moisten the mouth. There is no antidote for this and it
  must be tolerated, although sucking hard candy may afford
  some relief. The only real difficulty is that your parent may
  find this symptom particularly annoying and be prone to

discontinue the medication before it has a chance to reach peak effectiveness. If this is the case, remind them that this nerve-blocking proves that the drug has begun to do what it is supposed to do.

- *Orthostatic hypotension.* This is a drop in blood pressure which occurs when the patient rises from a sitting to a standing position, causing lightheadedness, dizziness, and even fainting, sometimes leading to falls and injuries. Make sure your parent understands to rise slowly and with caution, allowing his body to adjust itself to the change in position.

- *Cardiac effects.* This is an extremely important area and one that is much misunderstood, even by physicians and some cardiologists inexperienced in dealing with psychiatric patients. Occasionally, antidepressants may produce a tachycardia (fast heart rate), but generally this is not a major consideration. In fact, cardiac illness is generally not a contraindication to antidepressant therapy unless there is a specific abnormality in the electrical conduction system of the heart (a conduction defect or a degree of heart block). Such a situation can be immediately detected by a baseline electrocardiogram (EKG) which *must* be done if your parent is to be treated with antidepressant medication. Patients with this condition may develop complete heart block with tricyclic antidepressant medication with potentially fatal consequences. If the electrocardiogram shows no evidence of an electrical conduction disorder, antidepressant medication is safe. Cardiac arrhythmias (irregular or extra heart beats) present no particular difficulty and, in fact, antidepressants have been shown to have an antiarrhythmic effect.

- *Urinary retention (difficulty or inability to void).* This is a particular problem for elderly men with enlarged prostate glands, which already constrict the urethra (urinary canal). These medications can further narrow the passageway and interfere with urination.

- *Constipation.* This is a common side effect, particularly annoying because constipation is frequently already a problem in depressed patients. If ignored, constipation can progress to complete paralysis of the intestine, a condition known as ileus. The patient may become impacted, requiring manual cleaning by a physician.

- *Glaucoma.* Patients with certain types of glaucoma (narrow angle glaucoma), should not take tricyclic antidepressants because these drugs can further increase intraocular pressure by interfering with the outflow tract. An elderly parent with glaucoma must be cleared by an ophthalmologist before antidepressant medications can be ordered.

- *Sedation.* Any medication can cause sedation, particularly in the elderly, and antidepressants are no exception. If your parent does become excessively sleepy, a solution may be found by lowering the dosage, or by switching to a less sedating choice of antidepressant (desipramine—Norpramin—is actually energizing as a rule), or by administering the medication only before retiring.

Listing all these side effects together may give you the impression that these medications are particularly dangerous, which is not so. When carefully administrated by an experienced physician who is fully aware of these potential difficulties, these drugs are essentially safe. However, because of the possibility of developing any of these side effects, they cannot be taken lightly. Supervision, monitoring, and regular office visits are essential to proper treatment. The fact is that severe depressions can only be alleviated through the use of these medications. Withholding them out of the fear that your parent will develop side effects, deprives her of a potentially life-saving treatment.

Monoamine Oxidase Inhibitors

This second category of antidepressant medication includes phenelzine (Nardil) and tranylcypromine (Parnate). For many years these drugs were used infrequently because of fears of producing dangerous increases in blood pressure when taken with certain restricted foods, and because of a variety of complicated interactions with other drugs, particularly for geriatric patients. Currently, however, they are more in vogue and may be particularly useful for elderly patients with cardiac disease or for those sensitive to the side effects of tricyclic antidepressants. They produce much less difficulty with constipation, urinary retention, and may be the only safe medications for patients with glaucoma. Furthermore, they may be used in patients with the cardiac conduction defects discussed before. Like tricyclic antidepressants, they also require a two- to three-week lag time before becoming therapeutically effective, and must be taken with a special diet which avoids food containing tyramine because they may interact to cause dramatic rises in blood pressure (hypertensive crises). The special diet is not difficult to follow, but must be adhered to:

Foods to Avoid When Taking Monoamine Oxidase Inhibitors. Foods to be avoided include all strong and aged cheeses (cream cheese and cottage cheese are allowed); all fermented or aged foods (salami, certain sausages, pickled herring); all spoiled fruit; and certain alcoholic beverages (red wine, sherry, vermouth, cognac, beer, and ale). Specific foods to avoid are broad bean pods (fava beans, Chinese pea pods); figs, raisins, and other dried fruits, liver and liverwurst; and meats or yeast extracts.

Foods to Limit When Taking Monoamine Oxidase Inhibitors. The following foods need not be avoided completely, but should not be eaten in excess: chocolate, anchovies, caviar, coffee, colas, curry powder, sauerkraut, licorices, mushrooms, nuts, rhubarb, shellfish, soy sauce, and Worcestershire sauce.

Unlike tricyclic antidepressants, these drugs interact with many other medications and can cause difficulties for those unaware of these complications. As a general rule, they cannot be taken safely with antihistamines, narcotics, anticholinergics, other antidepressants, blood pressure medications, diabetic medications, anticoagulants, or L-dopa used in the treatment of Parkinson's disease. They must be stopped prior to any surgical or dental procedure requiring anesthesia or narcotic painkillers. To ensure safe use, a comprehensive list of dangerous drug interactions follows:

Allergy medication
Amphetamines
Asthma inhalants
Cold medication (e.g., Dristan, Contac)
Diet medications
Epinephrine or other sympathomimetic amines
L-dopa and dopamine
Local anesthetics with epinephrine
Meperidine (Demerol)
Nasal decongestants, sinus medication

Obviously careful monitoring is absolutely essential with this type of antidepressant medication. As a result, these drugs are generally not the treatment of first choice, but a severely depressed patient who does not respond to tricyclic antidepressants probably merits a trial on monoamine oxidase inhibitors. It must be remembered that when switching from a tricyclic antidepressant to a monoamine oxidase inhibitor, or vice versa, your parent must wait for an extended period until the first antidepressant is entirely out of his system, as they can have serious interactions when taken at the same time.

Other Antidepressants

In recent years, a series of new antidepressants have been produced which do not have the same chemical structure as either the tricyclic antidepressants or the monoamine oxidase inhibitors, but, nonetheless, seem effective in relieving the symptoms of depression. While these drugs are often touted by drug companies, and sometimes by physicians excessively impressed by advertising or pressure from drug detail men, their advantages over the more standard antidepressants have been exaggerated, and tend to be less effective in general. That is not to say, however, that they have no place in treatment, and in certain situations present definite advantages over the more typical medications. Of these, doxepin (Sinequan or Adapin) is used most frequently and seems to produce fewer cardiac side effects, although it may be somewhat sedating. Others include tranzoclone (Desyrel) which also has fewer cardiac side effects and presents somewhat less difficulty with constipation, urinary retention, and other so-called anticholinergic side effects; maprotiline (Ludiomil) which causes less hypotension and anticholinergic difficulties, but can be quite sedating; and amoxapine (Asendin) which has the advantage of sometimes producing a quicker response although it may be responsible for some reversible, but irritating, neurologic side effects. The one new antidepressant that may well prove to be extremely beneficial is fluoxetine hydrochloride (Prozac). So far, this medication seems to be equally effective while producing fewer side effects, making it potentially ideal for elderly patients. However, as with all relatively new drugs not yet widely tested among geriatric patients, the jury is still out.

Psychostimulants

Psychostimulants (amphetamines, generally methylphenidate or Ritalin) for older patients increase alertness and activity and speed up the brain, and, as a result, have a special place in the treatment of depression in elderly patients. They are particularly useful in the treatment of medically ill, weakened patients, and those with severe dementias who may not be able to tolerate regular antidepressant medication. They may be also used in combination with other antidepressants, making them even more effective. Despite their usefulness, however, they are addicting and administration must be carefully supervised by a physician. They are never the first drug to be used.

Lithium Carbonate

Lithium has been very prominent in recent years. Originally this medication was thought to be most useful in treating manias (high periods of excitment and euphoria), but it has been found to be of dramatic help in preventing mood swings in patients who go both high and low (manic-depressive cycles) and even for those with only recurrent bouts of depression. When it works, lithium can be extraordinarily effective and prevent recurrence of such episodes without any of the annoying side effects of antidepressant and antipsychotic medication. Unlike other antidepressants, lithium must be regulated carefully with blood tests until the proper therapeutic dose is arrived at. This is because the therapeutic dose is very close to a dose that would be toxic to the patient. Once the correct blood level is established, however, patients can be monitored with repeat measurements of blood levels every three months. Side effects are generally mild, but if the blood level rises too high, nausea, vomiting, diarrhea, constipation, tremor, ataxia, or severe fatigue may result. Rarely, patients may develop a severe neurologic syndrome, which if untreated, can lead to confusion, lethargy, and even coma. Occasionally, long-term use of lithium can cause diminished thyroid function, and this should be re-evaluated periodically by use of blood tests. Patients with severe heart or kidney disease should not be given lithium, while those on diuretics (water pills) must be monitored with great care because diuretics can raise the lithium level in the blood. Anti-inflammatory medications may also produce unexpected increases in blood lithium. As with other medications, particular caution must be used with elderly patients to avoid variations in lithium level and consequent toxic side effects. In all cases, baseline kidney and thyroid functions must be determined before lithium therapy is begun.

Potentiators

These are drugs which, when used in combination with the primary antidepressants, enhance their effectiveness. Such potentiators include small doses of lithium, thyroid hormone (L-triiodothyronine), and amphetamines.

Electroshock Treatment

While antidepressants are generally effective in the treatment of the vast majority of depressions, sometimes they do not provide relief. In such instances, there is another treatment which is even more effective, yet still strikes fear into the hearts of the general public: shock treatment. Never has so benign and tremendously effective a treatment been so misunderstood. It is understandable, since no one likes the idea of having electrodes put to a parent's head, and an electric shock administered. It sounds primitive, it sounds brutal, it sounds like the brain will be destroyed, but it works. And, if the truth be told, it works better and quicker than all of the medications and probably with fewer side effects.

The fact is that electroshock treatment (ECT) is a highly effective treatment fro a very serious life-threatening illness and should be evaluated rationally. In the proper hands, it is a totally painless and safe method and does not produce any long-term memory impairment or brain damage. The patient is anesthetized, so that she is asleep and feels nothing. She is given a muscle relaxant so that she does not thrash about and injure herself during the convulsive therapy. A seizure is produced in the brain, but because of the additional medication, one does not experience the body seizure seen in epileptics during a natural seizure. The electric jolt takes one second and the patient is awake again in about 20 minutes without any memory of the procedure. The main danger of ECT is only the anesthesia itself, which has the same relatively minimal risk as any anesthesia for surgical procedure. The only side effect is a temporary loss of memory during the period of the electric shock treatment, which generally takes between two and three weeks (for about four to twelve treatments, generally three per week scheduled every other day). Memory impairment may be minimized by the use of unilateral ECT (to the nondominant side of the brain). This is particularly helpful to geriatric patients who may have some degree of confusion already. But even with conventional, bilateral ECT there is no long-term memory loss and no dementia, unless the method is abused by constant use over a long period of time. Temporary memory loss is to be expected, as well as some permanent amnesia about the events of the two to three weeks of electricshock treatment.

It is often thought that physical frailty and old age make ECT a poor choice for the elderly. In fact, the opposite is often the case, and frequently older patients, who are unable to withstand the side effects of antidepressant medication, can be safely and effectively treated with ECT.

SUICIDE: A REAL DANGER

No discussion of depression can be ended without a brief mention of its most ominous consequence: suicide. Suicide is a common outcome of severe depression at any age and, as mentioned earlier, dramatically increases with age. Elderly, lonely men are the most likely patients in the entire population to successfully commit suicide, while suicide rates for older women are among the highest for women of any age group. Even more frightening is the fact that elderly patients are more likely to commit suicide without first making the warning threats so common in the case of younger patients.

As a result, any significantly depressed elderly parent must be viewed as a potential suicide risk and taken very seriously. Particularly ominous are the following situations: lack of interest by family or caretakers so that your parent sees no hope for help; isolation without expectation for increased social contact; recent bereavement; recent institutionalization or change in living situation; physical illness, either new or chronic without hope of cure; alcoholism; severe symptoms of depression (anorexia, insomnia, weight loss); previous suicide gestures; and finally, when it occurs, the verbalized threat of suicide or of having no hope left. If you notice any of these signs, your parent requires immediate attention and treatment to alleviate his despair and give his hope through attention, treatment, and cure. He must be placed in a safe situation (a hospital or the home of a relative where he will have constant supervision) while a treatment plan is formulated and put into immediate effect. Care, concern, and recognition of the problem will in itself often provide the support needed to allow the treatment process to proceed.

MANIA: THE FLIP-SIDE OF DEPRESSION

Before we conclude this discussion on depression, a few words should be said on the opposite but closely related mood disorder: mania.

Mania is the opposite pole to depression and this accounts for the term bipolar depression, used to describe patients who cycle between low periods (depression) and high periods (mania). Far less common than depression, mania is characterized by a triad of symptoms: hyperactivity (nonstop activity), pressured speech (rapid, constant talking), and euphoria (exaggerated happiness). Typically such patients are very excited, somewhat funny, sometimes nasty and irritable, expansive and grandiose, jumping from one idea to another so quickly that it is hard to follow them (tangential thinking), and racing about in a constant state of motion. Such episodes often start abruptly, reach a peak quickly, and can be even more troublesome than depression because the patient is much harder to control and tends to deny his illness. Manic patients may exhaust themselves because they stop sleeping, and are constantly on the move. They frequently get themselves into trouble because of their characteristic grandiose plans which they try to put into effect, without judgment or any sense of reality.

Treatment of such conditions is similar to the treatment of all psychotic states, usually requiring hospitalization and treatment with antipsychotic medication. Mania responds especially well to lithium which may be used in the acute period and later on as a prophylactic measure.

Generally, these manic episodes alternate with depressive ones, and you may see such a person cycle from one to the other in rapid succession. As patients age, this cycling may be so rapid that affected patients are regularly ill. Again, lithium can be very helpful with those who need ongoing psychiatric care and constant monitoring of their psychological state until they are stabilized for a period of time. Once stabilized, such patients may have very long periods of remission and return to their previous level of functioning. If lithium is not effective, recent clinical studies have demonstrated that other drugs like carbazepine (Tegritol) divalproex sodium (Depakote), and valproic acid (Depakene) have been useful in controlling the wide mood swings of this disorder.

·7·

Paranoid Disorders

Paranoia is the fixed belief in a false set of ideas. Frightening as these ideas may often be, they are held onto with unshakeable conviction.

WHEN A PARENT BECOMES PARANOID: THE CASE OF MRS. S.

After depression, paranoia is the most frequently encountered psychiatric disturbance in the elderly. It certainly is the one that is most dramatically troublesome for patients, their families, and the professionals attempting to manage them. The extent of the problem may be relatively minor, with the parent offering vague and inconsistent complaints ("They don't like me at the senior center, I'm a different type") which may only minimally interfere with living; more moderately severe ("People have started gossiping about me." "Did you see how she looked at me when I walked by?" "Mrs. A. took my sweater when I turned my back!"), which can lead to the avoidance of others and periodic quarrels with friends or neighbors. In extremely severe cases, the affected person's entire existence may revolve around his paranoid orientation to the world:

> Mrs. S. lived in terror of her son. She had persistently called her community's crime victims program, the local police precinct, various community organizations, and had pleaded with the office of her local state senator for protection. She was in a constant state of panic and saw no solution. Changing her will

had made no difference. Her son continued to harass her, keeping watch on her apartment and regularly burglarizing her residence.

She seldom left her apartment now, and when I visited her at home it was under the uncomfortable pretense that I was a city investigator looking into her son's activities. This wasn't completely untrue. My services had been requested by several of the community agencies she had beleaguered with her daily phone calls.

At first she was suspicious of my credentials, but with a little prodding she was quite willing to fill me in on her situation. She wasn't exactly sure what her son was up to. She hadn't seen him in several years, but she was convinced that he was watching her and playing tricks on her. In the days when she was not afraid to leave her apartment, she would come home to find her drawers and closets in disarray. She locked her bank books and jewelry in a safe deposit box, changed the locks on her apartment many times, even added a police lock, but somehow he managed to find entry. At first, she explained, he only looked around, but then things began to disappear. Little pieces of costume jewelry, an ash tray memento from a Florida vacation, and even an evening dress with a matching sequined jacket that she had worn to her grandson's bar mitzvah.

She painstakingly recorded his activities and documented "break-ins" in a disorderly journal. The entries were in a cramped, minute handwriting. The later entries had become more alarming and coincided with her mounting terror and attempts to secure police protection. Some of her entries are presented here:

June 5th. C. shone a flashlight into my window, blinked it on and off twice.

June 9th. I had to go out to shop. I watched carefully at the door, didn't see the gray car, so I went to the grocery. Back in 20 minutes, but my coral necklace was missing and wires were pulled out behind the TV set???

June 15th. The gray car is back. It circles the block with one headlight out. I think another car takes turns so I won't know. I'll have to watch more carefully.

June 27th. The TV is giving me the story. It said, E., take Christ into your life . . . Maybe it's C.'s wife who put him up to this.

July 10th. It is harder, but I will fool them. Something was put in the food. I have three boys now to get me take-out; each day I send a different one to a different take-out so they won't know where they will go, and even if they work for C., he won't be able to get to the stores. This way I don't have to leave my apartment ever and I can protect myself. What does C. want?

When her son was contacted, he turned out to be a pleasant and concerned family man living in the suburbs who didn't know what to do with or where to turn for help for his mother. He explained that she had began to show this behavior from her early sixties, after his father's death, but that her brother had been the original object of her suspicion until his death three years ago. Up until then, her son had been the good one. He had learned to endure her endless phone calls attacking his uncle for all the malice of which he now found himself accused.

He had tried for years to get help for her. She naturally rejected all offers and he began to replace, in her eyes, his uncle as the object of her suspicion, even to having to prove that he had not stolen the bar mitzvah dress. His mother could be very convincing, and instinctively could tone down her wilder accusations when she wanted to make her point.

In recent years it had become intolerable. Three lawsuits she had started against him had finally driven his wife to desperate fury and soured his attitude toward her. He had not seen his mother in 18 months, and if not for his concern that she was now so totally absorbed by her paranoia that she no longer left her apartment, he would have been content to leave her alone for the rest of her life.

This story, dramatic as it sounds, is not uncommon, or even unusual. Severe paranoid states, uncomplicated by dementia, account for 10 percent of first admissions to psychiatric hospitals of persons after age sixty, and have been found to be present in more than 3 percent of residents in nursing homes, where they are always the most difficult conditions to manage.

UNDERSTANDING PARANOIA

Like the term depression, paranoia is used in various and confusing ways. Paranoia may be a secondary symptom of dementia; this will be discussed in chapter 10. It may be a symptom of schizophrenia, an even more serious chronic illness which begins in adolescence or early adulthood. What I am discussing now, however, is a primary illness of its own, and, for some unknown reason, it is more prevalent in women. This chronic condition typically does not begin until later life, generally after age sixty. It does not clear up on its own, and is characterized by paranoid delusions, that is, a set of fixed, unchangeable, false beliefs that someone is trying to hurt them. A paranoid parent is completely convinced that she is correct, no matter how unlikely or bizarre her accusations. She cannot be "talked out of" her belief, and will actively resist all attempts to help her, no matter how miserable she might be. She never sees herself as ill and will become incensed by any such suggestion. In fact, anyone who offers such an idea may soon find himself looked upon as an agent of the "conspirators." Sometimes these patients isolate themselves, living out their lives in fear and bitterness, often becoming increasingly terrorized as their paranoia takes over every function of their life. Others will be quite vocal, endlessly accusing friends, relatives, and neighbors, of trying to "get them." They harass police and social service agencies for assistance to combat their persecutors. Occasionally they become violently obsessed with their fantasies of constant persecution. In the final stages, they may begin to hallucinate, claim to hear voices of their enemies, and imagine that recording devices are in the walls. They listen for every sound, convinced that "they are coming."

Unlike other psychiatric illnesses in the elderly, this is not a disorder which seems to "come out of the blue." A parent who develops this illness in later years generally was somewhat disturbed throughout her life, often being isolated, unsociable, and quick to take offense. Looking back, you may realize that she had few friends, and seemed a bit cold or acted oddly in social situations. An affected parent may have been subtly paranoid for years, misinterpreting innocent remarks, causing family feuds, and gradually losing contact, however marginal, with relatives or acquaintances. Despite these interpersonal difficulties, she may have been highly competent in her career and very well able to handle her life, albeit alone, cold, and often embittered.

As paranoid patients age, alienate whatever contacts they have had, and retire their condition usually deteriorates. Out of the work force, there is no need for them to interact with co-workers or customers, and they may become increasingly isolated. This seems to exaggerate their natural tendency toward paranoia. The more they are cut-off from the real world, the more they create a world inside themselves which seems real to them. Some people think that these paranoid symptoms are a way of reaching out for contact, although in a negative and frightening way, as if being under surveillance is better than being totally cut off from others. In this regard, it is interesting to note that significant hearing loss is especially associated with developing paranoid tendencies, further underscoring the idea that increased isolation and lack of contact with others for any reason may be a major factor in their illness.

TREATMENT FOR A PARANOID PARENT

Treatment of paranoia is hampered, and sometimes made impossible, by the patient's determined resistance to any sort of help. Not only are these patients convinced that they are correct in their paranoid view of the world, they become even more agitated when their beliefs are questioned. No matter how many people tell them that it is their imagination, no matter how close the person is who attempts to reassure them (and these people seldom have anyone who is really that close), no matter how authoritative the physician or therapist, they remain fanatically convinced about their delusions. As a result, most of these patients go untreated until their paranoia and their reactions to it land them in a situation where treatment is forced on them by some third party. When this happens, it may necessitate involuntary psychiatric hospitalization, which at first naturally exaggerates their paranoid belief that someone is after them.

Once they are in a treatment setting, however, this disorder responds relatively well to treatment. Patients' paranoid ideas are controlled to the extent that they can function without disturbing others. This is accomplished through the combined use of antipsychotic medication, the development of an ongoing supportive relationship with a therapist, and sometimes, the use of behavior modification.

Medication is of primary importance in the treatment, but the patient often actively resists. If they can be convinced to take the first few doses of medication, however, very often they will continue to accept medication even if the basic paranoid symptoms remain intact for some time. Long-term exposure to antipsychotic medication will generally diminish the symptoms and, in many cases, eliminate them altogether. An even greater problem is the difficulty in getting patients to continue taking the medication once they leave the hospital setting. Even when they know the maintenance dose will be roughly half of the dosage they received at the hospital, almost always, patients will deny that the medication had anything to do with making them feel better and, unfortunately, they will discontinue it as soon as possible. Because the paranoid symptoms will not return immediately, they are even more convinced of the correctness of their decision. Within a few months, though, the symptoms invariably return, and we meet with the same resistance to treatment, despite th evidence of its previous success.

When a patient continues to resist treatment, it may be time for you to consider long-acting injectable medications [fluphebazine hydrochloride (Prolixin); or haloperidol (Haldol)]. These can be administered by injection only every 2 to 3 weeks by an internist or general practitioner, which lessens the stigma attached to psychiatric follow-up. Later, it progress is maintained, oral medication can be substituted if the patient seems more willing to comply.

If your parent suffers from paranoia, the most successful treatment to encourage is a positive supportive relationship with a therapist, which will provide the nonthreatening social contact an isolated, paranoid person secretly craves but fears. A relationship like this works as long as the therapist does not attack or ridicule the delusional ideas, but rather points out the problems that will result if the patient acts on her paranoid thoughts, or commiserates with the patient, urging the patient to take her tranquilizers to calm herself. Sometimes it may simply be more effective to accept the patient's ideas, but advise her to keep them to herself so as not to create more adverse attention, or, even more hopefully, to divert the patient's attention from her paranoid concerns toward other activities that the patient can tolerate and that will help distract her from her psychotic preoccupation.

Sometimes psychotherapy directed toward understanding underlying problems can be effective, especially when the likely psychologicial cause of the paranoia can be determined, and the patient seems motivated toward understanding:

> Miss L., an elderly, very intelligent woman, came to my office mystified by radio transmitters which had been placed in the walls of her apartment. Not only did she feel the building vibrate, but they seemed to transmit their radio waves into her body, causing odd sensations, particularly in the genital area. A careful history of recent events revealed that her younger sister had died two months before, leaving behind her husband of many years, to whom the patient admitted she had long been attracted.
>
> It seemed now plausible that the genital vibrations might represent some unacceptable sexual response to her now-available but unattainable brother-in-law, feelings about which she was likely to be guilty.
>
> Discreetly asked about this possibility, the patient flushed, lowered her eyes and said, "That might be a possibility . . . I had some fantasies actually."

One week later, the sensations had ceased without medication or other intervention.

Subtle behavior modification techniques may also be used to reward a parent's efforts to interact in a socially acceptable way with people and social contacts, for instance by participating in senior citizen centers or volunteer groups. Ignoring your parent's paranoid ideas can be a form of negative reinforcement.

As a concerned child of a paranoid parent, you should follow a similar approach when dealing with your parent. What works for therapists will work best for you, and even assist in her recovery. Never try to talk your parent out of a "crazy idea" and don't get involved in pointless confrontations about "accepting reality." Instead, try to tolerate her strange ideas while learning how to redirect her attention into healthier areas. Don't go overboard and think you can remake an isolated, socially inhibited individual. Remember, a paranoid person generally cannot accept too much closeness or personal contact, so don't try to force her into frightening social situations which she has never been able to handle. Rather, try to strike a balance between a reasonable amount of social contact which she needs to break down her isolation and excessive closeness which she may not be able to tolerate. Above all else, as best as you can, make sure that your parent continues in therapy and takes her medication, even when she is sure she is "entirely cured."

Finally, keep in mind that, occasionally, paranoid delusions have a basis in reality, although almost always greatly exaggerated. In these days of tenant harassment, for instance, the landlord may not be entirely innocent. More important, if your parent's accusations toward you and other family members strike a resonant chord in you own observations, examine the situation honestly, let your parent's therapist know, and be willing to make reasonable concessions.

Mrs. S., whose son was the object of her delusional beliefs, was involuntarily hospitalized at a psychiatric facility. During the first days of her treatment, she was convinced that she was not actually in a hospital, but in a fake setting orchestrated by her son while he rifled through her possessions. She was unsure whether the psychiatrist and staff were actively in league with, or only unwitting dupes of, her son and his friends. She passively accepted haloperidol, albeit with amused disdain, which was started at a low dose and cautiously raised. She was carefully monitored for side effects. Initially refusing to become involved with other psychiatric patients or group activities ("that's for sick people," she smiled tolerantly), she slowly accepted some limited involvement and actually became friendly with one of the social workers with whom she shared a mutual interest in sewing. After two weeks she abandoned her staunch refusal to allow her son to visit, and after a stormy and accusative initial meeting, allowed follow-up casual visits, and began expressing some renewed interest in the activities of her grandchildren.

She remained in the hospital for about five weeks altogether, but never quite abandoned her ideas. She decided instead to "forgive" her son because he seemed to have changed and grudgingly agreed to let him renew his visits to her at home. She never quite accepted the treating psychiatrist, but thought she might visit the social worker on occasion to "give her some pointers on sewing." She even agreed to take her medication to "humor" us.

Although they never really established a close relationship, Mrs. S. and her son did keep in touch, and, occasionally spent some mutually comforting time together during her last years.

·8·

Other Psychiatric Syndromes Common in Elderly Parents

Depression and paranoid disorders are the most severe of the common psychiatric illnesses that may affect elderly parents. However, several other psychological disturbances merit special attention because of the frequency with which they occur.

ANXIETY DISORDERS

Feelings of overwhelming anxiety, sometimes reaching panic proportion, are common at any age, but may be particularly intense in later life, especially when those affected are isolated and have no one to reassure them. This kind of anxiety is generally not related to any obvious precipitating event or situation which the patient can consciously recall. And because it seems to "come out of the blue," it is quite terrifying. The true anxiety or panic attack is one of the most frightening of human experiences. There is an intense feeling of panic and dread, and physical symptoms of a fast heart rate, shortness of breath, hyperventilation, and chest pain, so profound that the person often believes that he is dying.

When such symptoms occur at a less intense but more chronic level, it is known as a generalized anxiety disorder. Such individuals have feelings of anxiety and tension most of the time, and never feel truly comfortable or at ease. When the symptoms are more intense, and occur in acute episodes, it is referred to as a panic disorder. In a related syndrome, known as a phobic disorder, the focus of the underlying anxiety is restricted to a single dreaded situation, activity, or object (for example, fear of bridges, elevators, or the fear of going outdoors—agoraphobia). In its extreme form, a phobic individual, in an effort to avoid confronting that dreaded situation, may so completely constrict his life to the point where he may become totally housebound.

The causes for such extreme anxiety symptoms are not yet at all clear. Recent scientific evidence suggests that people who are prone to these severe anxiety attacks have an underlying biochemical disorder. Classical psychoanalysts feel more at home with the idea that they result from a person's unsuccessful attempts to curb emotional impulses within himself which he finds unacceptable. Such impulses may be sexual (wanting to have sex with a married person or relative), or aggressive (wishing some hated person was dead), and are quite normal, but are unacceptable and intolerable for that person. Such forbidden impulses can produce an enormous degree of anxiety. If these underlying unconscious concerns can be discovered through psychotherapy, chances are your parent may be able to accept and understand his excessive reaction.

Unfortunately, most elderly parents tend to avoid such in-depth soul-searching. If your parent shows an interest, you should definitely pursue a course of psychotherapy. More often though, you'll find yourself settling for simple forms of medication. Minor tranquilizers or low doses of antidepressant medication can be very helpful. These medications will relieve your parent's chronic anxiety and may avoid or interrupt panic attacks in most situations. Obviously you must remember that chronic use of minor tranquilizers is addictive. Eventually your parent will require higher and higher doses to achieve the initial effect. Be aware, also, of the sedative effects of these medications and the fact that they may precipitate depression. If your parent is taking these medications, he should receive some supportive psychotherapy to try to help him understand the psychological bases of his symptoms.

SUBSTANCE ABUSE (ALCOHOL AND DRUGS)

"I guess it's just another case of Alzheimer's," said the overwhelmed social worker who cared for the residents of a large apartment complex for senior citizens. Mr. W., a retired Norwegian merchant seaman, had been found walking down the halls of the building, in a disoriented and confused state, and naked as well. He was taken back to his apartment, which was filthy and obviously had not been cared for in quite some time. A refrigerator stood empty except for some moldy frankfurters. The next morning, Mr. W. could give no further account of himself. He just smiled nervously and said over and over again that the social worker "must have made a mistake."

My psychiatric assessment showed all the usual signs of confusion and memory loss, and his physical examination was unremarkable except for multiple cuts and bruises indicating that he had taken many falls. A telephone call to his son, however, provided the real explanation: "Look under the bed," he suggested. We did. Lined up rather neatly, given the apartment's general condition, were rows of vodka bottles, carefully stored, mostly empty.

Alcohol and drug abuse are not uncommon problems in elderly parents, often made more troublesome because they go undetected. Symptoms like confusion, impaired judgment, and mobility disturbances are too frequently dismissed as consequences of old age, senility, or chronic physical illness. Studies show that doctors forget to ask, while families are ashamed to tell of these abuses. Sometimes the person doesn't even know himself, the problem having started slowly and built up without anyone really recognizing it for what it was.

Alcoholism in the aged tends to fall into two categories: those who have been alcoholic for years, and simply grew old (this is more common now than in the past, since medical intervention has helped alcoholics live longer); and those who begin drinking in later life, often in reaction to some psychological stress. It is now estimated that between 2 to 10 percent of the elderly have significant problems with alcoholism, with an even higher incidence in widowed or medically ill patients. Elderly widowers have the highest rate of alcoholism of all age groups.

Alcohol is a central nervous system depressant which slows people down, diminishes their intellectual abilities, increases memory loss, impairs judgment and muscular coordination, and obviously adds to any degree of mental impairment already present in an elderly person. Prolonged abuse over years will cause an irreversible organic mental syndrome because of toxic effects on the brain and liver, contributed to by vitamin deficiency and malnutrition which are typical additional consequences of prolonged alcoholism.

Early detection of abuse is always important. Advise your parent's doctor if you notice any of the following clues: the rapid onset of confusion with periods of lucidity alternating with more severe impairment, unexplained falls, personality changes with angry outbursts, memory lapses, insomnia, uncontrolled hypertension, or problems with controlling symptoms of gout.

If detected before there is irreversible brain damage, treatment is especially effective for a parent whose drinking has begun in later life. These people will often respond to psychotherapy (individual, family, or group, depending on the situation), particularly if the source of the unhappiness is discovered and can be alleviated to some extent. Isolated individuals can be urged to become involved in senior citizen centers where activity and socialization can replace isolation and the craving for alcohol. Difficult family situations, aggravated by undiscovered alcoholism, can often be resolved, repairing relationships that have broken down. For a motivated parent whose alcoholism is severe, disulfiram (Antabuse) can be prescribed. This medication causes an extremely unpleasant reaction (intense nausea and vomiting, a pounding heart, and elevated blood pressure) when alcohol is consumed. The knowledge that drinking will immediately and invariably produce so severe a reaction is enough to make some people refrain from further abuse. Unfortunately, the craving is so strong for some that they will drink anyway and become quite ill, a dangerous situation for an elderly parent, especially one with heart disease or hypertension. Antabuse can be used safely by a motivated patient who understands the potential dangers involved. If the drinking bouts can be linked to a true major depression, antidepressant medication can sometimes reverse the situation. In addition to drug management, support groups and Alcoholics Anonymous are now more aware of this problem in the elderly and can be tremendously useful in maintaining abstinence.

Drug abuse is another common, often undiscovered problem. The danger is even greater and ironic because it frequently occurs by gradual overuse of medications prescribed by doctors in the first place. As a result, your parent may vigorously deny his addiction and feel justified in saying that such medication is "medically necessary." While the use of "street drugs" like heroin or cocaine is less typical (although there are more elderly addicts than you might suspect), the abuse of minor tranquilizers (Valium is the most popular) and sedatives (barbiturates) is of growing concern and of potentially staggering proportions. No one knows the frequency with which this occurs, but if you notice any changes in your parent's level of awareness and intellectual functioning, you should carefully investigate his medicine cabinet and night table for such seemingly innocuous medications. If you find evidence of abuse with addiction, your parent should be enrolled in a suitable detoxification program, under a doctor's strict supervision. Such a program should include monitoring participants for withdrawal symptoms.

INSOMNIA

One of the most frequent complaints among the elderly is difficulty in falling asleep. Surveys indicate that as many as one in three elderly people are affected by insomnia. Older people tend to take longer to fall asleep, have more frequent waking episodes during the night, and seem to need less sleep in any case. Whether these changes in sleep patterns are related to normal aging is not clear, but even such minor variations can be extremely upsetting to parents who have been ingrained with the idea that they must get eight hours of uninterrupted sleep. Frequently these relatively

minor sleep difficulties are greatly exaggerated, though not delib-
erately; and many sleep studies, performed in laboratories, have
shown that insomniacs report far more time spent awake than
actually occurs. Despite all of this, there is no question that sleep
disturbances of any sort can be tormenting problems for many
elderly parents.

Even though it is quite common, surprisingly there are as yet no
really good long-term studies of the treatment of insomnia in the
elderly. There are, however, a number of possibilities which
should be looked into in attempting to remedy this situation.

Since physical illness, severe depression, and drug dependence
all commonly contribute to insomnia, make sure your parent has
been checked carefully by his physician to rule out these potential
underlying causes. Prompt discovery and treatment of such conditions frequently resolves the entire situation. All sorts of medical
problems can cause physical discomfort which becomes more pronounced at bedtime when your parent is alone and attempting to
relax, an essential prelude to falling asleep. Depression is particularly notorious for being at the root of sleep disorders. If this is the
case, an antidepressant medicine taken by your parent an hour
before bedtime, can be particularly effective. Another common
problem is overusing sleeping medication, which can backfire.
Such abuse of sedatives builds a tolerance to the drug (the need for
even greater doses to create the same sedative effect). Self-withdrawal
from the abused drug results in even greater sleeping problems,
and a dangerous cycle can be established. In such a situation,
careful supervised withdrawal of sleep medication is essential before
the sleep disorder itself can be tackled.

If your parent's physician cannot identify any specific underlying
problem, and the insomnia seems to be a pure and isolated symptom, you can still make some commonsense suggestions which can
make a major difference.

Using techniques developed by behavior therapists, you can help
your parent break bad sleeping habits. Suggest to him that he only
go to bed when he is sleepy, rather than at a specified time. If you
can, try to discourage daytime napping, or even lying down to

rest, read, or watch TV, and emphasize that bed should be reserved for nighttime alone. After all, you can point out, a person only needs a certain amount of sleep in 24 hours, and daytime napping will only mean nighttime sleeplessness. Daytime exercising can be very effective, making your parent physically tired enough to fall asleep easily at night. Be sure to tell him though that exercising just before retiring tends to be stimulating, and defeats the purpose. Some doctors suggest that when people are unable to sleep, they should move into another room for the night, rather than spending an agonizing night of tossing and turning.

If your parent's problem is more severe, techniques of deep muscle relaxation can be used before going to sleep, and during the day to relieve tension. Such techniques are best learned from an experienced therapist, and involve tensing and then relaxing groups of body muscles in succession.

Psychotherapy can sometimes be useful in uncovering sources of anxiety and stress and, when successful, is the most effective and long-lasting strategy.

Finally, the judicious use of sleep medication does have its place. Intelligent use of short-acting minor tranquilizers such as alprazolam (Xanax), triazolam (Halcion), or chloral hydrate can be effective, especially if drug holidays (avoiding the drug two days in a row each week) are used to avoid building tolerance. It cannot be stated too often, however, that constant use will lead to abuse and addiction as a result of the need for increasing doses to produce the same effect, and a more serious sleep problem in the future.

HYPOCHONDRIASIS

One of the most frequent emotional disorders of later life is hypochondriasis, a condition in which a parent is not only convinced that he is physically ill, when nothing is in fact wrong with him, but will determinedly refuse to accept any reassurance or information to the contrary. Sometimes only one body system is affected, often the gastrointestinal tract. Sometimes the entire body, either in turn or all at once, may be the object of pain and discomfort.

To be frank, those affected are among the most annoying patients, both to physician and family, because of the incredible persistence of their beliefs and their endless perseverance in seeking a medical answer. If you find yourself in this situation, you may understandably be at your wit's end or "burnt out" by the entire experience. Such elderly parents are unstoppable, holding steadfastly to their mistaken conviction. In their search for a "cure" these seniors will make the rounds of doctors and specialists. Sometimes they stay with one for a while, who gratifies them with workups and examinations, but always, in the end, leaving dissatisfied. If one physical ailment is temporarily resolved, another will immediately appear in its place. And psychological explanations are never accepted.

In effect, the reason that this illness is so persistent is that it often is more than an illness; in fact, it's almost a way of life. Often starting in childhood, this hypochondriacal preoccupation has many positive aspects for an elderly parent. It permits an enormous degree of control over his surroundings and those around him. While it is hardly an effective way to live, it is a powerful "weapon for the weak" who have abandoned other more assertive ways of functioning. Some "benefits," as perceived by the parent, are that chronic illness bestows power and control over others; family members can be manipulated, often at will; and responsibilities, conflicts, and tension can be avoided with illness an ever-ready excuse.

Rather than acknowledge his own doubts, a "sick" person can use his illness to rationalize his failures and his unwillingness to make an effort. These "professional patients" actually take pride in their disability. Sickness allows a parent to be taken care of, with dependency needs met by a concerned caretaker. Their symptoms provide an outlet for their emotions and mask deeper psychological pain. Visiting doctors and clinics can become a way of life, a sort of retirement hobby for many. At its worst, hypochondriasis can consume a parent's entire identity.

Given the unconscious "benefits," it is easy to see why such patients are so reluctant to allow their symptoms to be cured, let alone face the possibility that a psychological problem is the true cause.

Treatment methods are notoriously ineffective and such persons frequently spend their entire lives absorbed with the ills inside their own bodies. One potentially treatable condition, which often overlaps or is confused with hypochondriasis, is depression, which may present with physical symptoms in the forefront. If your hypochondriacal parent does seem to be depressed, or has other symptoms of depression, for instance, an acute onset of pain or illness rather than a lifelong pattern, diminished functioning, lack of energy, or disturbances of appetite or sleep, a trial of antidepressant medication will often clear the "hypochondriacal" picture.

However, straightforward hypochondriasis offers limited treatment possibilities. Occasionally antidepressant medication or minor tranquilizers do offer some diminution of symptoms. More frequently, family counseling can be somewhat effective in reducing general tension, exploring your parent's true psychological situation, assisting family members to help him see what is truly bothering him at times of stress, and even teaching him better ways of getting results. At the very least, some of the more pleasurable secondary benefits of his symptoms can be removed. Individual counseling is notoriously ineffective, as a confrontational approach will only lead to further and more vigorous denial.

·9·

Approaches to Psychiatric Treatment

Once a diagnosis of psychiatric illness has been made, arranging for your parent's treatment may still be difficult and confusing. Many questions frequently come to mind, but no simple answers. What if my parent refuses to see anyone? Who should I call? A psychiatrist? Psychologist? Social worker? Do they need to specialize in geriatrics? Can my parent be helped at his age?

We can dispel some of the confusion so that appropriate treatment can be planned by having a basic general understanding of the therapeutic possibilities available.

The most common concern that I hear in my practice is the fear that a parent will simply deny that there is a problem and refuse to see anyone at all. Many families are so convinced of this that they never broach the subject at all, closing the door to any possibility of treatment. In my experience, the particular concern often has much more to do with a family fear and protectiveness than it does with the parent. A firm, united, and caring family can almost always convince a fearful or stubborn parent to accept at least one consultation. Once the initial, face-to-face contact has been made with a professional, the parent's fears usually will subside and treatment can begin. After all, establishing a trusting relationship is a professional's job, so leave it to him and stop worrying. Just use a simple, direct approach to get your parent to that first visit. Nine times out of ten, you will succeed. If not, consult a professional yourself for advice: as in the following case report.

Dr. R., a hostile, paranoid, retired physician, had recently disinherited his three daughters, convinced that they were only after his money. His arrogant disdain for "headshrinkers" had convinced them in advance that he would never accept psychiatric treatment, especially since he denied any problem in himself. After several consultations with the sisters, I suggested that we make use of their own genuine distress in order to involve their resistant father. Picking up the phone in front of them (as they cringed in anticipation), I called the elderly gentleman, introduced myself as a physician consulted by his three daughters who were emotionally distraught because he was so angry with them, and suggested that he come in to talk to me so that we could calm them down. While his daughters awaited an outraged response, he readily agreed, eager to tell his "side of the story" so that we could "help them out." He came to see me the very next day, and quickly established a friendly bond. Although never exactly acknowledging that he had any problem, he drifted into regular treatment, saying "For a headshrinker, you're not so bad."

I tell that story to demonstrate that there is almost always a way. You probably know how best to handle your reluctant parent, and if you don't, see someone else who can suggest a strategy. You wouldn't give in to a child who refused a vaccination; the same holds here.

Once your parent agrees to accept help, who do you go to? This can be a much more confusing decision than in the case of a physical problem because the mental health field has so many different types of professionals, all trained in different ways. Don't make it so hard on yourself. If at all possible, find someone who specializes in geriatrics, referred by a responsible source (medical center, physician, community agency) with well-documented professional credentials. If the problem is serious and may require medication, start with a consultation with a geriatric psychiatrist (an M.D. who can prescribe medication if indicated). He can always refer you to another professional if appropriate and suggest a variety of treatment approaches. It is always important to choose someone with whom your parent is comfortable, and who seems knowledgeable and flexible enough to respond to the specific needs of an aged individual.

Even so, alternatives for psychiatric treatment may be so confusing and varied that you still might not be entirely sure what to do. So that you can intelligently assess the choices, I offer a basic framework for decision making. One word of advice: Whatever approach you decide on, it must take into account all contributing sources of difficulty including physical illness and social problems. The overall approach must be flexible enough to make use of a variety of techniques. There is no room for narrowmindedness; whatever works should be used. Once a treatment plan is agreed upon, it should be coordinated by one person, but all those involved in the treatment (you, your parent, home attendant, social worker) must understand as fully as possible both the underlying problem and their specific role in the treatment program.

COUNSELING

Individual counseling for the elderly can be an extremely helpful tool in alleviating many areas of psychological distress. I can't say too often that one of the most wrongminded and saddest ideas is that the elderly cannot benefit from psychotherapy because they are "too old"; or, "it's too late to change." This all too frequently expressed notion stems not from any insurmountable difficulty in dealing with the elderly in psychotherapy, but from our own fears and prejudices. More often, the fact is that therapists, who are generally much younger, are often afraid themselves to get that close to an older person, and psychotherapy is as close as you can get. Young people are afraid to hear what an old person has to say. Their own fears of death, aging, deterioration and physical illness, all the unpleasant facts of daily life with which an elderly person has to deal bring their own mortality too close for comfort. The elderly are actually quite willing to talk; often it is the therapists who are afraid to listen. Instead, it has always been easier to dismiss them, even as Freud did at the beginnings of psychoanalysis, by the faulty suggestion that they are simply too old, too inflexible, and that their patterns are irreversible. Not so.

The state of affairs regarding psychotherapy for the aged (and, by the way, this situation had been buttressed up until recently by Medicare's refusal to pay beyond a limited amount for psychotherapy, limiting it alone among medical treatments for the elderly) is particularly sad because care is so vital. As discussed in earlier chapters, later life can be an especially difficult time, with areas of profound psychological stress rarely encountered by younger people. To say that such difficulties are just an expected part of later life does nothing to relieve the pain and suffering engendered by the loss of loved ones, physical disability, financial pressure, diminished social position and productivity, all in the face of the ever-looming specter of death that can no longer be denied. Not only are these issues so prominent and constant in advanced age, but solutions are harder to come by. An aged parent cannot just find a new wife, have another child, or get a better job. These are problems of enormous proportions and to deny psychological help to those who need it most is a sad and unfortunate commentary on our society's treatment of its elderly.

The fact is that while emotional problems can be severe and solutions seem limited, there is almost always, at the very least, a way that the situation can be improved and substantial solutions worked out. I offer an example:

> Loneliness, especially for the frail homebound elderly, can sometimes seem like an insoluble situation, and I have often despaired at the possibility of promoting some beneficial change.
>
> Speaking at a conference on loneliness to these same homebound elderly, I decided to point out that their situations were not as hopeless as they felt, and that they themselves had to accept the responsibility to make positive changes.
>
> I should not have worried. Before I spoke, a ninety-four-year-old, blind, wheelchair-bound woman was brought to the microphone. As a past president of the New York Gray Panthers, a political action group promoting the rights of the elderly, she proceeded to lambast those in the audience who

had the audacity to feel sorry for themselves. Pointing to her own seemingly insurmountable infirmities, she regaled us with stories of her activities which she now conducted by telephone, continuing her involvement in various political organizations, speaking at conferences, training others to carry on her work. Glaring at her audience through sightless eyes she said what now seemed obvious: "Don't come to me and whine. You have no one to blame but yourselves!"

The fact is, with determination, perseverance, and creativity, there is always a way to cope.

Psychological counseling has a major part in the treatment repertoire for elderly patients. Before describing specific techniques, some general advantages of individual counseling should be understood and noted. Considering the various stresses of later life and the potential isolation of an elderly parent, psychotherapy is particularly advantageous for those who need to have someone to simply listen to them, to whom they can express their true feelings without fear of being negatively judged or rejected. Unlike a friend or family member, a therapist has no personal ax to grind and is in a position to both listen objectively and offer potential solutions which benefit the patient alone. How much better it is for your parent to discuss with an interested third party, decisions about moving into your home, than it would be to explore these issues with you. Nothing allows for a more honest, nonthreatening discussion, with all areas of potential conflict in the open. Not only can the therapist bring unselfish objectivity to the discussion, but training and skill in both anticipating difficulties and providing insight so that a workable solution can be found.

Once your parent's trust is established, so that communication can be open and honest, the basic work of psychotherapy involves coming to an understanding of disturbing psychological issues about which he is often unaware. Such conflicts, hidden in the recesses of our minds, what the psychoanalysts call our unconscious, can cause profound disruption in our daily lives, and bringing them into conscious awareness can be a great relief. The elderly are no different from younger generations in this; both are able to understand what has been secretly bothering them and to make constructive use of such insight. It is a great relief to finally know the cause of one's anxiety and depression, made even more frightening and overwhelming by its mysterious nature.

> Mr. D., a widower and retired attorney, was mourning the death of his eldest son who had been his business partner and friend, and who had died in a car accident two years before. His younger son, a school teacher, had made valiant and constant efforts to console his father but had only met with resistance and anger. In fact, far from filling the void in his father's life as he had hoped to do, the son was beginning to get the idea that his father couldn't stand to have him around. Their relationship had always been a reasonably good one, not a close one like that of his older brother, but loving and concerned. It was as if the brother's death was not only a tragedy in itself, but that it had somehow disrupted the remaining father-son relationship.

> The father, however, disagreed. Of course he loved his remaining son, as he always had. Naturally he was irritable and depressed, but saw no reason for his son's hurt feelings. After all, a son had died and you don't get over something like that, not ever.

> As the grieving father talked about his dead son, the emotion that was most evident was not that of depression but of anger, and as my psychotherapy session with him proceeded, that anger became palpable and intense; and, despite his denial, was clearly directed toward the living son. It was as if he couldn't control himself, was totally unaware of how strongly he felt, and was under the influence of a force beyond his control.

> When he finally worked himself up into a towering rage at the stupidity of his remaining son for continuing to imagine that he was angry at him, I simply asked, "Do you think that you might be angry at him because he is still alive, and because the wrong son died?"

> Suddenly, there was no more denial, no more resistance, only tears and the beginning of an understanding of what he

was honestly feeling and what had stood between him and his only remaining child.

Counseling, then, can uncover and clarify intensely troubling emotions and ideas about which your parent is essentially unaware. Such unconscious issues can cause anxiety, depression, phobias, or a variety of other symptoms that will respond to the understanding achieved through insight-oriented counseling. Such insight can be used in combination with medication and environmental changes in your parent's living situation to maximize the outcome of treatment. Without it, even a very positive response to medication, for instance, may be shortlived and fragile.

There are other psychological approaches to counseling in addition to the insight-oriented model just described. Counseling methods that focus on changing maladaptive behavior through a process of reeducation and instruction (behavioral and cognitive techniques) have been used to target specific symptoms and focus on undoing learned maladaptive behavior. For instance, an elderly parent who has become afraid to walk or leave his home can be taught to regain his lost ability through a carefully monitored desensitization technique. He learns to overcome his fears through a graduated series of exercises which start with the easiest first positive step and progress through increasingly difficult maneuvers until the final outcome is achieved. Relaxation techniques can be particularly useful in combatting increased anxiety as these gradual steps are taken.

Psychological counseling can be enormously effective in some situations, but not all forms of emotional distress will respond to "talking therapy." So that you don't lead your parent in the wrong direction, trying to interest him in psychotherapy for conditions that simply do not respond, let me point out those situations for which therapy is most useful:

Extended grief reactions. A prolonged mourning period during which a parent is unable to function for over three months, remaining obsessed with the death of a loved one, and unable to imagine going on with his life.

Difficult adjustment reactions to new situations. The inability to deal with retirement, loneliness, loss of loved ones, physical illness, chronic disability, illness in a spouse, the dilemma of whether or not to move into a retirement community or a nursing facility, problems about children moving away or questions about moving in with children, financial distress, legal concerns. All of these can be exceedingly difficult and coping with any of these situations can cause psychological paralysis or breakdown in a vulnerable parent. Should such a situation arise, a good therapist can be instrumental in finding solutions to problems that seem overwhelming, and alternatives where none seemed to exist. You may be asked to play a role by providing your parent's therapist with an honest appraisal of the situation from your point of view, so that he can carefully consider all of the issues and be aware of potential solutions.

Problematic marital and family problems. Marital discord is certainly not a problem reserved for the young, although an elderly parent may often find it difficult to admit and talk about, particularly with an adult child. Parents are obviously entitled to the same disappointments and dissatisfactions with each other that you experience with your spouse, and the fact that the elderly tend to feel that it is less acceptable, makes these difficulties more intense and less accessible to assistance and resolution. Not only are marital disputes at issue. Disagreements with you and your siblings can be similarly disruptive for your parent and may lead to endless friction and discontent. Financial matters are regularly issues of family dissension and an elderly individual may rightfully feel battered, needing an outside friend and protector to inform him of his rights.

If marital discord does exist, you may want to suggest joint counseling or couple therapy to your parents. Similarly, should there be disruptive tension in the parent/child relationship, consider family therapy which may actually lead to better communication than ever before.

Parents with chronic psychiatric disturbance, especially while taking regular medication. It is simply a bad idea for physicians to place elderly patients on psychotropic medication, no matter what the psychiatric disorder, and to think that the problem is solved. Parents with serious emotional difficulties require ongoing support and assistance in understanding themselves and their illnesses, and adjusting to life's difficulties given their particular vulnerabilities. While the underlying illness may or may not be biologic, such persons are clearly more susceptible to stress and will be greatly benefited if a counselor can pick up on areas of difficulty and prevent them from intensifying, minimizing the potential for further breakdowns.

The therapist you or your parent selects for counseling should have proper credentials and training. A psychiatrist, licensed psychologist, social worker, or psychiatric nurse, any of these is well qualified, especially if they have demonstrated some interest and expertise in geriatrics. A trained mental health worker, as part of a geriatric psychiatric team, usually can perform the same function successfully. It is always important to chose someone with whom your parent is comfortable, and who seems knowledgeable and flexible enough to respond to the specific needs of an aged person.

MAKING CHANGES IN YOUR PARENT'S ENVIRONMENT

Often the best therapeutic results can be achieved in the simplest of ways, by making needed changes in a parent's living situation. Often the emotional distress is primarily a result of increasingly unmanageable conditions. Such supportive changes may make an overwhelmed parent comfortable enough to cope again, so that symptoms of anxiety and depression may be relieved, allowing him to function more effectively, without the need for psychotherapy or medication. For a complete discussion of possible environmental adjustments see chapter 4: Looking at the Home Environment: When It's Time for a Change. The suggestions and variations thereof offer almost endless possibilities for supportive care to bolster those suffering from emotional distress. When these environmental supports are used in conjunction with psychotherapy and medication, your parent's chance of a successful resolution is maximized fully.

DRUG THERAPY

Psychotropic medication (medication that affects the mind) is so prevalant in the treatment of psychiatric disorders in the elderly that its use is estimated to be as high as 35 percent in patients over the age of sixty-five, and even higher in nursing home residents.

While drug use has almost become a national pastime, a great deal of confusion exists about its values and drawbacks. Clearly, something so widely used should be better understood.

The fact is that proper administration of such medication can be extremely useful in treating psychiatric illness in the elderly, but only when used intelligently and with caution, with a full awareness of the special problems associated with the aging body. Improper use can cause more harm than good, while random self-medication, which is so common, can have lethal consequences. (See the section in chapter 3 on "Medication and Your Parent: Avoiding Unnecessary Complications and Side Effects" for a general discussion of the special considerations involved in medicating the elderly.) At this point, let us focus on the proper place for psychotropic medication in a treatment plan for a parent with psychiatric illness.

Categories of Psychotropic Medication

Psychotropic medications fall into several categories according to their therapeutic actions.

Major tranquilizers. These drugs are also known as neuroleptics or antipsychotic medication. The name "tranquilizer" here is something of a misnomer, misleading at best, and has caused endless confusion between these medications and minor tranquilizers like Valium which are more correctly thought of as calming agents. Major tranquilizers include chlorpromazine (Thorazine), thioridazine (Mellaril), trifluoperazine (Stelazine), fluphenazine

(Prolixin), haloperidol (Haldol), and many others. They are used in the treatment of severe psychiatric illness of a psychotic or agitated nature. They are quite different from minor tranquilizers like Valium which are simply used to relieve anxiety. While they also calm patients who are frightened by their psychotic ideas and hallucinations, they are basically used to organize fragmented thinking, to reduce or eliminate hallucinations and delusional ideas, and to diminish severe agitation and violent behavior. In young patients these drugs are used primarily in the treatment of schizophrenia and are tremendously effective, far reducing the numbers of patients who previously had to live out their lives in state hospitals. In the elderly, these same drugs are used, although in very small doses, to treat paranoid disorders as well as agitation and assaultive behavior secondary to organic mental states. These problems are so common among the senile elderly that they account for most of the vast numbers of nursing home residents on psychiatric medication, and are frequently used to maintain patients at home in a more manageable state. Typical choices for elderly patients include haloperidol (Haldol) and trifluoperazine (Stelazine), which are the least sedating, or chlorpromazine (Thorazine), or thioridazine (Mellaril), which can make a patient sleepy, a frequently desired side effect for patients who are agitated and difficult to control at night. These drugs are not addicting, which means that a patient does not go into withdrawal when they are stopped, and does not need more and more to produce the desired effect over time. Side effects are relatively minimal and generally include dry mouth, occasional abnormal body movements which are controllable with antiparkinsonian medication, sedation or diminished blood pressure if the dose is too high. Because side effects tend to be so minimal, these medications can be prescribed for use at home without much difficulty, providing caution is exercised initially to find the proper dosage. Since a patient with an organic mental state will deteriorate over time, the dose will have to be continually evaluated and regulated under the supervision of an experienced psychiatrist.

Minor Tranquilizers. Various derivatives of these drugs have been proliferating in recent years and are so popular that they are now virtually household words. These antianxiety agents include diazepam (Valium), chlordiazepoxide (Librium), alprazolam (Xanax), clorazepate dipotassium (Tranxene), lorazepam (Ativan), oxazepam (Serax), triazolam (Halcion), and temazepam (Restoril). These medications are now the most frequently prescribed in the United States and are not only extremely effective in reducing tension and anxiety and treating insomnia, but the most frequently abused.

All of these medications are addicting, a fact that was unknown up until several years ago, and must be used with caution, particularly in the elderly. Addicting means that patients will develop a tolerance to these medications and require increasing doses to produce the same effect over time. Discontinuation of an addicting medication will produce a withdrawal syndrome which can be dangerous and is notoriously prevalent in these medications. Abuse over a long period of time requires slow detoxification (that is, gradual withdrawal of the medication by slowly decreasing the dose), to avoid such a withdrawal syndrome. Another danger of these drugs is that because they are so commonly used and were thought for so long to be so safe, people tend to swap them indiscriminately. While younger people can probably get away with this without much difficulty, the aged are particularly vulnerable and indiscriminate use may induce sedation, depression, and addiction.

Given all the warnings about abuse and addiction, however, these medications should not be discredited. Used properly, they are extremely effective, both for relieving tension and for treating insomnia. Neurotic symptoms in the elderly, caused by unrelieved anxiety, manifest themselves in overt anxiety, insomnia, hypochondriasis, and agitation. While psychotherapy is most useful in understanding the underlying causes, some people will reject such treatment, while others will require some calming agent to relieve their distress while the underlying causes are explored. Not only are these medications very effective in relieving the symptoms already described, they can be especially useful in relieving episodes of acute agitation and crippling panic attacks.

Although side effects of these tranquilizers for younger patients are very minor and infrequent, in the elderly they may produce drowsiness, impaired motor coordination, and even a significant depression if used over a long period of time. Because drug levels gradually build up in the body, it is generally better for an elderly parent to choose a medication with a short half-life. This means that a drug moves through the body and is excreted in a shorter time. As a result, a drug like alprazolam (Xanax) is now considered a better choice than diazepam (Valium) for elderly patients because of its much shorter half-life.

In order to minimize the danger of addiction, I advise using these medications in as low a dose as possible, omitting doses whenever feasible (at least one dose every other day) and avoiding nightly use of sleeping medications (two nights in a row each week without medication is optimal). Increasing usage must be recognized immediately and gradual reduction in dosage initiated even over a parent's objections.

Barbiturates and Other Hypnotics. For many years people relied on barbiturates (including phenobarbital, amobarbital, secobarbital) to relieve anxiety and treat insomnia. These early barbiturates were joined by meprobamate (Miltown) and similar compounds like methyprylone (Noludar) and ethchlorynol (Placidyl).

While all of these medications are somewhat effective and were popular in their time, they were soon found to be extremely dangerous, especially for elderly patients for whom there is an enormous potential for producing tolerance, physical dependence, life-threatening withdrawal syndromes, as well as ease of fatal overdose. While they are still used, these medications have no place whatsoever in the treatment of anxiety or insomnia in the elderly. Minor tranquilizers, as described in the previous section, are not only far safer, but more effective.

Antidepressant Medication. This category of medication includes the tricyclic antidepressants, monoamine oxidase inhibitors, psychostimulants, and lithium. Their role in the treatment of depression, as well as their side effects, have already been described in detail in chapter 6: Depression.

Side Effects

Despite the best efforts, all psychotropic medications have some side effects. While this does not preclude their use, side effects should be understood so that you and your parent are prepared for their consequences and can spot them early on.

Cardiovascular Side Effects. The most common side effect in this category is lowered blood pressure, a particular worry as low blood pressure may precipitate dizziness or falls in fragile patients. Fractured hips are a frequent consequence of a fall after over-medication; the incidence is so high in fact, that it is now estimated that 20 percent of people who live beyond the age of eighty will break a hip at some time in their life. A particular blood pressure problem with medication is orthostatic hypotension. This means that when a person rises from a sitting to a standing position, or from a lying to a standing position, the body takes a longer period of time to adjust to the change and the blood pressure falls drastically. As a result, particularly when your parent gets up to go to the bathroom during the night, there is the danger of lowered blood pressure and a consequent fall.

Therefore, if your parent is taking psychotropic medication, be sure he has his blood pressure monitored regularly, in sitting and standing positions. If this difficulty occurs, he should be instructed to use caution when changing from one position to another.

Cardiac side effects are much less frequent, but must be considered. The most dangerous situation is for those who have heart disease which interferes with the heart's electrical conduction system causing a heart block. Such a condition will be picked up on an electrocardiogram so that this test is always a prerequisite of antidepressant medication in elderly. Use of antidepressant medication in elderly persons with heart block presents the only potentially fatal consequence of these medications.

Sedation. This effect is so simple that it may be overlooked, but it is a common difficulty which must be evaluated over time. A good therapeutic effect obviously makes no sense if your parent is too drowsy to enjoy the achievement. Doses must be regulated cautiously to avoid sedation, or reverse it when it occurs.

Neurological Side Effects. An elderly parent who is taking a major tranquilizer is far more susceptible to neurologic difficulties known as extrapyramidal side effects. This is a fancy name which means that these medications may produce abnormal body movements of one sort or another. These side effects begin generally at 4 to 21 days after the onset of treatment, and are infrequent after 3 months. They are reversible by discontinuing the offending medication, but they can also be controlled by the additional use of low doses of antiparkinsonian medications such as trihexyphenidyl (Artane) or benztropine (Cogentin). Frequently, antipsychotic medication is given in combination with antiparkinsonian medication, the latter's purpose is to control these common but irritating side effects. The only serious, and often irreversible, neurologic side effect, is tardive dyskinesia, a syndrome in which the mouth and tongue move uncontrollably in a chewing-like motion. This side effect is most common when high doses of antipsychotic medication have been used for a long period of time. At the first sign of this side effect, medication should be immediately discontinued if the psychotic illness is not too severe to disallow it.

Anticholinergic Side Effects. These most common side effects are generally minor, but most annoying. The term "anticholinergic" simply means that since these medications are so active in the nervous system they also interfere with other nervous system functions. The results include: dry mouth (by blocking the action of the salivary glands); lowered blood pressure; constipation (by blocking the motility of the bowel); urinary retention (by blocking bladder emptying, a particular concern for elderly men with enlarged prostates); and the aggravation of glaucoma (by blocking the outlet canal for ocular fluid).

All of these are quickly and easily reversible if the medication is stopped in a timely fashion.

Allergic Reactions. Even allergic reactions tend to be more common in the elderly. These are relatively rare but include suppression of the bone marrow, leading to severe anemias, liver damage, and dermatitis. These are so infrequent that they should not be frightening or a major consideration in accepting their use.

DRUG INTERACTIONS

Families, patients, and physicians must always be on the lookout for potentially dangerous drug interactions, a particular concern for the elderly because of the greater likelihood of multiple prescribed medications.

While a complete list of potential interactions would be difficult to provide, and overwhelming as well, the most commonly encountered difficulties should be mentioned:

Drug Interactions with Major Tranquilizers

Cholinergic Blocking Effects. Many elderly patients take drugs which have the same tendency to interfere with certain nervous system functions as do the major tranquilizers. When such medications are administered along with a major tranquilizer, they have an additive effect. As a result, dry mouth, urinary retention, and severe constipation, can become serious problems. Potential interacting drugs include belladonna alkaloids (including Donnatal), anticholinergics, antihistamines, and tricyclic antidepressants.

Alpha-Adrenergic Blocking Effects. This is a second category of nervous system functions which can be severely affected if major tranquilizers are administered at the same time as reserpine (Serpasil), phenoxybenzamine (Dibenzyline), phentolamine (Regitine), and methyl dopa (Aldomet).

Antihypertensives. Major tranquilizers prevent certain high blood pressure medications (antihypertensives) from reaching the receptor site where they work, thereby reducing their therapeutic effect. Potential difficulties have been found with guanethidine (Ismelin or Esimil), bethanidone, and clonidine (Catapres).

Sedatives. If your parent is already taking a sedative, that is, a medication which depresses the central nervous system, adding a major tranquilizer to his drug regimen may precipitate extreme sedation. The effects of the combination are additive.

Anticonvulsants. Major tranquilizers tend to lower the seizure threshold in patients with convulsive disorders, and may precipitate seizures in patients who had been stable prior to their administration.

Drug Interactions with Tricyclic Antidepressants

Far more than the major tranquilizers, these drugs block certain central nervous system functions and produce the same interactions mentioned in the previous section, only to a far greater extent.

Tricyclic antidepressants will reduce and delay the absorption of phenylbutazone (Butazolidin) and levodopa (L-dopa), which reduces the therapeutic effect of these drugs.

Estrogens may enhance the effect of antidepressants by interfering with their metabolism and breakdown.

Thyroid drugs will stimulate antidepressant activity.

Tricyclic antidepressants interfere with certain antihypertensives (guanethidine, bethanidine, and clonidine).

Seizures can break through in patients who have been previously controlled with anticonvulsant medication, though this is rare.

Drug Interactions with Monoamine Oxidase Inhibitors (MAOIs)

As discussed in chapter 6, Depression, these drugs are particularly likely to interact adversely with other medications and even certain foods, by inhibiting the breakdown of catecholamines. Increased levels of catecholamines raise the blood pressure, sometimes dangerously, and can result in hypertensive crises, fast heart rate, fever, agitation, delirium, and even stroke. As a result, foods containing tyramine, dopa, or serotonin must be avoided. A complete diet including foods to avoid has already been presented in chapter 6.

Because MAOIs increase the level of catecholamines, obviously medications which similarly increase catecholamines are strongly contraindicated. These include cold medications, nasal decongestants, asthma inhalants, many allergy and hay fever medications, various narcotics especially meperidine (Demerol), amphetamines, antiappetite or diet medications, adrenaline, local anesthetics with adrenaline, as well as L-dopa for Parkinson's disease.

Because of the range of interactions, if your parent is on a monoamine oxidase inhibitor, you must check with his physician before using any other medication. Dental and surgical procedures can be performed only after these medications have been discontinued for a period of time.

Lithium

The main drugs which interact adversely with lithium are the diuretics (water pills). Diuretics will interfere with the kidneys' excretion of lithium and cause the drug to build up in the system, potentially to toxic levels. Any patient on lithium who uses diuretics must be carefully monitored by the treating psychiatrist.

Alcohol

One of the most common concerns is the combination of alcohol with any medication. While this is a complicated area, a simple rule of thumb is that alcohol is only prohibited with barbiturates (sleep medication like Seconal and phenobarbital which elderly patients should never use in any case). Otherwise, alcohol can be consumed in moderation with all other categories of psychotropic medication without danger. However, remember that alcohol does exaggerate the action of drugs by interfering with their metabolism (breakdown by the body) and may increase their action. Moderation is the key.

In short, the area of drug interaction is a complex one, especially in the case of an elderly parent on a variety of medications. Administration and supervision by a knowledgeable physician will avoid these difficulties, so that these drugs may be carefully administered, as long as all pertinent information is brought to the doctor's attention. Perhaps most important, an elderly parent must avoid self-medication, and the use of multiple drugs prescribed by different physicians at different times, and used indiscriminately. Families should periodically check night tables and medicine cabinets for outdated or excessive medications and dispose of them.

Having outlined all of the pitfalls of drug therapy at the outset, I hope you are not left with the impression that psychiatric drug treatment is particularly dangerous, or fraught with unmanageable side effects. The truth is that, used with caution and knowledge, these medications remain highly effective, are remarkably safe, and can bring enormous relief to an elderly parent in emotional distress. The fact that they are so commonly used is testimony to their success. They work!

PSYCHIATRIC HOSPITALIZATION

There may be times when an elderly parent suffering from a severe mental disturbance requires hospitalization for psychiatric evaluation or treatment. Justifications for hospitalization are varied and may be essential to provide a safe environment for:

- A parent who may wish to harm or kill himself.
- Someone who is so disturbed that he is unaware of his actions and may unintentionally be a danger to himself.
- A parent who is a clear danger to others.

- A parent who has medical problems severe enough to make outpatient treatment with psychiatric medication potentially hazardous.
- A parent who has not responded to outpatient treatment and needs a more comprehensive approach including hospital supervision with nursing attention, group therapy, occupational and physical therapy, and daily counseling in an environment conducive to recovery.
- Complex diagnostic issues which require daily observation, evaluation, and testing as well as joint assessment by professionals with a wide variety of backgrounds.
- Substance abuse with the need for supervised detoxification (withdrawal).

Psychiatric hospitalization can be a thorny issue, resisted by parent and family alike because of the stigma traditionally attached to it. While this is understandable and must be dealt with, avoidance of necessary hospitalization may be just as life-threatening as the refusal to accept hospitalization for acute medical illnesses. This is a prejudice which must be overcome. Furthermore, brief hospitalizations can frequently be arranged in psychiatric units within a general hospital facility, reducing the "stigma" for your parent, as well as your nightmares about "snake pits" and state hospitals.

Hospitalization in a psychiatric unit will naturally have some potentially frightening aspects. The unit may be unlocked; the windows will be secured; mirrors may be made of special glass; there may be only community pay telephones; and no individual television sets. There may be some frightening looking patients on the unit; and there may be a seclusion room for agitated patients. On the other hand, no one has to remain in bed; people are dressed in street clothes; there are professionals available 24 hours a day to talk to; there are regular activities to attend, and group meetings. Dining is generally in a communal dining hall and there are ample lounge areas for socialization. After overcoming the initial concerns, most people find such situations relaxing and therapeutic.

At the hospital, you will find professionals from a wide range of disciplines who bring their individual expertise to bear on the treatment program. There will be psychiatrists, with expertise in both psychotherapy and the use of psychotropic medications and their adverse side effects; consulting internists and subspecialists for any concomitant physical problem; psychiatric nurses who understand psychiatric illness as well as the medications required; psychologists available for testing; social workers to provide additional counseling, work with families, and offer information and assistance about postdischarge resources in the community; activity therapists who provide a range of art, dance, music, and movement programs to supplement and further recovery. These specialists will confer with one another in assessing and treating your parent in the hospital, and deciding on discharge planning to continue the progress achieved during the hospital stay. Involved family members should be included in all decision making, and counseling and support groups for families are almost always available. The emphasis nowadays is on short-term hospital stays. This reduces the fear that your parent may have that he is going to be locked away for an extended period of time. Any lingering fears of being "put away forever" are no longer justified.

In special circumstances, where continued maintenance at home may be dangerous or impossible to implement, consideration may be given to extended care in a nursing home or health-related facility. More frequently, your parent will be returned to the home situation, sometimes with auxiliary help to permit better functioning and an improved quality of life.

Admission to a psychiatric hospital can be arranged in accordance with several different procedures which vary from state to state. Psychiatric hospitalization, unlike other medical hospitalization, can be a particularly thorny legal area, because, so frequently the patient is unaware of his illness, resists treatment, and must be hospitalized against his will. The basic underlying problem is how best to protect the patient's rights without endangering him or the community. Understandably, people will have different ideas about this and when people disagree it becomes a legal question. Because it is such a common concern, each state has worked out its own legal procedures to guide those involved, and to adjudicate conflicting opinions when they arise. Despite years of experience, this remains a difficult decision to make, and recent court hearings over the involuntary hospitalization of questionably disturbed homeless people have brought this problem again to the forefront of legal and psychiatric concern.

If the psychiatric hospitalization is voluntary, that is, your parent is willing to sign himself into a hospital, there is little difficulty or confusion. Signing a document agreeing to psychiatric hospitalization permits the hospital to retain your parent unless he requests discharge. Even then, generally the hospital has a period of time (often 72 hours) to decide on the safety of release from a psychiatric facility. The facility may comply, but it may also decide to change the person's status to an involuntary one, a decision about which you and your parent have legal redress.

If the hospitalization is involuntary, or if a voluntary status is changed to an involuntary one, then the legal apparatus is naturally far more complex. Again, the rules vary from state to state, but generally an involuntary hospitalization can be arranged through a combination of family petitioners who feel that hospitalization is necessary, and licensed doctors who attest to a person's need for involuntary retention. City and state facilities also have the right to retain individuals against their will. The rules governing involuntary retention depend basically on whether the person represents a danger to himself or others, but the degree of menace may have to be decided upon ultimately by the courts. The degree of psychiatric disturbance will be taken into account.

This may all seem cumbersome, but every state does have a system and experienced psychiatrists know how to work appropriately within legal bounds. In most cases a parent can be hospitalized either through the action of relatives and physicians, through a court order obtained by the family, or through city or state hospitals who are so empowered. Once hospitalized, patients have state-established legal resources to advise them as to their rights and which will arrange a court hearing within a limited period of time. At a court hearing, evidence is presented and a judgment can either release the individual or retain him for a specified length of time. Such decisions are reviewed periodically, so that no one can be retained indefinitely against his will.

Geriatric patients present a special situation within the general psychiatric-legal framework. Frequently, they are less aware of their rights and, frankly, attorneys and courts are less likely to vigorously advocate for them. While this makes it easier for families and psychiatrists to hospitalize a disturbed parent, their rights must be considered and their wishes taken into consideration whenever feasible. It is too easy to ride roughshod over the wishes of elderly patients, particularly those with diminished mental faculties, when careful attention can often lead to a resolution which is satisfying to all parties concerned. Sometimes this is not possible and then you must have the courage to make appropriate decisions to protect your parent's well being.

Involuntary psychiatric hospitalization of an elderly parent may be indicated in the following situations:

- Suicidal depressions, especially if your parent is isolated, has expressed the desire to die, and is so hopeless that he cannot be involved in any outpatient treatment approach.
- A severely depressed parent, who has stopped eating and caring for himself to the point where he is at risk, even without specific active suicidal intent.
- An agitated and aggressive parent with poor judgment who may attack others, either as a result of senility, mania, or paranoia.
- A paranoid parent whose psychotic ideas about others may be potentially dangerous.
- A parent with severe dementia who is totally unable to care for himself is at obvious imminent risk, but is unaware of his predicament and refuses assistance despite vigorous efforts on his behalf.

All of these situations may require urgent psychiatric hospitalization for which your parent may see no need. Despite objections, this can and must be accomplished through legal procedures established by your state. It is never "impossible" to arrange if you are determined, concerned, and willing to follow through. Failure to do so can lead to far greater and even potentially fatal consequences.

Part III

Caring for
Parents with
Physical
Illness

·10·

When the Mind
Begins to Fail

- *Understanding the Process*
- *What to Do and How to Go About It*

As discussed in an earlier chapter, some degree of memory loss is probably unavoidable in later life and should be anticipated without undue alarm. While you can honestly reassure your parents that such memory lapses are typical and most elderly people live out their lives in complete control of their mental abilities, some unfortunately will develop what others only fear: a true dementia.

Frightening as it may be, if your parent is beginning to show signs of significant memory loss and confusion, you must face up to the possible implications and arrange for an immediate evaluation by an experienced physician. Attempts to deny or cover up may be completely understandable for an affected parent, but not for a concerned family member.

A thorough medical evaluation is vital for the simple reason that, while some forms of dementia are untreatable, others respond very nicely, and all the more so if they are caught at an early stage.

In order to diagnose the treatable types of dementia, doctors have made a sensible distinction between its two forms: reversible and irreversible. The reversible dementias have been subdivided into three categories: delirium, normal pressure hydrocephalus, and pseudodementia (a form of depression already described). The irreversible dementias include Alzheimer's disease, which is now so much in the public eye, and multi-infarct dementia (caused by atherosclerosis, the same process responsible for heart disease and strokes), plus a few less common neurologic disorders.

REVERSIBLE DEMENTIAS

Reversible dementias are particularly important to recognize since prompt treatment is the key to a satisfactory result.

Delirium is the most common form of reversible dementia and refers to a state of severe mental confusion which, unlike the situation in most irreversible dementias, seems to give no warning. One day your parent will be perfectly all right and, the next, he may be utterly confused. In this case, your index of suspicion should be very high for a treatable, reversible dementia.

In addition to its rapid onset, a number of other clues help distinguish delirium from chronic irreversible dementia. For instance, in states of delirium, the person has a "clouded sensorium." This means that a person has a reduced awareness of his environment and seems to be in a "fog" or "out of it." He cannot focus his attention on the world at large, and drifts in and out of touch with reality.

At other times, far from being "out of it," he may be hyperaroused, anxious, and restless.

He develops "illusions" or visual misinterpretations. Illusions are not hallucinations; when a person hallucinates, he hears voices or sees things that are not there, in an illusion, there is only misrepresentation of what actually *is* in the room; for instance, he may think that the blanket is a person or that the window shade is a ghost.

In reversible dementia, the person is highly distractable. Psychomotor activity is altered, meaning that he is either overactive or stuporous.

Although disoriented with impaired memory, he appears to be perplexed by what is going on. He neither takes his confusion in stride nor denies it as an irreversibly demented person is often prone to do.

Finally, normal sleep cycles are disturbed and frightening night-mares are common.

Delirium, or acute brain syndrome, as it is also commonly known, can be the consequence of almost any significant medical problem to which the elderly are naturally and particularly prone. If the underlying disorder can be determined early and reversed, the mental confusion which accompanies it may gradually or even rapidly disappear. If the underlying problem is not discovered, the mental change can often become permanent, or the person's mental state will deteriorate from the underlying medical illness. A sudden onset delirium is a *signal of illness* and must be investigated vigorously. While almost any underlying medical problem can cause a delirium, the most common causes are listed below:

- The number one offender is medication. Always evaluate your parent's medication, especially if a new medication has been prescribed recently. Never let anyone tell you that a medicine is safe and has no side effects. That is never true for everyone, and particularly for the elderly who are highly susceptible to medication side effects. Even if your parent has been on the same medication for a long time, medication levels tend to build up in the body overtime and can cause confused states in elderly people. In his confusion, there is a danger that a parent may self-medicate or overmedicate himself. Always check your parent's medicine cabinet to see what medications he may be using.

- Malnutrition. Delirium can result from poor eating with vitamin deficiency developing over a period of time. Many elderly have poor eating habits, and some will stop eating during periods of mental stress. In time, this will result in severe confusion.

- Dehydration in elderly parents can happen very quickly, just as it does in infants. This can occur because they simply do not drink enough liquids because of hot weather, or after an extended period of diarrhea or vomiting. Dehydration is a very common occurrence, and can be reversed in less than a day through the administration of intravenous fluids.

- Anemia is a low blood count with diminished red blood cells, which means less oxygen for the brain. Less oxygen means that the brain does not function well and confusion ensues.
- Infections in the body have the capacity to cause a confusional state, especially if your parent already has some borderline mental impairment. Venereal diseases are still occasional possibilities and should not be overlooked.
- Heart and blood vessel disease, such as irregularities of the heart can intermittently affect a parent's mental state. Any heart or blood vessel disease can cause confusion and some of these disorders are easily treated with medication or even surgery. Atherosclerotic clogging of blood vessels in the neck and brain can cause episodes of confusion, known as transient ischemic attacks (TIAs). Blockages in the large carotid arteries in the neck altering circulation to the brain are particularly amenable to surgical intervention, a situation which can easily be detected during a routine physical examination.
- Brain tumors are always dreaded, but are seldom the cause of a confused mental state. Some are benign and can be excised surgically with excellent result.
- Trauma, even a minor head injury, in an elderly person can sometimes cause internal bleeding which may not be obvious. Symptoms may not occur for a week or more in a subdural hematoma, a blood clot in the brain which can be surgically removed with full return of functioning.
- Lung diseases, such as emphysema and related disorders, diminish the supply of oxygen to the brain.
- Cirrhosis of the liver or other liver disease poses a significant threat for the elderly. The liver excretes body wastes. If it is not functioning properly, these wastes will build up, make a person toxic, and cause delirium.
- Kidney disease, similar to liver disease, results if the kidneys malfunction and do not rid the body of waste products.
- Thyroid disorders affect the body's metabolism which is essential to normal mental functioning.

- Substance abuse should never be dismissed. Remember that an elderly parent may secretly abuse alcohol or drugs. Frequent misdiagnoses are made because this is not considered. Substance abuse and the concomitant withdrawal states can be readily relieved if they are acknowledged, or they can lead to increasing confusion which may become irreversible if left untreated.

In short, it should be obvious that almost any medical problem affecting the physical state of the body can cause acute dementias. Many of these can be reversed if detected and treated early. The rapid onset of a confusional state should never be ignored or dismissed as hopeless senility. Unfortunately, this is an all too common assumption, and such reversible conditions remain untreated.

With all of these possible underlying causes, it might seem particularly difficult to determine the true culprit. In reality, a careful assessment by an experienced physician, preferably one who specializes in geriatric medicine, can rather quickly detect any of these problems, even though the list may seem long to a layperson. Except in occasional complicated cases, it is not even a particularly hard diagnosis to make.

An assessment of an acute delirium starts with a careful and attentive medical history, consisting of an investigation of the presenting problem, all previous medical conditions, hospitalizations, and use of medication. Under these circumstances, the patient is is obviously incapable of giving this history himself. As a result, the physician must make do with material gathered from all significant people available and you must offer what assistance you can. This careful history-taking is followed by a complete physical examination, and a series of laboratory tests which screen for most of the possible underlying difficulties described earlier. These tests have been mentioned in chapter 5 on assessment.

These basic tests will be followed up by more specific procedures should any abnormalities be detected. Treatment for a reversible brain disorder depends on discovering and correcting its underlying cause. Sometimes this can be done on an outpatient basis; but, if the delirium is severe, emergency hospitalization may be required. In such severe cases, hospitalization permits the patient's circulation and oxygen level to be maintained, glucose given intravenously, and vital signs checked frequently to evaluate body temperature, pulse rate, respiration, and blood pressure. Never forget that a patient in such a situation is frightened and confused. His anxiety can be reduced substantially if a familiar person remains with him, and if he is placed in a quiet room and is not exposed to excessive outside stimulation. Always try to avoid restraints which may create further anxiety, but do not be afraid to use them if, for example, you fear your parent can injure himself severely while in such confused, agitated states.

While delirium is the most frequent form of reversible dementia, two other conditions bear special mention because they are not uncommon and frequently forgotten.

The first is a condition known as normal pressure hydrocephalus. This complicated name refers to a neurologic disorder in which excessive fluid accumulates in the brain because of faulty reabsorption causing pressure which results in gradual destruction of brain tissue. Its characteristic symptoms include a progressive confusion, difficulty walking, and urinary incontinence. This particular triad of symptoms does not occur early in Alzheimer's disease, with which this condition is too frequently confused, and if these symptoms are present, an immediate neurologic evaluation should be performed. Surgical intervention by shunting the excessive brain fluid results in some improvement in about half the cases, with cessation of further deterioration.

Another form of fully reversible dementia, which is even more frequently ignored, is pseudodementia, in which the patient seems grossly confused, but there is no medical basis for their condition (see page 118). As discussed, such patients characteristically develop their dementia rapidly; their confusion is not progressive but sudden and full-blown. These patients are actually suffering from a "masked" depression, not dementia, and their confusion is accompanied by other symptoms of depression, making proper diagnosis possible. This syndrome responds well to antidepressant medication with complete remission of the confused state. Since reversible dementias in the elderly are probably responsible for *upward of 20 percent of all new dementias,* they are the most important of all to identify early, because they can effectively be treated.

IRREVERSIBLE DEMENTIAS

Irreversible dementia, the understandable dread of the elderly, may be overwhelming for you as well. There is no denying that this is a terrible disease, and as the name says, it is truly irreversible.

The irreversibility of this disorder is understandably difficult for patients and families to accept, and it is particularly sad, and unfortunately all too common, to see people who are still searching for a more knowledgeable doctor who is up on the latest medication and will have an antidote. No such antidote exists, and there is no evidence to suggest that any cure will be forthcoming soon. If a dementia is irreversible, you must accept and adjust to the fact, and deal with it intelligently. To do so, the first step is to understand the illness with which we are dealing.

As with reversible dementias, the basic problem is that of intellectual deterioration and memory loss. Unlike reversible dementias, however, irreversible dementias:

- Generally, but not always, have a relatively slow (insidious) onset. The patient gradually becomes confused and forgetful, and early signs can be detected months in advance of any significant confusion.
- There is no "clouding of consciousness." Patients are perfectly alert, just confused. Nor is there any abnormal body activity.
- The intellectual decline progresses inexorably in a common pattern. Often the first signs are personality changes, or a marked exaggeration of previous trends in your parent's regular personality. Paranoia and depression can be early symptoms, emerging even before obvious decrements in intellectual functioning are apparent. Your parent will be anxious and try to "cover up" his own early awareness of memory deficit and

slowed thinking. He will be moody and prone to aggressive outbursts.

Soon after, the more ominous and undisguisable memory defects begin. Your parent will forget recent events and be unable to retain new information. Later, he will experience disorientation to time, followed frequently by disorientation to place. General information, particularly having to do with current events, is also soon lost.

Further on, and by now the dementia should be obvious to everyone, there will be verbal changes such as perseveration (repeating phrases over and over) and confabulation (making up entire stories in response to questions). Motor unrest, pacing, wandering, and the inability to sit still may become prominent, sometimes followed by apathy, complete dullness, and the inability to recognize even close family members. In the end there is a complete loss of memory and even the sense of one's own identity may be lost, accompanied invariably by incontinence and occasionally by erratic, uncontrolled body movements.

Perhaps a typical case history would be useful:

When I first met her, Mrs. W. was a sophisticated, stylish society matron in her middle fifties. She was accompanied by her husband, her poise marred only by her tense anticipation of our meeting. She was afraid of the questions she could no longer answer.

Her excellent memory, it seemed, was no longer what it had been. Although she reassured herself that she still remained exquisitely acute in recalling the slightest detail involved in the upbringing of her two sons, she showed alarming gaps in recalling simple everyday things, gaps which were beginning to embarrass her in social situations. An avid bridge player with several master points to her credit, she had completely forsaken tournament play, and her errors at friendly neighborhood games left her friends perplexed, and discreetly questioning her as to whether she was distracted. But she knew that she was not distracted. More frightening than that, she knew she could no longer remember the cards. Intelligent and shrewd, with a lifetime of social graces eminently intact, she gamely tried to hide from me those same disturbing lapses in memory and thinking, and attempted to portray herself as controlled and intact. But when questioned more exactly, she could no longer maintain her facade and even her worried and intuitive husband was surprised to see that her arithmetic would no longer be acceptable to a sixth grader, and that she could no longer quite remember the name of the president, although it was just on the tip of her tongue.

I had occasion to see her over the next few years as her thinking became more confused and her world more constricted. Bridge was a thing of the past, and she avoided even her dearest friends who treated her in a new way: "kindly, perhaps, but as if I am no longer one of them." She picked up on the unintentional slights, the overly concerned comments, which she immediately recognized as patronizing. Their extreme kindness was cruel in emphasizing her differentness, and she was humiliated in their company.

Pretense was not quite forgotten, but her memory became so bad that she no longer questioned it and reluctantly agreed to hire her housekeeper as a full-time companion, remarking with poignant regret that she only dimly understood: "Our roles seem to have changed, almost reversed somehow, as if I were a child and she needed to guide me."

She uncertainly appreciated her husband's concern in drawing her a map from her apartment to my office, and gamely followed it with intense concentration, never allowing her companion to guide her. She knew enough to hide it from others and was still aware in a vague way that the map itself was something to be ashamed of, but was no longer quite certain of what she was ashamed.

One day she remarked with sadness that her husband had moved into the spare bedroom, and was annoyed as well, but she made excuses for him and was afraid to ask why. She seemed no longer to hear when her companion murmured to me that she was incontinent at times. She seemed to tune things out when people whispered in front of her.

She occasionally pretended interest when she thought it was

expected of her, but no longer had any, not even for our occasional talks. She seldom recalled my name, and was no longer embarrassed about it. Finally, she came no more. Several months later her husband called to tell me that he had found her playing with her own feces, smearing herself with great delight as she talked aimlessly to herself. He had decided to take steps to institutionalize her, despite his loyalty and misgivings.

When she was finally admitted to a carefully selected nursing home she was not aware of the change.

She died there, three years later, at the age of sixty-one.

The chronic progressive irreversible dementias are essentially of two basic types: Alzheimer's disease and multi-infarct dementia—although there are also several other less common neurologic disorders. While the brain pathology is quite different in all of these distinct illnesses, the course and outcome are similarly bleak: a gradual downhill progression to complete dementia and death within three to ten years, sometimes even more rapidly.

Alzheimer's Disease

In 1907 Alois Alzheimer, a pathologist, autopsied the brains of a series of patients who had become demented at an early age. He discovered certain typical examples of brain damage, specifically, a gross atrophy (shrinking) of the brain, particularly in the cerebral cortex (where intellectual functions are carried on) and in the hippocampal area (a section deep in the brain involved in emotion). On microscopic examination of brain tissue, he discovered the now classic findings of neurofibrillatory tangles (dying or degenerating nerve cells) and senile plaques (twisted masses of nerve tissue and amyloid) which are the hallmarks of what is now known as Alzheimer's disease. Simply stated, he found that the disease resulted from the unexplained and rapid death of nerve cells in the brain, a form of primary neuronal degeneration. It is now understood that the neurons which are particularly affected belong to brain sections known as the locus coeruleus and the nucleus basalis of Meynert, areas involved with the production of acetylcholine, the neurotransmitter vital to memory processes.

Although Alzheimer's original work dealt with early, so-called presenile dementias, it was long known that elderly patients also suffered from a clinically identical illness and on autopsy showed the same brain lesions. The only difference seemed to be that the earlier onset Alzheimer's disease ran a quicker and more virulent course. As a result of the basic similarities, it was decided to drop the old differentiation between earlier presenile dementia and senile dementias of later life, and to call them all Alzheimer's disease. As we all know, this name captured the public's imagination in the early 1980s and by the time it made the cover of the weekly news magazines, it had secured its place in the medical and public nomenclature.

In any case, what we are dealing with is the rapid acceleration of brain cell death in particular areas of the brain, as well as the depletion of brain neurotransmitters that carry nerve impulses from one brain cell to another (acetylcholine and the enzyme responsible for its synthesis, choline acetyltransferase) all of which are involved in promoting memory and thinking.

Alzheimer's disease accounts for 50 to 70 percent of irreversible dementias making it the fourth leading cause of death in the United States, responsible for 100,000 deaths each year. A recent study at Boston's Brigham and Women's Hospital suggested that 10 percent of people sixty-five and older and 50 percent of those over eighty-five were suffering from the illness, which may seem terribly ominous if you do not recall that less than 3 percent are affected under age seventy-nine. I suggest that you be cautious about these statistics. My hunch is that many elderly people (especially those over eighty-five) suffering from the "normal" memory loss expected in advanced age are being lumped in and may be inflating the numbers. The most relevant factor about these new population studies is the evidence that Alzheimer's disease seems to run in families far more often than originally believed.

Details of genetic transmission are still unclear, but seem more likely to occur in cases of dementias with an early age onset, with some suggestion that close relatives of affected patients may have as much as four times the chance of developing the illness as does the general population. An estimated 10 to 30 percent of victims have the type which is inherited.

The cause of Alzheimer's is entirely unknown, although there is no want for theories. These include: infection with a slow virus (a virus that takes many years to cause illness, similar to the situation suspected in multiple sclerosis); higher concentration of metals in the brain (particularly aluminum); an autoimmune phenomenon (in which the body attacks itself); head trauma; or the most recent idea, a defect in the twenty-first chromosome.

Daniel Carleton Gajdusek, a Nobel Prize–winning researcher, has unified all of these theories by suggesting that not one but a variety of different insults to the nervous system may interfere with axonal transport of neurofilament leading to their piling up in the neuron, with cell death resulting. That is, many different causes can have the same effect on the central nervous system. In short, no one knows the cause and the possibilities raised are the same possibilities that researchers bring up for every other disease whose origin is unknown. It may well be years before any answer is found.

Sadly, there is still no cure for patients with Alzheimer's disease, a fact which is hard for people to accept, particularly for the families of those affected. To make things more confusing, various "cures" have been touted through the years, even by respected members of the medical profession, only to be retracted quietly after their day in the sun. None of these "cures" has ever panned out.

In all honesty, when you consider the underlying problem in Alzheimer's disease, it is easy to understand why a cure will not be forthcoming so readily. After all, brain cells are rapidly dying for no clear reason. Since the body has no way of replenishing dead nerve cells once they have died, there is nothing to do.

Because no one understands just why the cells die at an accelerated rate, scientists have not been able to devise a cure for preventing early cell death. The treatments to date have been aimed at maximizing the function of the brain cells that still survive, or trying to increase the amounts of chemical transmitters available in the brain. These attempts include the use of

- Vasodilators (Pavabid), drugs that expand the blood vessels, bringing increased blood flow to damaged areas of the brain.
- Metabolic enhancers (Hydergine), which increase the metabolism (activity) of the remaining nerve cells.
- Hyperbaric oxygen chambers (in which people are exposed to pressurized oxygen) which would increase the oxygenation of the brain.
- Neurotransmitter precursors (choline) which would increase the amount of acetylcholine available, the neurotransmitter depleted in this illness.
- Physostigmine, an anticholinesterase, which blocks the breakdown of acetylcholine.
- Arecholine or oxotremorine, which attempt to bypass the damaged neurons and stimulate the receptor nerve cells.
- Piracetam, which increases the activity of brain cells and perhaps their firing rate.

All good ideas that do not work.

The latest drug in this series is tetrahydroaminoacradine (THA), and there may just be a glimmer of hope about its usefulness. THA is an anticholinesterase (like physostigmine) which also blocks the breakdown of acetylcholine, the neurotransmitter depleted in Alzheimer's and necessary for the transmission of brain impulses. This medication enjoyed some interest in the early 1980s with positive claims, but these were quickly refuted while clinical trials demonstrated some associated liver damage. Recently, however, some unpublished preliminary studies seem to demonstrate some appreciable gains without excessive side effects; and there are stories of pending FDA approval. Whether or not anything truly positive has been shown is still unclear; and, even if so, this is no major breakthrough. At the very most, THA just may slow the decline. It does not reverse deterioration; and it is certainly not a cure.

There is no cure.

While this is a sad and, at present, bleak outlook, it is better to know and accept the truth than to run around looking for wonder cures that do not exist.

Although there is no treatment for Alzheimer's disease, there are many things that can be done to assist in the intelligent management of those affected, making things a bit easier for both parent and caretakers. I will describe these recommendations following the next section on multi-infarct dementia and you will see that both irreversible dementias can be handled in much the same way.

Multi-infarct Dementia

Multi-infarct dementia is the second leading type of irreversible dementia, accounting for about 15 to 20 percent of cases. This is also commonly called "hardening of the arteries" which earlier was thought to be responsible for most dementias.

This illness results from atherosclerotic changes (plaques) in the blood vessels which carry blood to different areas of the brain. These changes narrow blood vessels, reducing the circulation, and cause ministrokes throughout the brain (multiple infarcts) which destroy small discrete areas. It is exactly the same situation as a heart attack or a major stroke, but those conditions involve large blockages, and this situation is created by multiple small blockages.

Multi-infarct dementia does not run in families, is more frequent in men than in women (as are all blood vessel diseases), and occurs more frequently in patients with untreated hypertension and diabetes. It is often associated with other forms of vascular disease, particularly heart attacks. It also occurs when emboli (small blood clots) travel into the brain from plaques in the large carotid arteries of the neck, and from diseased valves in the heart. These last two conditions are potentially treatable, surgically and medically, if detected before brain damage occurs. Examples of treatment include removal of the atherosclerotic plaques in the external carotid arteries of the neck, and good control of hypertension and diabetes.

Because multi-infarct dementia results from many small strokes over a period of time, its course varies a little from Alzheimer's disease. In this condition, the onset may be more acute. Deterioration occurs with every new ministroke and, therefore, the course will follow a stepwise pattern. For some unexplained reason, multi-infarct dementia patients are also known to be more labile (emotional) than Alzheimer's patients, and even more likely to develop explosive tempers with violent outbursts.

If the ministrokes occur in certain parts of the brain (this is random and varies from patient to patient) there may be a predominance of certain specific symptoms, depending on the area of the brain affected: apraxia (forgetting how to perform a simple action); agnosia (inability to remember familiar object); ataxia (lack of coordination); aphasia (loss of speech or the ability to understand what is said).

These symptoms may occur alone or in combination, or may not be obvious at all. Clinically, these patients may seem identical to those with Alzheimer's disease and, in any case, follow substantially the same downhill course with the same drastically reduced life expectancy.

OTHER IRREVERSIBLE DEMENTIAS

These less common dementias account for a relatively small percentage of those affected, and often can only be diagnosed by a neurologist with sophisticated tests or by autopsy after death. Their course is similar, there is no cure, and I include them only briefly:

- Pick's disease is very similar in course to Alzheimer's and frequently indistinguishable until autopsy. Atrophy of the brain is particularly prominent in the frontal and temporal lobes of the brain, with characteristic Pick bodies seen on autopsy. It frequently occurs even earlier in life than Alzheimer's and even more clearly runs in families.
- Huntington's disease is a genetic disease, accompanied by severe chorea (uncontrollable "jerky" body movements).

- Parkinson's disease is predominantly a motor (body movement) disorder, with stiffness and tremor, later accompanied by dementia. In this well-known illness, the motor difficulty precedes the dementia by many years and will be detected early in the course.
- Creutzfeld-Jacob's disease is a dementia caused by a virus, with a life expectancy of only one year, accompanied by other neurologic deficits.

Taking Care of Your Parent with Irreversible Dementia

While there is no cure for dementia, or even any method of stopping or slowing the deterioration, steps must be taken to provide your parent with proper care in order to ease his situation without placing undue stress on you or other caretakers. Such a balance is difficult to arrive at, but if careful and informed planning is done, solutions can be achieved which are practical and tolerable for all involved. Most of the management techniques are quite simple and just take some common sense based on a good understanding of the illness.

Recognize and accept the illness, and your parent's limited mental capacity. Do not expect him to do more than he is capable of, and certainly do not tease him or get angry about his failings, as if it is his fault and in his control. Too frequently, family members want to deny the progress of the illness, make believe it is not happening, and wind up taking it out on the parent himself, as if he is putting on an act or not trying hard enough to remember. Don't add to your parent's distress by burdening him with your own difficulties.

Respect the need to "cover up" failings and attempts to disguise symptoms to save face. It makes no sense to rub your parent's face in his own forgetfulness and confusion. Help him over embarrassing moments by discreetly protecting his self-esteem and gently pointing him in the right direction when necessary. It is not a crime, and it is not demeaning, to humor a confused parent if he takes a foolish stand about something he has forgotten. Let it be.

When a confused parent "gets caught" in some intellectual

failing, he will often argue and become outraged and abusive, insisting that he is correct in his assertion, however faulty. Do not argue back. It will get you nowhere and needlessly upset him. When you think about it, if he accepts what you say, he is admitting to his own confusion. No one wants to accept the fact that he is losing his mental processes.

Keep the living situation simple, safe, and structured, and make sure your parent gets the assistance that he requires. Sometimes families will leave a confused parent alone all day without supervision, which is about the same thing as leaving a young child alone to function independently. This can be terribly frightening to a confused person, and lead to potentially dangerous situations: He may leave the house in a panic and wander aimlessly in the streets, set a fire through improper use of the stove, leave the gas on, etc. Supervision is essential at all times, no matter what your parent says or the family wants to believe.

Make sure that you are in tune with the progress of the disease. It is easy to deny your parent's increasing incapacity, but it will lead to problems if you do. If he starts to get lost on unsupervised walks, arrange for someone to accompany him, and have him wear an I.D. or Med-Alert bracelet at all times. If he attempts to leave the home at night, install a lock which can only be opened with a key from the inside. Just as you would with a child, try to anticipate difficulties and modify the environment to suit him so that he can carry on in safety with some measure of independence and dignity.

You may want to make use of some psychotherapy techniques. While conventional psychotherapy has little place in the treatment of dementia, some work can be done to strengthen your parent's sense of control over certain areas of his life, despite his increasing helplessness. Also, reality orientation is a useful technique through which your parent is constantly reminded and reoriented to the date, time, and place in his environment. Such reminders seem to slow deterioration, keep the person in better contact with reality, and maximize his self-esteem.

While the increasing confusion and memory loss may seem bad

enough, unfortunately your parent may also become agitated, assaultive, or paranoid as a consequence of the dementia. These secondary psychiatric symptoms invariably become problems at some point, as the dementia progresses.

Why do these secondary symptoms occur? As your parent becomes more confused and forgetful, he may become distraught, angry, and frustrated with himself, and with those around him. When a person can no longer function as he used to and no longer understands exactly what is going on around him, it is easy for him to be easily provoked, agitated, and even to strike out, sometimes violently. Try to avoid provoking your parent whenever possible, although this is not always easy to do. One frequent error, which can lead to agitation, is unnecessary arguing with an elderly parent, especially by a well-meaning family member who feels he has to point out "reality" just when a parent is trying to cover up his confusion. Such a situation is antagonistic and may lead to a violent response.

Another way in which your parent may disguise his confusion and memory loss is to become paranoid. For instance, when he mislays a valuable object, rather than accept his mental lapse, he may say "I didn't misplace my bank book. My daughter stole it!" Or, "I can't find my ring, the only one with a key to my apartment is the superintendent. He must have it!" Upsetting as these paranoid ideas are to others, they afford some measure of relief to the patient. Obviously, by believing that someone else is responsible, he does not have to accept his own forgetfulness.

Disturbing and even dangerous as these symptoms are, they represent the only relative "bright spot" in the treatment of dementia because, while nothing can be done about the underlying confusion, these secondary psychiatric symptoms can rather easily be modified with psychotropic medication (drugs that modify behavior, thinking, and mood). In fact, this is one of the most easily treated problems in all of geriatric psychiatry and no patient should be deprived of such treatment when needed.

Symptoms of agitation and paranoia will respond to certain tranquilizers which have the effect of diminishing the anxiety about the confusion. As your parent becomes less frightened and his frustration diminishes, he can actually accept his memory loss with more equanimity. Medication counteracts the outrage or paranoia, so that, using the example of the misplaced bank book or ring, your parent may say instead, "My memory isn't what it used to be. I'll have my daughter look for it."

The best medications for relieving these symptoms are known as major tranquilizers or neuroleptics. This same class of medication is used in treating young psychotic patients, but doses in the elderly are very low. Families are often afraid that such medications will turn a parent into a "zombie" and frequently avoid them for this reason. This is not the case. The therapeutic goal is to tranquilize or calm the patient without sedating him, a result that can be achieved if medications are carefully prescribed and regulated. Haloperidol (Haldol), trifluoperazine (Stelazine) and thioridazine (Mellaril) are a few examples of these medications, which can often very quickly bring these symptoms under good behavioral control. If your parent is agreeable to taking medication, much of the problem is already solved. After about a week on medication, very often there will be no further problem. If, on the other hand, your parent is very reluctant to comply with taking medication and the situation is difficult, these medications are available in liquid form and can be administered in any liquid, hot or cold. Haloperidol, in particular, is tasteless and odorless. Sometimes families have difficulty with the idea of giving medication without a parent's consent or under false pretenses, but confused people are not always competent to make a reasonable decision. You would not deprive your child of immunization because he didn't like to take an injection. No more should you deprive a demented parent of such safe and effective medication. Sometimes, when patients are even more reluctant and suspicious, more complicated devices are necessary to ensure compliance. There is always a way, however, if caretakers are determined and inventive enough. An interesting example follows:

I visited a confused eighty-five-year-old woman who had come to believe that her husband was involved in an extramarital affair. Not only was she paranoid, she had become violent and physically assaulted him whenever he left the apartment to go food shopping or visit the local senior citizen center. Convinced of the accuracy of her suspicions, she naturally refused to consider taking medication or accepting any sort of medical intervention.

Her daughter, frightened by the repeated attacks on her frail father, saw no solution and was considering placing her mother in a nursing home. She consulted with me as a last resort. I made a house call, which the elderly lady accepted rather easily despite earlier refusals to consider visiting a doctor in his office. While she still adamantly refused to consider taking any medication (after all, it was her husband, not she, who had the problem), I couldn't help but notice the plentiful supply of vitamins prominently displayed on the kitchen table at which we sat. Offering her "the latest in vitamin supplements," she accepted my prescription. Nighttime haloperidol (Haldol) was ordered, admittedly without the conscious consent of the woman, and the daughter quickly agreed to make daily visits to administer the medication and observe her mother's condition. In just three days, she reported that her mother was doing well, allowing her husband to come and go without complaint. Over the next months, the situation stabilized further with only mild episodic outbursts which were easily controlled with occasional extra doses of "vitamins."

Not only are these medications safe and effective, they have relatively few side effects and can usually be continued with relatively little monitoring by a physician once the correct dosage is established. The only problem likely to be encountered is some degree of sedation or walking difficulty. If these side effects do occur, they can be modified by discontinuing medication temporarily until the side effect diminishes and then resuming it at reduced dosages. The initial period of finding the right dose, one which calms the patient without sedating him, can be a little tricky but will be achieved in time with perseverance and guidance by an experienced geriatric psychiatrist.

There can be a few other side effects, although these are uncommon at the low doses generally needed to control these situations. These additional side effects include an annoying dryness in the mouth, constipation, mildly blurred vision, decreased blood pressure, and difficulty urinating, particularly in elderly men with enlarged prostate glands. Stiffness and abnormal body movements occasionally occur. All of these side effects are easily reversible by simply discontinuing the medication and rechecking with your physician who may alter the dosage or try another tranquilizer.

Another secondary psychiatric symptom of dementia is depression, a not unexpected consequence of this terrible illness. While depression is understandable, this does not mean that it should be ignored or untreated when it becomes extreme. If your parent withdraws to the point of total isolation or refusal to eat—a not uncommon occurrence—antidepressant medication should be tried. If administered cautiously, started at low doses, and increased slowly, there should be no major difficulty. If it works, the patient may become far more responsive, begin to eat, and again be manageable at home. If not, the medication can always be discontinued without difficulty. Side effects include sedation, lowered blood pressure, and if there is a pre-existing heart condition, rare cardiac difficulties. Antidepressant medication in patients with dementia must be carefully monitored by a skilled and experienced geriatric psychiatrist.

Taking care of a parent with Alzheimer's disease is an extremely difficult and trying ordeal for the primary caretaker. If it is to be done successfully, it must be sensibly geared to the parent's capabilities and continually modified as his mental status deteriorates. Even in the best of circumstances, such care is an enormous burden and measures must be taken to preserve not only the affected parent but the primary caretaker, especially when it is an elderly spouse.

If other family members are available, they should provide regularly scheduled periods during which the main caretaker can be relieved of his responsibilities, to pursue his own pleasures. If either the caretaker or the patient resists, the other involved family members should persevere. If guilt is binding the caretaker to constant attendance on the patient, in time, guilt will turn to anger or depression. No one can maintain this taxing twenty-four-hour, seven-day-a-week job indefinitely.

In many communities there are day centers which can provide temporary respite. Sometimes there are day hospital programs for Alzheimer's patients and, almost always, there are senior centers where both patient and spouse can go to spend part of the day. Especially in the earlier stages of the illness, there will be activities in which the patient can still participate, freeing up the spouse to socialize independently. It is better for both to have some relief from each other.

As the condition further deteriorates and the patient becomes more confused and needs physical care, you should take advantage of additional resources. Depending on your parent's level of functioning, it is an excellent idea to have a part-time or full-time home attendant to provide assistance (see chapter 4, in the section on "Personal Care in the Home"). Trying to provide all the care will wear down the spouse or adult child so that all parties will suffer in the end. Home attendants can be provided by agencies who screen and train them. If cost is a factor, less expensive attendants can be found privately through an advertisement in a local paper or through church and synagogue bulletin boards. Such attendants must be screened and interviewed personally so that the proper person can be chosen. In my experience, there are many excellent attendants who can be found, but it may be difficult to keep someone for extended periods of time, considering the burdens of the job. As a result, families must be prepared to supervise and replace attendants periodically. If you are lucky enough to get someone for an extended period, treat her extremely well and with understanding of the difficulties she may face, and she may well stay throughout the entire course of the illness. Once a good home attendant is in place, your parent will often accept her and the well parent should take advantage of the situation to get involved in at least some independent activities, outside of the home.

If all of this becomes overwhelming, there are often social agencies, funded privately, through religious groups, or the government, to assist in advising, overseeing, and supervising the patient's care, as well as Alzheimer's support groups for families facing similar difficulties. Such agencies are important resources for guidance, planning, and assistance both with day to day difficulties and emergency situations. They will generally provide home attendants and meals-on-wheels; they may employ and select home attendants and offer cleaning services; they may advise as to eligibility for various government supportive entitlement programs. These agencies have a great deal of experience in this area and are invaluable in providing information and support in managing such situations.

Finally—and this is the hardest part—there may be a time when it is no longer possible to care for a demented parent at home. At such times it is necessary and proper to consider institutionalization. While such a decision is always difficult, it must be faced. Some families recognize their own limitations and the extent of their capacity, realizing that when things reach a certain point, they can no longer cope. Others will unfortunately be bound by guilt and loyalty far beyond the point where such devotion makes any sense. Each person must decide for himself and understand that there are no perfect choices. Caretakers can only do their best, and eventually institutionalization must be considered. Considerations involved in making that selection have already been covered in chapter 4, in the section on "Placement in a Long-Term Institutional Setting."

There is also the matter of finances in the care of the demented patient. The magnitude of the expense involved in the proper care of such patients is staggering and the situation must be understood and handled as carefully and seriously as all other areas. If this is attended to in a sensible manner, with planning and thoughtfulness, it can always be worked out. If not, I have seen chaos result. First, one must know the expenses, what one is entitled to and what one is not. While much of what follows has already been covered in some detail in various sections of chapter 3, I will highlight the important issues, specifically in relationship to a parent suffering from dementia.

Medicare will cover most hospital and physician fees, but not much else. Home care, attendants, medication, and nursing homes are not covered by Medicare. For these services the family is on its own. Home attendants cost from $6 to $10 an hour through agencies, depending on the area. The cost may be far less if acquired privately, and less yet if a live-in arrangement is arrived at. Nursing homes vary widely from state to state and charge according to the level of care. In New York, for example, skilled nursing facilities (the highest level of care for the most deteriorated patients) charge in excess of $5,000 per month; health-related facilities for more independent patients charge over $3,000 a month. And the rates go up annually. You must check these fees for your area. They are all state regulated.

As with most things financial, there is less of a problem if one is very rich or very poor. If you or your parent is financially secure and financial aid is not an issue, the most extensive basic care in a nursing facility will require up to $60,000 per year. Hospitalization, private duty nurses, private attendants, and some doctors' fees, are additional.

Lawyers specializing in this area can be especially helpful in working out the finances and protecting both the parent's and the family's assets. They can do this in a variety of ways. Often a conservatorship is necessary in which the patient is deemed to be incompetent, so that a family member can utilize the patient's assets for paying whatever fees are required. More complicated arrangements are also possible and have been discussed in detail in chapter 3, in the section on "Legal Decisions."

Certainly, when there are substantial financial resources at stake, an attorney experienced in such matters should be consulted. It will save you and your parent a good deal of money in the long run.

At the other end of the spectrum, if your parent has no money or very limited resources, each and every state has a variety of entitlement programs which are provided to fill the gaps left by the Medicare system. The most important of these is Medicaid. Financial prerequisites vary from state to state, but can be explained by local social service agencies specializing in assistance programs for the elderly, or by local Medicaid and social welfare offices. Medicaid pays for home attendants, for nursing homes, for ambulances, for medication, for almost everything basic that one needs. If your parent has no financial resources, Medicaid should be applied for immediately. If his money is running out, it should be applied for as soon as he approaches the financial level accepted. One must not delay! Care is expensive and it has to be paid for by someone. Medicaid applications can take several months to be approved, which can leave you and your parent in a desperate situation during the waiting period.

All of this may be terribly confusing. Again, assistance for such planning may be provided by either an experienced attorney or, more likely, by a social worker associated with social welfare agencies catering to the needs of the elderly.

For all such planning, especially for those families in the vast middle income spectrum, very careful consideration must be given to provide for the patient while also protecting the spouse. While these plans must be geared to the individual situation, the general idea is to "spend down the assets" to the Medicaid level so that financial assistance is available, opening the door to resources and entitlement programs. It doesn't make much sense to scrimp and save every penny, particularly because one may well be in a far better situation once the money is gone and Medicaid and other entitlement programs are available. This is a very hard thing for many people to accept, so they must be guided by interested and concerned family members. If nursing home placement is indicated, assets are generally split between patient and spouse, although the spouse will be permitted to retain the family home. All of this must be individualized to the specific situation and done in a timely fashion. Refusal to plan ahead can lead to untold and unnecessary difficulties. Consult chapter 3, the section on "Medicaid," for more specific information as to options.

In the end, in every area of care for a parent suffering from dementia, one must plan and gear a strategy to the condition as it deteriorates. To do so will make this most difficult of all medical situations at least tolerable. You are not alone, and because this is so common a problem, answers to every situation do exist if one has the drive and determination to find out what is available.

·11·

When the Body Begins to Fail

- *Understanding the Basics*
- *Knowing How to Help*

As parents age, it is inevitable that their bodies will gradually weaken in a variety of ways, making them increasingly susceptible to physical illnesses that can affect every organ system.

Among the many indignities to which the aged are subjected is the dawning awareness of the inexorable deterioration of their own body. As the realization grows that there is no escape, the aging individual must try to find some way to come to terms with the disturbing new reality: diminished physical capability; a growing awareness of one's vulnerability and mortality; a sense of helplessness which cannot be overcome by any action, however forceful and intelligent; a need to rely on others; and a loss of one's sense of independence. For many, this may be an almost intolerable situation, and a successful adaptation to these new limitations may be hard to manage.

A healthy, realistic attitude must include some degree of unhappiness and distress, but the reaction should not be so overwhelming that physical problems cannot be dealt with as they arise. While it is an emotional burden, it can be accepted, especially if caring family members and thoughtful health care professionals offer emotional and physical support without being demeaning.

Unfortunately, many older people are unable to maintain a

realistic and accepting outlook, and develop a highly distorted approach to illness. Two reactions are very common and represent opposite extremes: for some, a chronic and constant preoccupation with illness, real and imagined, resulting in emotional invalidism; for others, a complete denial of real physical symptoms which may put them at great risk.

Two brief examples should suffice:

Case 1. An athletically active man in his early sixties developed a minimal tremor of his leg and was diagnosed as being in the early stages of Parkinson's disease. He was told that his prognosis was uncertain, but that he could probably expect many years of good health before any significant deterioration. Rapidly becoming obsessed with his illness, despite no real interference in his daily functioning, he became a textbook expert on his illness and soon developed every symptom of his disease, as well as every side effect of the medication on which he had been started. An active billiards enthusiast, he dropped out of competitive play, convinced that he would soon be the butt of jokes, or an object of pity and scorn, despite the fact that his leg disability had no bearing on his competitive play. He began to monitor his body day and night, focusing on his heart, one day, his bowels, the next; and started to make endless rounds of doctors. Convinced of his diminishing stamina, he considered early retirement and began to think of himself as an old man. His medicine cabinet became filled with pills for illnesses he did not have, and he measured his time between neurologic examinations to reevaluate the progress of his disease.

Case 2. A man in his late sixties developed Menieure's disease, an inner ear affliction which affected his balance and which could not be easily treated. While his symptoms interfered minimally in his life, he was an inveterate home handyman and could not be convinced by his increasingly concerned wife to abandon jobs which required a ladder. He became incensed at her suggestion that he limit his activities, telling her that she was an "overprotective old hen," and continued at an even more exaggerated pace. While retiling his roof, he became dizzy, fell, and fractured a hip.

The first case illustrates the danger of emotional invalidism, an excessive concern with one's health that can disrupt an entire life. Frequently such people will make "doctoring" a retirement vocation, become obsessed with normal body functions like bowel movements and sleep patterns, focus on any sign of deterioration, however minimal, and "listen" to their bodies in a vigilant way, attempting to discern any variation in what they consider optimal functioning. More often than not, they run into real trouble by abusing unneeded medication, and through unnecessary diagnostic testing. The second case is another common maladaption to illness, in which a person's self-esteem seems to depend on his ability to function as if he were still young, refusing to moderate his activity in any way, and thereby running the risk of dangerous complications. Both extremes are exaggerated reactions to physical illness and aging, and they require family intervention or even professional counseling so that a more realistic attitude can be achieved. Failure to attend to such a situation may lead to a permanent maladaption.

Even if so severe a reaction does not develop, physical illness can still be troublesome emotionally in terms of excessive anxiety or depression. Most helpful in avoiding such distress is to keep your parent fully informed should he develop an illness, preparing him for what he can reasonably expect, while maintaining a positive outlook. Hospitalization, especially surgery, can be especially frightening and it is essential for a physician to completely prepare your parent. Often physicians are unaware of the special needs of the elderly or, worse, may dismiss them as "too old to understand." In such cases, family members must step in to make sure that a proper explanation is forthcoming. It is almost incredible to realize what frightening medical procedures are regularly done to an elderly person without even basic explanations. Unfortunately, the more frightened a person is, the more silent he may become, giving others the idea that he does not want any information. This may result not only in unnecessary emotional distress, but in a poor treatment response as well.

In helping your parent cope with a physical illness, you should:

Develop a basic understanding of your parent's reaction to illness, whatever it may be, and try to put yourself in his shoes so that proper questions can be asked and fears allayed.

Keep your parent well informed about his illness so that he can participate in his own care and make his own decisions, and, most important, so that he does not develop exaggerated fears. At the same time, it is not necessary for him to hear every ominous statistic about his poor prognosis. An easy rule to follow is to keep a parent fully aware of those issues about which something can be done, while playing down the bad news.

Be sure to select an experienced and compassionate physician who you and your parent trust, and on whom you can rely for care and guidance whenever medical treatment is necessary. Do not hesitate to advocate for your parent whenever he may be too afraid or overwhelmed to do so for himself.

In order to be most effective, it is always a good idea to have a basic working understanding of those disease processes common to the elderly. If you are well informed, it will be more likely that you will be able to identify risk factors early on, preventing illnesses before they occur. Should an illness develop, you may even be able to detect it early in its course, enabling you to bring your parent in for prompt medical care, and, later on, to assist in the ongoing management of chronic medical problems.

While the specific details of medical treatment are well beyond the scope of this book, a certain degree of informed awareness is essential so that you can intelligently participate in your parent's care.

This chapter should provide the basic information required through a systematic investigation of the major illnesses which affect the elderly.

CARDIOVASCULAR DISEASES

Atherosclerotic Heart Disease

Living with heart disease is still the primary chronic health problem with which elderly parents must cope. Despite well-publicized advances and prolonged life expectancy, it remains the number one cause of death, and can be frightening and incapacitating, a constant reminder of approaching mortality. Knowing about the disease and its treatment is comforting in that it brings some measure of psychological control to the situation, as well as maximizing your ability to follow the medical regimens and enhance the quality of your parent's life.

What is atherosclerotic heart disease? Atherosclerotic heart disease, also known as coronary artery disease or colloquially as "hardening of the arteries" refers to the gradual buildup of cholesterol plaques on the inner walls of blood vessels. When this "narrowing" occurs in the coronary arteries which supply blood to the heart muscle itself, the heart may not get enough blood and oxygen, causing a sensation of pain or pressure, often traveling to the left arm or neck. This condition is known as "angina pectoris." Discomfort may arise with exercise or stress, or even with normal activity in cases of more severe coronary artery insufficiency. Moreover, patients with such narrowed coronary arteries are susceptible to complete blockage, resulting in a heart attack (myocardial infarction). In such a case, when the blood flow is entirely interrupted to a portion of the heart, the affected heart muscle dies, leaving a scar and some degree of heart damage, with diminished cardiac functioning.

As a result of these atherosclerotic changes the heart muscle weakens, becomes less efficient, and pumps less blood. Congestive heart failure, a condition caused by backing up of blood in the system, may develop. If the right side of the heart is affected, fluid may develop in the lungs (pulmonary edema). If the left side is damaged, the ankles and legs became swollen (peripheral edema).

Additionally, when scarring affects the electrical conduction system of the heart (the system that regulates the heart beat), cardiac arrhythmias (irregular heartbeats) may develop. Severe atherosclerotic heart disease may affect the heart valves as well, leading to increased heart failure.

Prevention. The best weapon against heart disease is a program of prevention, something with which you are probably already familiar in midlife. You and your parent can follow the same preventative programs which should include: treating hypertension (high blood pressure); lowering elevated cholesterol or triglycerides through diet or medication; stopping smoking; losing excess weight; exercising for at least 20 minutes a day, three days per week; controlling diabetes; and scheduling periodic medical checks which should include blood pressure monitoring, electrocardiograms, and stress tests when indicated.

When do you call the doctor? Whenever a symptom raises concern about the heart, it never hurts to call your physician, particularly if you have a good working relationship. Parents prone to cardiac anxiety have the right to medical reassurance whenever it is needed.

Specific causes for alarm include:

- Chest pain, especially if the sensation is that of a weight on the chest, or if the pain radiates to the left arm or neck. Other forms of chest pain, even indigestion, should not be dismissed.
- Fainting (syncope)
- Extreme confusion
- Shortness of breath (dyspnea)
- Worsening congestive heart failure
- Rapid deterioration of general health

If any of these target symptoms occur, do not hesitate to call your parent's physician to arrange for an immediate physical examination and electrocardiogram.

Treatment approaches. Despite the best attempts at preventive medicine your parent may still eventually develop atherosclerotic heart disease and need ongoing medical attention.

For optimum treatment your parent should continue all preventive measures; proper diet, a regular exercise program, no smoking; be checked regularly by a physician who may wish to periodically consult a cardiologist; and take corrective medication. Treatments for heart disease fall into several categories. The most commonly prescribed drugs are the nitrates: nitroglycerine (taken under the tongue and kept always available), which temporarily expands the coronary arteries, relieving episodes of "angina pectoris," and the longer-acting nitrates (administered as pills or worn as patches on the chest wall).

Nonnitrates that are also effective in preventing cardiac pain are beta-androgenic antagonists (Inderal and others), which are vasodilators and also slow the heart rate, decreasing the heart's need for oxygen, and calcium channel blockers (Verapamil, Diltiazem, Nifidipine) which act as local vasodilators for the coronary vessels. Digitalis is prescribed for strengthening the heart muscle and increasing its efficiency. Other medications correct congestive heart failure, such as diuretics which remove excess fluid from the system; and still others correct arrhythmias. If these medications cannot solve the problems, certain surgical procedures may be recommended. Inserting a pacemaker corrects problems with the heart's electrical conduction system and thereby prevents arrhythmias. Angioplasty is when an inflatable sac or "balloon" is surgically inserted to open up a clogged coronary artery. Bypass surgery involves transplanting blood vessels to the heart when regular arteries are clogged. Naturally, for acute espisodes, your parent will also need to be hospitalized. Only the careful monitoring available in coronary care units can detect life-threatening arrhythmias, which are reversible with intravenous medication.

Psychological management. To help your parents adjust, always remember the two cardinal rules of managing chronic illness:

- Don't let them deny the illness. Face the problems and seek proper and ongoing medical attention.
- Don't let them become so involved with the illness that it becomes the focus of their lives and they become emotional invalids.

In the case of atherosclerotic heart disease, the strategy is to have your parents seek regular medical care, stick to their dietary regimens, and take their medication properly, but not to monitor themselves too closely, for example, by constantly checking their blood pressure with home devices or being afraid to occasionally "cheat" on their diet, or pampering themselves with too much sedentary rest. The trick is to learn to live with sensible precautions, but without constant fear.

To maximize your effort, advise and counsel your healthy parent to treat your sick parent in this way. A constantly hectoring, nagging spouse, who fears any physical activity and restricts all enjoyment, will be far more detrimental to a cardiac patient than anything else. To live as normal a life as possible—even with heart problems—is the goal.

Stroke

A stroke, or cerebrovascular accident (CVA) is pathologically similar to a heart attack, in that it is generally caused by a blockage of blood vessels already narrowed by atherosclerotic plaques. The only difference is that the blood vessels affected are in the brain. When blood flow to part of the brain is interrupted, that part suffers damage. Sometimes the area affected is small, as in the situation of ministrokes (although if multiple ministrokes occur, they will accumulate to produce multi-infarct dementia). In other cases, a larger area is damaged producing a full-blown stroke. This may cause weakness or paralysis of one side of the body or face, interfering with speech or impairing intellectual functioning. Again, the body part affected is that which is controlled by the damaged portion of the brain (the body side opposite to the damaged brain section).

While a blocked blood vessel is the most common cause of stroke, it may also be caused by bleeding secondary to hypertension (cerebral hemorrhage), a weakened blood vessel in the brain which spontaneously bursts (aneurysm), or a blood clot which travels to the brain from a damaged heart valve or atherosclerotic plaque in the neck (embolus). Whatever the case, the result is basically the same—loss of neurologic functioning depending on the area of the brain affected.

Prevention. Because the underlying causes of strokes are basically the same as the causes of heart disease, similar preventive measures are recommended: control of hypertension, a healthy diet low in cholesterol and salt, weight reduction, regular exercise, diabetic control, diminished psychological stress if possible.

There are many warning signs for strokes. Your parent may experience lightheadedness, fainting, weakness or tingling of a limb or side of face, periods of confusion, speech difficulty, headaches, nausea and vomiting, or personality changes. These symptoms of neurological malfunction are really transient ischemic attacks (TIAs) caused by a temporary interference with the blood flow to the brain. A TIA is a warning sign for stroke much as angina pectoris or coronary artery insufficiency is a warning sign for heart attack.

Any evidence of a TIA calls for an immediate neurological examination, a CT scan and an EEG. If a TIA is diagnosed, your parent can be preventively treated for stroke with buffered aspirin (now used to prevent heart attacks as well) taken on a daily basis. Moreover, if the neurological exam traces the cause of the transient ischemic attack to plaque in the large arteries of the neck (carotid or subclavian), surgery may be needed to remove the plaque and prevent recurrences.

Treatment of stroke. When a parent suffers a stroke, hospitalization is immediately required. There is no direct treatment for a completed stroke (once brain cells die, they do not regenerate) but a patient must be monitored until symptoms partially clear, as they often do after the initial brain swelling recedes.

The first acute stage of hospitalization involves basic care to avoid further complications through: changing positions to avoid bed sores and pneumonia; repositioning joints so that contractures do not develop; and exercising muscles in bed to prevent stiffening and contractures.

When the symptoms of stroke have cleared as much as can be expected, your parent will be ready for the second stage: rehabilitation. This will include physical therapy (to strengthen muscles and improve tone); occupational therapy (to increase skills required for the activities of daily living, as well as writing and negotiating household chores); and speech therapy (to relearn speech and increase communication skills).

The psychological side of stroke. Stroke victims with residual disability are prone to severe adjustment problems. Poststroke depressions are common, often occurring six months to two years following the neurological damage. Such severe depressions should never be neglected and simply labelled as "understandable." They must be treated appropriately with antidepressant medication and psychotherapy.

Even if your parent does not develop a severe psychological reaction, you should remember how difficult it is to live with a chronic disability that interferes with everyday functioning, is so noticeable to others, is often humiliating, and generally, threatens one's self-esteem.

An affected parent must be involved as much as possible in his own rehabilitation to both increase his functional ability, maintain his self-esteem, and increase his feeling of control. Never treat a parent whose speech is affected as if he were confused, or demean him in any way. Involve him fully in family activities and keep him occupied according to his skills. Do not rely on therapists alone for rehabilitation; continue individual and family efforts. Throughout the recovery period, be patient, but firm and encouraging. Concerted rehabilitation efforts can and do make enormous differences, physically and emotionally.

Hypertension

Hypertension does not refer to a chronic state of anxiety, as many think, but to elevated blood pressure in the peripheral blood vessels. This strains the heart muscle which must pump against greater resistance, and gradually weakens it so that blood may back up (congestive heart failure) and even cause a heart attack. At the same time, uncontrolled hypertension can cause kidney damage, strokes, or retinal damage.

Hypertension is often dramatically referred to as "the silent killer," because, despite the damage it causes over time, it most often exists for many years without producing any symptoms. As a result, elderly parents should be checked at least annually for elevated blood pressure so that prompt treatment can begin, preventing unneeded stress on the heart.

Prevention is the same as with all diseases of the cardiovascular system, although a low salt diet is more vital here than in the other situations. Weight reduction, an exercise program, and avoidance of psychological stress can sometimes alleviate the condition without medication.

When hypertension cannot be reversed by more conservative measures, antihypertensive medication is essential. It must be regulated and monitored until adequate control is obtained. The first choice is generally an oral diuretic, which decreases the body's fluid volume thereby diminishing blood pressure. Other alternative choices with excellent results include beta blockers, methyl-dopa, and clonidine. Different medications work in different ways and may be used in combination to produce the desired effects. Side effects can be annoying and include fatigue, sexual impotence, and depression; but, by trying alternatives, through trial and error, satisfactory solutions can always be found. The primary problem is simply getting a parent to take medication faithfully for a condition which has no symptoms, especially because the medication may produce mild discomfort where none was experienced before. Still, through education, involvement, and a careful eye on the medication bottle to check compliance, even the most intransigent will generally come around in time.

WHEN WALKING BECOMES LIMITED

If your parents begin to develop problems with mobility for the first time, they need a careful and thorough assessment to determine the specific cause so that reversible or partially reversible conditions may be adequately treated. So that you have some basic understanding of the underlying illnesses involved, let us look briefly at the most frequent: arthritis, osteoporosis, hip fracture, and Parkinson's disease. (Stroke has already been discussed.)

Arthritis

While not life threatening, arthritis is certainly the single most prevalent chronic medical condition in the elderly. Actually, "arthritis" refers to not one, but to many different diseases, all of which cause pain, swelling, and stiffness of the joints, eventuating in potential deformities and diminished mobility.

If symptoms of arthritis do occur, it is important for a rheumatologist to pinpoint the specific disorder so that appropriate treatment can begin. Doctors usually divide arthritis into two categories: the most common and least severe form, osteoarthritis, and the more incapacitating inflammatory arthritides (such as rheumatoid arthritis or polymyalgia rheumatica). Osteoarthritis generally causes stiffness, particularly in the morning, which lasts for several minutes, as well as pain, with less frequent bouts of inflammation. The inflammatory arthritides involve more swelling, a longer duration of pain, increased stiffness, generalized fatigue, and eventually can be more deforming and incapacitating.

Treatment can afford a certain measure of relief but will not remove all symptoms. A comprehensive treatment regimen should include an exercise program optimally designed by a physical therapist, weight reduction when indicated to ease pressure on affected joints, a bed board, proper shoes, warm baths for severe bouts of pain, cold packs for inflamed joints, as well as medication. Buffered aspirin, effective and inexpensive, is still the mainstay of treatment, but anti-inflammatory drugs (Motrin, Indocin, Naprosyn, Clinoril) are useful in many cases. In all cases, parents must be watched for gastrointestinal upset and bleeding, confusion, and occasional liver and kidney sensitivity. For some severe arthritides, local injection of anesthetics or steroids may be necessary, and even systemic steroids or surgical joint replacement.

Additional information is available through The Arthritis Foundation, 1314 Spring Street, Atlanta, GA 30309 (404) 872–1000.

Osteoporosis

Osteoporosis is now popularly known as a bone problem in older women, although it is almost as common in men. It is estimated that upward of 30 percent of women and 20 percent of men over the age of sixty-five are affected by this illness which involves the degeneration of bone mass, causing weakening of the bones and increasing susceptibility to multiple spontaneous fractures. Generally, osteoporosis begins in the spine and pelvis, causing curvature of the spine ("shrinking") as the vertebrae are compressed. Later, osteoporosis may affect the long bones and ribs as well.

Osteoporosis is caused by inadequate intake of dietary calcium, diminished estrogen in postmenopausal women (necessary for bone production), decreased exercise and diminished exposure to sunlight (impairing Vitamin D metabolism), chronic use of steroids, as well as a variety of less common medical disorders which affect calcium metabolism (such as hyperparathyroidism, hyperthyroidism).

Diagnosis is easy by x-ray examination of the skeletal system, although there is some evidence that many cases may go undetected for some time until obvious lesions are seen. The best treatment is prevention through a good diet rich in calcium and protein, and a program of regular exercise. Once the disease has begun, it is harder to reverse, but some effect can be achieved through exercise, supplemental calcium (safe except for those who are prone to kidney stones), vitamin D, and estrogen therapy (although development of endometrial cancer is a concern), and fluorides. Check with your parent's physician to choose an appropriate regimen.

Hip Fracture

Falls resulting in fractured hips are notorious for causing severe disability in the elderly, which all too frequently, culminate in death. For all too many aging parents, a hip fracture can be "the beginning of the end," with mortality statistics as high as 50 percent within six months. For this reason, it is essential to do whatever can be done to avoid preventable falls, and to expedite aggressive rehabilitation should a fracture occur so that complications do not set in.

It should not be surprising that your elderly parents would be particularly prone to falls since they are likely to suffer from any number of conditions which make them vulnerable. It may be harder for them to get around because of arthritis, confusion, or neurologic impairment. A variety of medical illnesses may cause weakness, while osteoporosis specifically weakens bones. Moreover, medications may be unpredictably sedating or cause fluctuations in blood pressure, making them lightheaded or dizzy.

Should any of these conditions pre-exist, parents should be warned to exercise caution and use canes, walkers, or wheelchairs, while making their home as safe as possible (see chapter 2, section on "Physical Frailty").

Despite your best efforts, your parent may fall and fracture a hip. Surgical intervention depends on the injury; the head of the thigh bone (femur) may need to be replaced or a pin may need to be inserted. New techniques like the Austin-Moore prosthesis and the Richard's Screw have made immediate ambulation possible after surgery. In all cases, physical therapy should be aggressive, mobilizing your parent quickly through exercise, practice walking, and training in the use of appropriate mechanical ambulation devices. If fear of falling again becomes an issue and interferes with rehabilitation, as it often does, families must be firm and reassuring to insure cooperation. You must get your parent back on his feet as soon as possible. To do less can literally be fatal.

Parkinson's Disease

This slowly progressive disorder is the most common neurologic cause of immobility in the elderly. It can be readily identified when the full-blown classic triad of symptoms develop: a pronounced tremor when not moving (a "resting tremor"); rigidity with jerky movements; and bradykinesia (slowed motor ability). More often, it starts more subtly, sometimes with a mild one-sided tremor and some difficulty arising from a chair. It is important to make a diagnosis as soon as possible because this disease responds nicely to medication, especially in its early stages, and new evidence suggests that a new drug, deprenyl (Selegine) plus vitamin E may slow its progress. If the diagnosis is missed early on, it is always a consideration in cases of dementia and depression which are common later developments.

The underlying abnormality in Parkinson's disease is a relative decrease in the ratio of dopamine to acetylcholine (two chemical neurotransmitters in the brain), and treatment involves increasing the level of dopamine or decreasing acetylcholine. For some reasons, tremors respond better to lowering acetylcholine with anticholinergic drugs like Artane or Cogentin, while bradykinesia (sluggish physical and mental responses) and rigidity are best treated with dopaminergic drugs like L-dopa and Sinemet. Regulation of such medication is tricky and side effects prominent, so that careful monitoring by an experienced neurologist is essential.

Reassure your parent that Parkinson's disease progresses slowly and that he will be able to live a full life for many years. In fact, complete deterioration may never take place. You and your parent may want to seek out a community support group for people with Parkinson's disease and their families.

Rehabilitation and the Family

No matter what the underlying disability, intelligent rehabilitation begins with a careful assessment of your parent's underlying physical impairment, his psychological attitude, and his support system.

Once a plan is decided on, you and your family can play an important role in the ongoing therapy by motivating and supporting your parent, practicing exercise techniques, building his confidence and self-esteem through practice and small successes, providing reassurance during periods of despair, and involving him in the ongoing business of living.

Family assistance should be carefully supervised by a physical therapist expert in evaluating and treating immobility. Useful strategies include exercise techniques that strengthen muscles, increase endurance, and improve joint range of motions; training in ambulation techniques and the use of mechanical devices; using heat treatments; hydrotherapy; ultrasound; and transcutaneous electrical nerve stimulation.

An occupational therapist can teach your parent various techniques for performing activities of daily living and more complex independent activities. Both forms of therapy boost a patient's self-esteem.

WHEN WEAKNESS BECOMES DISTURBING

It is not uncommon for an elderly parent to start to decline, appear weaker, complain of chronic fatigue and malaise, and show signs of mental slowing. All too frequently, such a situation is attributed to "old age" without thorough clinical investigation. Such a dismissal is never appropriate. Your parent deserves a comprehensive medical evaluation including a complete physical examination, all essential blood work, x-rays, and an EKG.

The potential causes of your parent's general weakness are many and varied. While a full description of all possibilities is not possible here, you should be aware of the more frequent underlying causes so that you can secure prompt and thorough medical attention.

Diabetes Mellitus

Diabetes mellitus is a well-known, relatively common disorder that tends to be hereditary. In diabetics, the regulation of blood glucose (sugar) by insulin is disordered so that a high level of glucose is present in the blood stream. By far, the most common form of diabetes in the elderly does not develop until later life, and is known now as type II diabetes (previously referred to as adult or maturity onset diabetes). Such patients generally do not require insulin injections as do patients suffering from type I diabetes (juvenile onset diabetes), a far more severe illness, so that your parent probably can be regulated with oral medication alone. The increased incidence of this disease in the elderly seems unrelated to insulin disturbances and is now thought to be attributable to the aging process itself. As we age, the body has a diminished capacity to utilize and process glucose, so that increased intake leads to elevated blood glucose levels.

Unfortunately, diabetes is not just a disease of glucose regulation, but has complications which cause cardiovascular diseases (such as heart attack or stroke), impaired vision or even blindness, kidney failure, peripheral nerve damage, and gangrene. To avoid such consequences, it is important to manage the condition optimally.

The early signs of diabetes include generalized weakness and fatigue; the three "P's": polyuria (increased urination), polydypsia (increased drinking), and polyphagia (increased eating); weight loss; blurred vision; repeated infections with slow healing; and itching. If you notice any of these in your parent, a prompt medical examination is in order. Diagnosis is made very simply by a single blood test: a fasting blood sugar, drawn in the morning before eating. A level of over 140 mg/dl means that your parent is diabetic.

Once the diagnosis is made your parent's physician will outline a treatment program. An affected parent should lose weight and stick to a diet recommended by the American Diabetes Association, low in fat and sugar, and available from the physician. Your parent's doctor may prescribe oral hypoglycemics (medication like Orinase, Tolinase, or Micronase) to lower blood glucose levels, carefully avoiding lowering it too far. Fluctuations in blood sugar are dangerous since too high a level can cause coma, while too low a level will result in insulin shock. Obviously, a diabetic patient must be regularly followed by a physician. Furthermore, your parent will now have to monitor blood sugar levels, using home urine or blood tests (easily measured by a prepackaged dipstick test). Occasionally, insulin injections cannot be avoided and your parent will need careful instruction as to administration. If he has trouble with self-injection, or even with testing his urine and blood, you will have to find a way to assist him. Visiting nurses may be invaluable in this regard.

Further information is available from the American Diabetes Association, 2 Park Avenue, New York, NY 10016 (212) 683–7444.

Living with any chronic illness is difficult, especially one like diabetes which requires daily procedures and dietary restrictions. Affected parents will need a good deal of emotional support and personal assistance particularly in the initial stages. Proper management, however, can result in the resumption of a full and active life.

Thyroid Disease

Hypothyroidism, a disease caused by an underactive thyroid, mainly affects those in the fifty- to seventy-year-old age bracket, and can be diagnosed by simple blood tests showing a low (T4) and elevated thyroid-stimulating hormone activity (TSH) which are normally part of any good medical evaluation. Symptoms include fatigue, memory loss, depression, and decreased hearing, so it is easy to see how it can be dismissed as a sign of "old age," without any further investigation. Treatment is by oral replacement thyroid. Severe cases, intensified by the use of sedatives, may result in a life-threatening condition known as myxedema coma.

Hyperthyroidism, caused by an overactive thyroid, is also common in the elderly. Unlike younger patients, two-thirds of those affected will have an enlarged thyroid gland (goiter) which is easily detected by physical examination. Symptoms include the well-known triad of weight loss, anorexia (decreased appetite), and constipation, again frequent symptoms among the elderly and therefore so easily dismissed. Other indications include unexplained tachycardia (increased heart rate) or heart failure; the development of an arrhythmia; psychotic symptoms or muscle weakness. A diagnosis can be made routinely by laboratory blood tests for T3 and T4, and confirmed by radioactive iodine uptake studies. Treatment involves radioactive iodine ablation (a procedure which destroys overactive thyroid tissue) and sometimes surgery.

Hyperparathyroidism

Hyperparathyroidism, a not uncommon illness in the elderly, is caused by an overactive parathyroid gland. This gland regulates calcium metabolism and when it functions abnormally it causes bone demineralization, joint pain, and general weakness, mimicking other bone diseases. High calcium levels are revealed through blood tests and surgery may be recommended for those affected.

Anemia

Anemia, in which the red blood count is low, must be suspected whenever a parent complains of weakness, fatigue, fainting, pallor, confusion, chest pain, congestive heart failure, or increased heart rate. It is easily diagnosed with a CBC (complete blood count). Never let a physician who discovers a "mild anemia" dismiss it out of hand as unimportant and "acceptable" in an older person.

Anemia, common in the elderly, may be caused by poor diet (not enough iron, vitamin B_{12}, or folic acid); internal bleeding (from lesions of the gastrointestinal tract which result in the loss of blood and iron and can easily be tested for by stool blood test and a GI workup); a chronic underlying disease; low vitamin B_{12} levels (due to poor absorption as a result of gastrointestinal disorders or loss of intrinsic factor [pernicious anemia] necessary for absorption).

Treatment depends on the cause of the anemia, and is often quickly reversible with improved diet, supplemental iron, and folic acid, or, in the case of pernicious anemia, with monthly injections of B_{12}. (Routine B_{12} injections, commonly administered by some physicians, are not recommended unless this condition exists.)

Undetected Infection

Not infrequently, an elderly parent may suffer an infection without having fever or other overt symptoms. The aged are most susceptible to infection because of other chronic diseases which weaken them and more frequent hospitalizations which leave them open to contact with airborne infections.

If your parent has been bedridden for a long time, he has a greater risk of getting pneumonia. Urinary tract infections are also common, particularly when a Foley catheter has been inserted during a hospital stay. The elderly are even more susceptible to meningitis and septic arthritis.

Such unsuspected infections can often be diagnosed by chest x-ray (pneumonia); a simple urine analysis (urinary tract infections); or an elevated white blood cell count.

Nutrition

Proper nutrition is vital for us all, but is even more crucial for the elderly because malnutrition makes them particularly susceptible to other illnesses, intensifies symptoms of a chronic disease, and leads to generalized weakness and fatigue. The elderly are particularly prone to have poor diets for a variety of well-known reasons: diminished appetite, not uncommon for the aged; confusion; dismay at the increasing cost of food; loneliness, which may make them lose interest in eating; problems with dentures; depression; and, particularly in widowers, the inability to prepare food adequately on their own.

If your parent has lost weight and seems generally weak, you should suspect inadequate nutrition as a cause and start to take a greater interest in his eating habits. Question him, check the refrigerator, arrange regular shopping trips, encourage him to enjoy one meal per day at the senior center, enroll him in a meals-on-wheels program, or simply organize a regular meal with a neighbor, friend, or relative. If essential, supplement his diet with a high nutritional supplement like Sustecal or Ensur, available over the counter at your pharmacy.

CANCER

Frightening as cancer is to us all, it touches the elderly most. They see their ranks being depleted more frequently by this terrifying illness than by any other except heart disease. They see firsthand how much suffering accompanies both the disease and its treatment. In no other illness is family support so vital, not only as a psychological support, but in helping a frightened and despairing parent tolerate treatment and combat this disease.

As most people know, cancer may affect any organ system. It involves the rapid and uncontrollable growth of abnormal cells which not only affect the original organ but spread locally or through the blood and lymph nodes (metastasize) to other parts of the body. Once it has spread, cancer can no longer be readily treated surgically; and radiotherapy or chemotherapy will be necessary.

The best treatment for any cancer is early detection so that it can be removed before it spreads. Here the concerned family member may make the difference. Denial of illness or refusal to seek treatment, common occurrences in frightened parents, must be quickly overcome. Early warning signs identified by the American Cancer Society include:

- A change in bowel or bladder habits
- A sore that does not heal
- Unusual bleeding or discharge
- Unexplained weight loss
- Thickness or lumps in the breast or elsewhere
- Indigestion or difficulty swallowing
- Changes in a wart, mole, or freckle
- Persistent cough or hoarseness

The most common cancers found in the elderly affect the stomach, colon, rectum, prostate, breast, and lung.

Once a diagnosis is made, treatment should be immediate. Age is generally not a factor unless your parent is particularly infirm. Never let a physician dismiss a parent because he is "too old." On the other hand, make sure that aggressive treatment is warranted given your parent's overall condition.

In many cancer cases, the treatment plan is routine and well established; but in other cases it may be open to multiple strategies. If this is the case, your parent will need your assistance and guidance in making decisions. Consult an experienced oncologist for a second opinion if you have any doubt.

Psychological support for a parent afflicted with cancer is essential, but may be emotionally draining for both of you. Try to involve as many close family members and friends as possible in order to divide the responsibilities.

First, make sure your parent knows that you will not abandon him out of your own fear of the disease. Face the ordeal with him, emotionally in tune, but in control of yourself. Involve him in his treatment to the extent that he desires. Answer all of his questions, but do not force information on him that he does not want to hear. Let his questions be your guide.

Be as optimistic as the circumstances allow and help him continue to lead as normal a life as possible. Remember to involve him in your family's social activities, try to visit more often, and keep his spirits up as best you can. Remind him and others who are involved in his care that cancer carries no stigma, and that there should never be shame involved.

If treatment is unsuccessful, call on agencies which specialize in cancer care to assist you and your parent. Cancer Care, a visiting nurse service, and other organizations can provide essential support for home care. Hospices in the final weeks of illness are extremely beneficial, providing physical and emotional support for all, while allowing for a dignified death, as pain-free as possible. Further information can be obtained from the Cancer Information Services (800) 4-CANCER. Do not go it alone; get the necessary help.

HEARING AND VISION LOSS

Our sense organs keep us in touch with the outside world. When your parent's hearing and vision start to deteriorate, he may become increasingly isolated and withdrawn. This can precipitate intense emotional distress if it is ignored.

Upward of 30 percent of older people suffer from significant hearing impairment. Statistically, men are more frequently affected than women, probably because of greater exposure to industrial noise during their working lives. Such hearing loss (presbycusis) is caused by thickening of the eardrum and stiffening of the middle ear bones. It cannot be reversed through medical or surgical intervention and can only partially be relieved by use of a hearing aid.

Although hearing deficits are common and easy to take for granted, they create far more emotional difficulty than most adult children generally realize. Elderly parents may feel unbearably isolated, embarrassed, and may even shun others to hide their disability. Even if an elderly parent does try to mingle, he's often received with little sympathy, and often excluded by others who find his deficit annoying and perhaps even frightening, especially if they are concerned about developing a similar disability themselves. Sometimes, the hearing disabled are even regarded as "senile," just an easy way to dismiss someone you don't want to bother with.

In addition to becoming withdrawn, angry, and irritable, isolation from hearing loss may intensify an elderly parent's tendency toward paranoia, especially when social cues are misread and cannot be corrected through the usual verbal explanations. Depression, too, can be a regular consequence of this unwanted isolation, and situations of extreme withdrawal are not uncommon.

Early on, it may be difficult to recognize more minimal hearing loss, especially when parents attempt to disguise their disability to avoid embarrassment or to deny it to themselves. Once it is noticed, however, minimal hearing loss can initially be dealt with by speaking slowly, clearly, and directing your conversation at the person. If more severe impairment develops, an assessment by an otolaryngologist and audiologist is essential. If they resist, out of false pride or misinformation, you should apply pressure to get your parents to accept an evaluation by these hearing experts, since a hearing aid, despite the social stigma, can do a lot to improve the situation.

Hearing aids amplify sounds, but unfortunately they cannot increase resolution. In other words, they simultaneously amplify background noise which can be confusing. Despite their limitations, however, hearing aids are of enormous assistance. The devices that amplify best are those worn on the body; behind-the-ear hearing aids are less effective and those that fit in the ear provide the least assistance. In addition, telephone amplification devices are now easily obtained, and there are now even hearing aids fitted with telecoils electronically connected to telephone receivers. Information about such equipment is available from the AT&T Special Needs Center (800) 233-1222.

Mundane as it is, hearing loss must never be neglected. Improved communication with others can effect a marked change in a withdrawn, depressed, or paranoid parent, whose mental status sometimes improves far more drastically through this than through complex psychiatric intervention.

Interestingly, hearing loss tends to cause a greater degree of emotional distress than does visual impairment. Nonetheless, significant loss of vision can obviously be debilitating as well, especially because it affects 20 percent of the aging population. Total blindness developing later in life is fortunately far less common, though diabetics must be monitored closely.

To prevent potentially reversible eye conditions from worsening, ophthalmologists suggest eye examinations every two to three years for everyone over age sixty-five. Cataracts, which occur in 30 percent of the elderly, are a condition in which the lens is clouded and vision is impaired. Cataracts are easily treated by surgical removal and implantation of a plastic lens. Despite the ease of correction, it is not at all unusual to see elderly patients who are virtually blind because of their unfounded anxiety about undergoing the surgical procedure. In my experience, cataract surgery is a most benign surgical intervention, and complications very infrequent. Age is not a factor. There is a 90 percent success rate; results are immediate and dramatic.

More worrisome is glaucoma, the single most common cause of blindness. It is caused by the buildup of intraocular fluid pressure which damages the retina and optic nerve. It can develop without symptoms so that regular routine eye exams are essential, especially with a family history of glaucoma or a diabetic condition. Treatment consists of eyedrops which prevent further deterioration and damage.

Finally, there are several retinal disorders which affect the area of the eye that receives visual signals. Again, periodic eye exams will pick up difficulties early, which may be amenable to laser surgery.

Elderly parents who have uncorrectable visual impairment need not be deprived of reading material. Large print newspapers and books, as well as audio tapes, are available through direct mail for a nominal fee. Local librarians can help you locate appropriate services.

If your parent's condition worsens and he effectively becomes blind, you may wish to contact one of the numerous organizations which administer to the specific needs of the visually disabled. Audio tapes, records, and books in Braille are available in all urban centers. There are even specialized housing facilities which cater specifically to the needs of the blind. Further information is readily available from The National Library Services for the Blind and Physically Handicapped, Library of Congress, Washington, DC 20542; (800) 424-8567.

OTHER PHYSICAL PROBLEMS

Urinary Incontinence

Urinary Incontinence is a common problem for the elderly and is often so poorly tolerated by caretakers and families that it may be the "last straw" in deciding to place a parent in a nursing facility. Why this problem is so particularly abhorrent to others is an interesting question, especially because families will accept far more disturbing behavior in other areas. Perhaps the omnipresent smell is too constant a reminder of deterioration and approaching death; perhaps we have become too fastidious and obsessively concerned with toileting and hygiene. Whatever the psychological cause, the reaction is almost invariable: incontinence will not be tolerated.

One should never simply attribute incontinence to age and leave it at that, as there are several causes which are modifiable, the most common of which are:

Stress incontinence. Especially in women, the muscles that control the bladder outlet may be weakened, perhaps as a consequence of decreased estrogen levels or injuries which occurred during childbirth.

Urinary retention with overflow incontinence. Any blockage of the outflow tract of the bladder (large prostate glands in men, for example) causes difficulty with voiding. If urine is retained in the bladder until it is at full capacity, regular leaking occurs.

Functional incompetence. Even with no urological or neurologic deficit, poor bladder control may result from confusion, loss of brain function, or simply from immobility. The root cause may be psychological. A severely depressed person may regress and become incontinent or incontinence may be an expression of anger and hostility.

Medication. Medication prescribed to treat other conditions may inadvertently be responsible for incontinence. Diuretics may cause frequent urination, anticholinergics may cause urinary retention with overflow; alpha-adrenergic blockers may decrease bladder outlet control and urethral tone; and sedatives or hypnotics may dim a patient's awareness that he needs to void.

The first step is to determine the cause through a comprehensive physical examination by an internist, a neurologist, or a urologist who will do a urine analysis with a urine culture, and a blood test to determine blood sugar and calcium levels. Depending on the cause the physician may change your parent's medication; suggest that your parent's bathroom be made more accessible (improved lighting, bedside commodes, urinals); teach your parent and you techniques for better bladder control (by establishing routines, scheduling toileting, and doing conditioning exercises to increase bladder and urethral tone). He may also recommend certain drugs to control incontinence: anticholinergics; alpha-agonists and antagonists; cholinergic agonists; and, most typically, topical vaginal estrogen. (This is a highly controversial area; the drugs are all of questionable effectiveness and they all have side effects.) In some cases surgical intervention can be effective: For women with stress incontinence, a procedure called bladder neck suspension can be done under local anesthetic. Men with enlarged prostates can benefit from increasingly refined prostatectomy procedures, although permanent incontinence is an occasional unwanted result.

You should strongly avoid diapers for your elderly parent if possible. This is a signal for a parent to "give up" and regress to a child-like level. You should also guard against permanent (indwelling) urinary catheters which almost always lead to infection and often death. In fact, if a catheter is used by a hospital or nursing home without good reason, question the staff and your physician. Your parent should never be catheterized for "staff convenience."

Nothing is more demeaning than incontinence and you should encourage your parent to strive for increased bladder control through any of the above techniques. Even if there is only a slight improvement, any greater sense of control goes a long way in increasing self-esteem, confidence, and the willingness to relate to others.

Constipation

Morning rounds on the geriatric service at the hospital are sometimes jokingly referred to as "bowel movement rounds," so persistent is the obsession of many elderly patients with their bowel routines. Anyone connected with the field of geriatrics understands that Freud was on the mark when he wrote of anal fixations.

However, before dismissing your parents' bowel concerns by assigning them a purely psychological meaning, be sure to investigate any persistent complaint with an examination by a gastroenterologist. Anatomical obstruction as a result of a mass or fecal impaction are the most likely considerations, although medication side effects should also be considered. More serious concern is warranted if constipation is accompanied by pain, fever, blood in the feces, persistent nausea or vomiting, or any sudden change in bowel habits.

If no physical problem is discovered, there are some things you can do to help a brooding parent:

Explain that it is not necessary to have a bowel movement every single day and that exercise and just moving around will improve bowel regularity.

Advise a diet high in fiber which includes stewed fruits and prune juice. Avoid the regular use of laxatives and enemas which worsen the situation and create a dependency on them. Metamucil, an over-the-counter medication, is the most natural alternative, prescribed by giving one package in 8 ounces of water twice a day.

Colase, a stool softener, may also be useful. The occasional use of milk of magnesia (two tablespoons) and cascara (one teaspoon), commonly known as a "black and white" is not harmful, but it should not be made into a daily ritual.

Be sure that constipation and bowel preoccupation are not masking an underlying major depression. Such concern is frequently a symptom of a masked depression (see chapter 6).

If bowel preoccupation persists, find out what is really bothering your parent. Frequently, they may be expressing all sorts of psychological concerns in these terms: fear of loss of control, concern about body deterioration and diminishing physical functioning, loneliness, and withdrawal. It may also represent the simple need for increased connection and contact with you.

HOSPITALIZATION

While hospitalization is a frequent and often unavoidable experience for an elderly patient, it should never be taken lightly. For many, it is a profoundly terrifying and disorienting experience, the effects of which can be minimized with proper preparation and reassurance from an involved and responsive family. Try to maintain daily contact during your parent's entire stay.

While the field of medicine itself has made enormous advances, hospitalization for the elderly is not without its risks, especially nowadays with a nursing shortage of epidemic proportions. So severe are staff shortages that you might consider a private duty aide should it be financially feasible.

Even with the most adequate staff, however, there are potential problems with which you should be familiar. For the patient a hospital presents a foreboding environment. Private and personal fears are exacerbated by a situation in which one's identity is lost, one is often not allowed to function independently, strange rules limit freedom and ambulation, clothes and personal belongings are taken away, and one must deal with a variety of personalities who change, shift by shift. It should not be surprising then to find that even the most minimally impaired patient in terms of mental functions may be prone to confusion, disorientation, and even agitation. Such acute organic mental syndromes are well known in hospital settings, especially in the isolation of an ICU (intensive care) or CCU (coronary care unit), and may even be so severe as to require restraints, side rails, an d medication to prevent self-injury. Furthermore, in these days of rampant malpractice suits, hospitals are more likely than ever to err on the side of "excessive" safety, using procedures which confine and infantilize patients, limit their mobility, and lead to further regression, dependency, and confusion. Again, a private duty aide or family member, providing support and reality orientation, may avoid many of these unwanted liabilities.

Confinement to bed is not without its own dangers. It causes increased weakness, decreased mobility, incontinence because of the inability to get to the bathroom or commode, fecal impaction, and even thrombophlebitis. Airborne infections are more likely because of increased exposure, and medication errors are not unknown. Diagnostic and therapeutic procedures, as well as surgery, especially with general anesthesia, have their own risks.

Hospitals have only begun to make needed adjustments for the elderly, an interesting fact considering that they represent their major clientele. Perhaps this should not be so surprising, considering the subtle discrimination practiced against the elderly in all areas of life.

None of this is to say that one should avoid necessary hospitalization. Modern medical advances can do wonders in returning your parent to health and an improved quality of life. However, forewarned is forearmed. You can cut down your parent's risks by following a few simple rules:

- If it is not an emergency, choose your hospital and physician with care, checking on staff and reputation.
- Be available to your parent, his physician, and the hospital staff throughout the hospitalization.
- Visit daily and provide whatever additional support is needed.

- Assist the staff where possible, while discreetly checking that the care rendered is optimum.
- Be reasonable! Nothing interferes more with care than a family who is unrealistically and excessively demanding, never satisfied, and looking for trouble.
- Discuss the course of treatment with physicians and nurses at reasonable intervals. Report changes in your parent's condition which may otherwise go undetected.
- Make sure that discharge and follow-up plans are adequately prepared in advance. In these days of "cost effectiveness" patients are discharged "quicker but sicker." Make sure that you know what to expect when you take your parent home. Poor preparation can quickly undo all progress.

INFORMED CONSENT

Frequently an elderly parent will require a medical or surgical procedure that requires informed consent. Any procedure requiring consent contains some degree of risk and naturally your parent should understand both the procedure and the potential risks involved. If your parent has the mental capacity to comprehend, no matter what his age, he can simply sign the consent forms himself. If his ability to understand the situation is in question, a psychiatrist will be called upon to examine your parent, perform a careful mental status examination, and make a determination as to his mental competence.

If the psychiatrist is convinced that your parent is capable, he can then sign a valid consent. If not, then a decision can be made for him which will involve family members, a hospital administrator, and sometimes a court proceeding. States have different rules about making this decision, but they all have procedures which take both the patient's rights and his well-being into consideration. Unnecessary medical and surgical procedures can be refused by family members and generally only forced when such avoidance is determined to pose an immediate life-threatening situation.

*　　*　　*

Taking care of an aging parent who is physically ill requires an educated awareness of your parent's medical condition, a comfortable working relationship with a well-trained and accessible physician, and an ability to insure your parent's compliance in following medical regimens. But the most important gift you can give is emotional support. This requires compassion and firmness, the determination to fight for what is possible, and the courage to accept what can no longer be changed.

Epilogue: See Me!

There is a popular poem pinned to many nursing station bulletin boards in hospitals and nursing homes.

What do you see, nurse? What do you see?
What are you thinking, when you're looking at me
A crabby old woman, not very wise,
Uncertain of habits, with faraway eyes
Who dribbles her food, and makes no reply
When you say in a loud voice, "I do wish you'd try."
Who seems not to notice the things that you do,
And forever is losing a stocking or shoe.
Who unresisting or not, lets you do as you will,
When bathing or feeding, the long day to fill.

Is that what you're thinking? Is that what you see?
Then open your eyes nurse, you're not looking at ME.
I'll tell you who I am, as I sit here so still,
As I drink at your bidding, and eat at your will.
I'm a small child of ten, with a father and mother,
Brothers and sisters who love one another.
A young girl of 16, with wings on her feet,
Dreaming that soon now a lover she'll meet.
A bride soon at 20, my heart gives a leap,
Remembering the vows that I promised to keep.
At 25 now, I have young of my own,

Who need me to build a secure, happy home.
A woman of 30, my young now grow fast,
Bound to each other, with ties that should last.
At 40, my young sons, near grown, will be gone,
But my man stays beside me, to see I don't mourn.
At 50 once more, babies play round my knee,
Again, we know children, my loved one and me.

Dark days are upon me, my husband is dead,
I look to the future, and shudder with dread.
For my young are all busy, rearing young of their own,
And I think of the years and the love that I've known.
I'm an old woman now, and nature is cruel,
It's her jest, to make old age look like a fool.
The body, it crumbles; grace and vigor depart,
There now is a stone where there once was a heart.
But inside this old carcass, a young girl still dwells,
And now and again my battered heart swells.
I remember the joys, I remember the pain,
And I'm loving and living life over again.
I think of the years, all too few—gone too fast,
And accept the stark fact, that nothing can last.

So open your eyes nurse, open and see
Not a crabby old woman, look close—see me!!!

This poem was found among the effects of a patient who died at the Oxford University Geriatric Service in England, and serves to remind the staff of what is so easy to forget in their everyday work.

If any rule is of primary importance in understanding how to begin to help your aging parents, it is to always look and listen to them carefully. So frequently, the elderly are dealt with as if they were all the same: old. As if oldness dispelled a lifetime of whatever meaning and individuality it possessed. As the grown children of aged parents, you know them better than anyone else. Trust that special knowledge. If you can listen to them, put yourself in their shoes, recognize their needs, their worries and wishes, you will never be far off in comprehending their distress and being able to assist them.

Once you know where they are emotionally, and what they want, you can find out what is possible for them. The alternatives are many and must be selected with care; use your understanding of your parents as a constant guide. Plans may change with their changing needs, but they can be modified and modified again, as you stay in tune with them.

Not all choices will make them happy. There is no way to get around that, any more than there has been in raising your own children. Your choices may, at times, seem unreasonable to them at best, self-serving at worst. Despite areas of disagreement, realistic choices must be made and they will not always be perfectly satisfactory. You can only do your best. If you listen to what your parents have to say, make yourself aware of the alternatives and, if need be, consult with professionals for guidance, a realistic and acceptable solution can generally be found.

And when it is, you may be surprised to find that not only are your parents' lives improved, but that yours has been enriched by the experience through a deeper and more thoughtful relationship with them, through added awareness of yourself, and through unexpected insights into your interactions with your own children. For we are not only observers of the aging process; it will affect us all. The knowledge we gather by our own experience with our parents should remain with us as a hopeful guide for our own future.

Selected Bibliography

GENERAL RESOURCES

American Association of Retired Persons. *Miles Away and Still Caring.* Washington, DC, AARP.

Anderson-Ellis, Eugenia and Marsha Dryan. *Aging Parents and You.* New York, Master Media Limited, 1988.

Crichton, Jean. *The Age Care Source Book.* New York, Simon and Schuster, 1987.

Halpern, James. *Helping Your Aging Parents.* New York, Fawcett Crest, 1987.

Hedberg, Augustin. Caring for Your Aging Parents. *Money,* October 1989.

Jarvik, Lissy and Gary Small. *Parentcare: A Commonsense Guide for Helping Our Parents Cope with the Problems of Aging.* New York, Crown Publishers, 1988.

Levin, Nora Jean. *How to Care for Your Parents.* Washington, Storm King Press, 1987.

Metro-Dade County Elderly Services Division. *For Those Who Care.* Video series. (305) 375-5335.

National Council on Aging. *Family Home Caring Guide.* Washington, DC, N.C.O.A.

Shelley, Florence D. *When Your Parents Grow Old.* New York, Harper & Row, 1988.

Silverstone, Barbara. *You and Your Aging Parents.* New York, Pantheon, 1982.

HEALTH CARE

Arthritis Foundation. *Arthritis, Basic Answers to Your Questions.* Atlanta, Arthritis Foundation, 1986.

Colden, Susan. *Nursing a Loved One at Home.* Philadelphia, Running Press, 1988.

Kane, Robert L., Joseph G. Ouslander, and Itamar B. Abrass. *Essentials of Clinical Geriatrics.* New York, McGraw-Hill, 1984.

Katcher, Brian S. *Prescription Drugs: An Independent Guide for People Over Fifty.* New York, Atheneum, 1988.

Katzman, Robert. Medical Progress: Alzheimer's Disease. *New England Journal of Medicine,* 314 (15), 964–973, April 1986.

Lipton, Helene L. and Philip R. Lee. *Drugs and the Elderly: Clinical, Social and Policy Perspectives.* Stanford University Press, 1988.

Long, James W. *The Essential Guide to Prescription Drugs.* New York, Harper & Row, 1988.

Mace, Nancy L. and Peter V. Robins. *The 36-Hour Day: A Family Guide to Caring for Persons with Alzheimer's Disease.* New York, Warner Books, 1981.

Portnow, Jay. *Home Care for the Elderly.* New York, McGraw-Hill, 1987.

Public Citizen Health Research Group. *Worst Pills, Best Pills.* 1988.

Reisberg, Barry. *A Guide to Alzheimer's Disease for Families, Spouses and Friends.* New York, The Free Press, 1981.

Silverman, Harold M. and Gilbert I. Simon. *The Pill Book.* New York, bantam 1982.

Wetle, Terrie, ed. *Handbook of Geriatric Care.* Boston, Harvard Medical School, 1982.

HEALTH INSURANCE

American Association of Retired Persons. *More Health for Your Dollar: An Older Person's Guide to HMOs.* Washington, DC, AARP, 1983.

Health Care Financing Administration. Selected Pamphlets. *Guide to Health Insurance for People with Medicare* (HCFA Pub. No. 02110); *Medicare and Prepayment Plans* (HCFA Pub. No. 02143): *Your Medicare Handbook* (HCFA Pub. No 10050).

Health Insurance Association of America. *The Consumer's Guide to Long-Term Care Insurance.* Washington, HIAA, 1025 Connecticut Avenue, NW, Washington, DC 20036.

Inlander, Charles B. and Charles K. McKay. *Medicare Made Easy.* Reading, MA, Addison-Wesley. 1989.

Posniaszek, Susan. *Long-Term Care: A Dollar and Sense Guide.* United Seniors Health Cooperative, 1334 G. Street NW, No. 500, Washington, DC 20005.

FINANCES

Burdish, Armond. *Avoiding the Medicaid Trap.* New York, Henry Holt, 1989.

Shane, Dorlene V. *Finances After 50.* New York, Perennial Library, 1989.

Smith, Marguerite T. The Best Ways to Help Financially. *Money,* October 1989.

Wise, Dan. Rainy Day Plan. *New York Magazine,* December 4, 1989.

HOUSING

American Association of Homes for Aging. *The Continuing Care Retirement Community: A Guidebook for Consumers.* AAHA, 1129 20th Street NW, Suite 400, Washington, DC 20036.

Carlin, Vivian F. and Ruth Mansberg. *Where Can Mom Live?* Lexington, MA, Lexington Books, 1987.

Carlin, Vivian F. and Ruth Mansberg. *If I Live to Be One Hundred: A Creative Housing Solution for Older People.* West Nyack, N.Y., Parker Pub. Co., 1984.

Henning, Roy, ed. *Finding the Right Place for Your Retirement.* New York, 50 Plus Guidebooks, 1983.

Luciano, Lani. Finding Health Care and Housing. *Money* October 1989.

MENTAL HEALTH CARE

Butler, Robert N. and Myrna I. Lewis. *Aging and Mental Health.* St. Louis, The C.V. Mosby Co., 1982.

Gose, Kathleen and Gloria Levi. *Dealing with Memory Changes as You Grow Older.* Toronto, Bantam Books, 1985.

Jenike, Michael A. *Handbook of Geriatric Psychopharmacology.* Littleton, MA, PSG Publishing Co., Inc., 1985.

Kermis, Marguerite D. *Mental Health in Later Life.* Boston, Jones & Bartlett Publishers, Inc., 1986.

Lazarus, Laurence W., ed. *Essentials of Geriatric Psychiatry.* New York, Springer Publishing Co., 1988.

Levy, Michael T. Psychiatric Assessment of Elderly Patients in the Home. *Journal of the American Geriatrics Society,* 33 (9), 1985.

Shader, Richard I., ed. *Manual of Psychiatric Therapeutics.* Boston, Little, Brown and Co., 1975.

Zarit, Steven H. *Aging and Mental Disorder.* New York, The Free Press, 1980.

Appendices

Appendix A: State Agencies on the Aging

Alabama
Commission on Aging
State Capitol
Montgomery, AL 36130
(205) 261-5743

Alaska
Older Alaskans Commission
Department of Administration
Pouch C-Mail Station 0209
Juneau, AK 99811
(907) 465-3250

Arizona
Aging and Adult Administration
Department of Economic Security
1400 West Washington Street
Phoenix, AZ 85007
(602) 255-4446

Arkansas
Office of Aging and Adult Services
Department of Social and
   Rehabilitation Services
Donaghey Building, Suite 1428
7th and Main Streets
Little Rock, AR 72201

California
Department of Aging
1020 19th Street
Sacramento, CA 95814
(916) 322-5290

Colorado
Aging and Adult Services Division
Department of Social Services
1575 Sherman Street, Room 503
Denver, CO 80203
(303) 866-3672

Connecticut
Department on Aging
175 Main Street
Hartford, CT 06106
(203) 566-3238

Delaware
Division on Aging
Department of Health and Social
   Services
1901 North DuPont Highway
Newcastle, DE 19720
(302) 421-6791

District of Columbia
Office on Aging
1424 K Street NW, 2nd Floor
Washington, DC 20011
(202) 724-5626

Florida
Program Office of Aging and Adult
  Services
Department of Health and
  Rehabilitation Services
1317 Winewood Boulevard
Tallahassee, FL 32301
(904) 488–8922

Georgia
Office of Aging
878 Peachtree Street NE, Room 632
Atlanta, GA 30309
(404) 894–5333

Guam
Public Health and Social Services
Government of Guam
Agana, GU 96910

Hawaii
Executive Office on Aging
Office of the Governor
1149 Bethel Street, Room 307
Honolulu, HI 96813
(808) 548–2593

Idaho
Office on Aging
Statehouse, Room 114
Boise, ID 83720
(208) 334–3833

Indiana
Department of Aging and
  Community Services
Consolidated Building, Suite 1350
115 North Pennsylvania Street
Indianapolis, IN 46204
(317) 232–7006

Iowa
Iowa Department of Elder Affairs
Jewett Building, Suite 236
914 Grand Avenue
Des Moines, IA 50319
(515) 281–5187

Kansas
Department on Aging
610 West 10th Street
Topeka, KS 66612
(913) 296–4986

Kentucky
Division for Aging Services
Department of Human Resources
DHR Building, 6th Floor
275 East Main Street
Frankfort, KY 40601
(502) 564–6930

Louisiana
Office of Elderly Affairs
P.O. Box 83074
Baton Rouge, LA 70898
(504) 925–1700

Maine
Bureau of Maine's Elderly
Department of Human Services
State House, Station #11
Augusta, ME 04333
(207) 289–2561

Maryland
Office on Aging
State Office Building, Room 1004
301 West Preston Street
Baltimore, MD 21201
(301) 383–5064

Massachusetts
Department of Elder Affairs
38 Chauncy Street
Boston, MA 02111
(617) 727–7750

Michigan
Office of Services to the Aging
P.O. Box 30026
Lansing, MI 48909
(517) 373–8230

Minnesota
Board on Aging
Metro Square Building, Room 204
Seventh and Robert Streets
St. Paul, MN 55101
(612) 296–2544

Mississippi
Council on Aging
Executive Building, Suite 301
802 North State Street
Jackson, MS 39201
(601) 354–6590

Missouri
Division on Aging
Department of Social Services
Broadway State Office
P.O. Box 570
Jefferson City, MO 65101
(314) 751–3082

Montana
Community Services Bureau
P.O. Box 4210
Helena, MT 39604
(406) 444–3865

Nebraska
Department on Aging
301 Centennial Mall South
P.O. Box 95044
Lincoln, NE 68509
(402) 471–2306

Nevada
Division on Aging
Department of Human Resources
Kinkead Building, Room 101
505 East King Street
Carson City, NV 89710
(702) 885–4210

New Hampshire
Council on Aging
14 Depot Street
Concord, NH 03301
(603) 271–2751

New Jersey
Division on Aging
Department of Community Affairs
363 West State Street
Trenton, NJ 08625
(609) 292–4833

New Mexico
State Agency on Aging
La villa Rivera Building
4th Floor
224 East Palace Avenue
Santa Fe, NM 85601
(505) 827–7640

New York
Office for the Aging
New York State Plaza
Agency Building 2
Albany, NY 12223
(518) 474–4425

North Carolina
Division on the Aging
708 Hillsborough Street
Suite 200
Raleigh, NC 27603
(919) 733–3983

North Dakota
Aging Services
Department of Human Services
State Capitol Building
Bismarck, ND 58505
(701) 224–2577

Northern Mariana Islands
Office of Aging
Department of Community and
   Cultural Affairs
Civic Center
Susupe, Saipan, Northern Mariana
   Islands 96950
Tel: 9411 or 9732

Ohio
Department on Aging
50 West Broad Street, 9th Floor
Columbus, OH 43215
(614) 466–5500

Oklahoma
Special Unit on Aging
Department of Human Services
P.O. Box 25352
Oklahoma City, OK 73125
(405) 521–2281

Oregon
Senior Services Division
313 Public Service Building
Salem, OR 97310
(503) 378–4728

Pennsylvania
Department of Aging
231 State Street
Harrisburg, PA 17101–1195
(717) 783–1550

Puerto Rico
Gericulture Commission
Department of Social Services
P.O. Box 11398
Santurce, PR 00910
(809) 724–7400 or
(809) 725–8015

Rhode Island
Department of Elderly Affairs
79 Washington Street
Providence, RI 02903
(401) 277–2858

(American) Samoa
Territorial Administration on Aging
Office of the Governor
Pago Pago, AS 96799
011–6848–633–1252

South Carolina
Commission on Aging
915 Main Street
Columbia, SC 29201
(803) 758–2576

South Dakota
Office of Adult Services and Aging
Kneip Building
700 North Illinois Street
Pierre, SD 57501
(605) 773–3656

Tennessee
Commission on Aging
715 Tennessee Building
Nashville, TN 37219
(615) 741–2056

Texas
Department on Aging
210 Barton Springs Road, 5th Floor
P.O. Box 12768 Capitol Station
Austin, TX 78704
(512) 475–2712

Trust Territory of the Pacific
Office of Elderly Programs
Community Development Division
Government of TTPI
Saipan, Mariana Islands 96950
Tel: 9335 or 9336

Utah
Division of Aging and Adult Services
Department of Social Services
150 West North Temple
Box 2500
Salt Lake City, UT 84102
(801) 533–6422

Vermont
Office on Aging
103 South Main Street
Waterbury, VT 05676
(802) 241–2400

Virgin Islands
Commission on Aging
6F Havensight Mall
Charlotte Amalie, St. Thomas,
    VI 00801
(809) 774–5884

Virginia
Department on Aging
James Monroe Building, 18th Floor
101 North 14th Street
Richmond, VA 23219
(804) 225–2271

Washington
Bureau of Aging and Adult Services
Department of Social and Health
    Services
OB-34G
Olympia, WA 98504
(206) 753–2502

West Virginia
Commission on Aging
Holly Grove—State Capitol
Charleston, WV 25305
(304) 348–3317

Wisconsin
Bureau of Aging
Division of Community Services
One West Wilson Street, Room 663
P.O. Box 7850
Madison, WI 53702
(608) 266–2536

Wyoming
Commission on Aging
Hathaway Building, Room 139
Cheyenne, WY 82002–0710
(307) 777–7986

Appendix B: Specialized Agencies

Administration on Aging
Department of Health and Human
   Services
200 Independence Avenue SW
Washington, DC 20201
(202) 245–0724

Aging Network Services
4400 East West Highway,
   Suite 907
Bethesda, MD 20814
(301) 657–4329

Alcoholics Anonymous (AA)
P.O. Box 459 Grand Central Station
New York, NY 10163

Alzheimer's Disease and Related
   Diseases Association (ADRDA)
70 East Lake Street, Suite 600
Chicago, IL 60601
(800) 621–0379
(800) 572–6037 in Illinois

American Association for Geriatric
   Psychiatry
1440 Main Street
Waltham, MA 02254–9132
(617) 984–7030

American Association of Homes for
   the Aging (AAHA) and
   Continuing Care Accreditation
   Commission (CCAC)
1129 20th Street NW,
   Suite 400
Washington, DC 20036
(202) 296–5960

American Association of Retired
   Persons (AARP)
1909 K Street NW
Washington, DC 20049
(202) 872–4700

American Cancer Society
4 West 35th Street
New York, NY 10001
(800) 4-CANCER

American Diabetes Association
2 Park Avenue
New York, NY 10016
(212) 683–7444

Diabetes Information Center
1660 Duke Street
Alexandria, VA 22314
(800) ADA-DISC
(800) 232–3472

American Foundation for the Blind
15 West 16th Street
New York, NY 10011
(212) 620–2000

American Heart Association
7320 Greenville Avenue
Dallas, TX 75231
(214) 750–5300

American Health Care Association
1200 15th Street NW, 8th Floor
Washington, DC 20005
(202) 833–2050

American Hospital Association
840 North Lake Shore Drive
Chicago, IL 60611
(312) 280–6000

American Lung Association
1740 Broadway
P.O. Box 596
New York, NY 10019
(212) 245–8000

American Medical Association
535 North Dearborn Street
Chicago, IL 60610
(312) 751–6426

American Society on Aging
833 Market Street, Suite 512
San Francisco, CA 94103
(415) 543–2617

American Speech-Language Hearing
Association
10801 Rockville Pike
Rockville, MD 20852
(301) 897–5700

Association of Sleep Disorder
Centers
604 2nd Street SW
Rochester, MN 55902
(507) 287–6006

Children of Aging Parents
2761 Trenton Road
Levittown, PA 19056
(215) 945–6900

Commission on Legal Problems of the
Elderly
American Bar Association
1800 M Street NW
Washington, DC 20036

Consumer Information Center
P.O. Box 100
Pueblo, CO 81002

Council of State Housing
Agencies
400 North Capital Street NW
Suite 291
Washington, DC 20001

Gray Panthers
311 South Juniper Street, #601
Philadelphia, PA 19102
(215) 545–6555

Life Safety Systems, Inc.
2100 M Street NW, #305
Washington, DC 20037

Manufactured Housing Institute
Public Affairs Department
1745 Jefferson Davis Highway
Arlington, VA 22202

Medic Alert
Turlock, CA 95381
(800) 344-3226
(For bracelets with personal medical information. Also, this organization will make your medical data available for emergency help.)

NARIC
National Rehabilitation Center
4407 Eighth Street NW
Washington, DC 20017
(800) 34-NARIC

National Arthritis Foundation
1314 Spring Street NW
Atlanta, GA 30309
(404) 872-1000

National Association for Ambulatory Care
5151 Beltline Road, Suite 1017
Dallas, TX 75240
(214) 788-2465

National Association for Spanish-Speaking Elderly
1412 K Street NW
Washington, DC 20005
(202) 393-2206

National Association of Area Agencies on Aging (N4A) and National Association of State Units on Aging (NASUA)
600 Maryland Avenue SW, Suite 208
Washington, DC 20024

National Association of Home Care
518 C Street NE,
Washington, DC 20002
(202) 547-7424

National Association of Housing and Redevelopment Officials
2600 Virginia Avenue NW
Washington, DC 20037

National Association of Mature People (NAMP)
2212 NW 50th Street
P.O. Box 26792
Oklahoma City, OK 73126
(405) 848-1832

National Association of Private Geriatric Case Managers
Box 6920 Yorkville Station
New York, NY 10128
(212) 831-5582 (office)
(212) 831-5101 (messages)

National Association of Rehabilitation Agencies
1700 K Street NW
Washington, DC 20009
(202) 842-0440

National Association of Retired Federal Employees
1533 New Hampshire Avenue NW
Washington, DC 20036
(202) 234-0832

National Association of the Deaf
814 Thayer Avenue
Silver Spring, MD 20910
(301) 587-1788

National Caucus and Center on Black Aged
1424 K Street NW, Suite 500
Washington, DC 20005
(202) 637-8400

National Clearinghouse for Alcohol
Information
P.O. Box 2345
Rockville, MD 20802
(301) 468–2600
(Distributes written materials and
answers public inquiries.)

National Clearinghouse for Mental
Health Information
Public Inquiry Section
National Institute of Mental
Health
5600 Fishers Lane
Rockville, MD 20857
(202) 436–4515

National Consumers League
1522 C Street NW, Suite 406
Washington, DC 20005

National Council on Alcoholism
733 Third Avenue
New York, NY 10017
(Write for information and referrals for treatment services in your
area.)

National Council of Senior Citizens
925 15th Street NW
Washington, DC 20005
(202) 347–8800

National Institute on Adult Day
Care
Dept. P, 600 Maryland Avenue SW
West Wing 100
Washington, DC 20024

National Interfaith Coalition
on Aging
298 South Hull Street
P.O. Box 1924
Athens, GA 30603
(404) 353–1331

National Kidney Foundation
2 Park Avenue
New York, NY 10016
(212) 889–2210

National League for Nursing
10 Columbus Circle
New York, NY 10019
(212) 582–1022
(Includes regional Visiting Nurse
associations)

National Mental Health Association
1021 Prince Street
Arlington, VA 22314
(703) 684–7722

National Pacific/Asian Resource
Center on Aging
1341 G Street NW, Suite 311
Washington, DC 20009
(202) 393–7838

National Policy Center on Housing
and Living Arrangements for Older
Americans
University of Michigan
200 Bonistrel Boulevard
Ann Arbor, MI 48109

National Senior Citizens Law
Center
2025 M Street NW, Suite 400
Washington, DC 20036

The New York City Alzheimer's
Resource Center
280 Broadway, Room 214
New York, NY 10007

Older Women's League (OWL)
1325 G Street NW (LLB)
Washington, DC 20005

Parkinson's Disease Foundation
640–650 West 168th Street
New York, NY 10032
(212) 923–4700
(800) 457–6676

Share-A-Home Association
701 Driver Avenue
Winter Park, FL 32789

Volunteers of America
340 West 85th Street
New York, NY 10024
(212) 873–2600

Appendix C: References for Nursing Homes

Alabama
Fred Draper
Executive Vice President
Alabama Nursing Home Association
4140 Carmichale Road
Montgomery, AL 36106
(205) 271–6214

Alaska
Dennis L. DeWitt
President
Health Association of Alaska
319 Steward Street
Juneau, AK 99801
(907) 586–1790

Arizona
William Walker
Executive Director
Arizona Nursing Home Association
124 W. Thomas Road, Suite 101
Phoenix, AZ 85013
(602) 277–0813

Arkansas
Jack Riggs
Executive Director
Arkansas Long Term Care
  Association
1324 W. Capitol Avenue
Little Rock, AR 72201
(501) 374–4422

California
Ronald M. Kurtz
Executive Vice President
California Association of Health
  Facilities
1401 21st Street, Suite 202
Sacramento, CA 95814
(916) 444–7600

Colorado
Arlene Linton
Executive Director
Colorado Health Care Association
1390 Logan Street, Suite 316
Denver, CO 80203
(303) 861–8228

Connecticut
Louis Halpryn
Executive Vice President
Connecticut Association of Health
   Care Facilities
131 New London Turnpike,
   Suite 18
Glastonbury, CT 06033
(203) 659–0391

Delaware
Rev. Richard Stazesky
Executive Director
Delaware Health Care Facilities
   Association
3801 Kennett Pike, Building 200
Wilmington, DE 19807
(302) 571–0822

Florida
Bill Phelan
Executive Director
Florida Health Care Association
215 S. Bronough Street
Tallahassee, FL 32301
(904) 224–3907

Georgia
J. Wendell Brigance
Executive Vice President
Georgia Health Care
   Association
3735 Memorial Drive
Decatur, GA 30032
(404) 284–8700

Hawaii
Lynda Johnson
Vice President
Hospital Association of Hawaii
320 Ward Avenue, Suite 202
Honolulu, HI 96814
(808) 521–8961

Idaho
Dale C. Shirk
Executive Vice President
Idaho Health Care Association
820 W. Washington, Suite 206
Boise, ID 83701
(208) 343–9735

Illinois
Rick L. Middleton
President
Illinois Health Care Association
1029 S. 4th Street
Springfield, IL 62703
(217) 528–6455

Indiana
Richard L. Butler
Executive Director
Indiana Health Care
   Association
One North Capitol,
   Suite 1115
Indianapolis, IN 46204
(317) 636–6406

Iowa
Larry L. Breeding
Executive Vice President
Iowa Health Care
   Association
950 12th Street
Des Moines, IA 60309
(515) 282–0666

Kansas
Richard (Dick) Hummel
Executive Director
Kansas Health Care
   Association
221 Southwest 33rd
Topeka, KS 66611
(913) 267–6003

Kentucky
James S. Judy
Executive Vice President
Kentucky Association of Health
  Care Facilities
9403 Mill Brook Road
Louisville, KY 40223
(502) 425–5000

Louisiana
Steven E. Adams
Executive Director
Louisiana Health Care Association
7921 Picardy Avenue
Baton Rouge, LA 70809
(504) 769–3705

Maine
Ronald Thurston
Executive Director
Maine Health Care Association
303 State Street
Augusta, ME 04330
(207) 623–1146

Maryland
Fred D. Chew
Executive Director
Health Facilities Association of
  Maryland
10400 Connecticut Avenue,
  Suite 300
Kensington, MD 20895
(301) 933–5500

Massachusetts
Ned Morse
Executive Director
Massachusetts Federation of
  Nursing Homes
886 Washington Street
Dedham, MA 02026
(617) 326–8967

Michigan
Charles Harmon
Executive Vice President
Health Care Association
  of Michigan
501 S. Capitol Avenue,
  Suite 335
Lansing, MI 48933
(517) 371–1700

Minnesota
Rick Carter
Executive Vice President
Minnesota Association of Health
  Care Facilities
2850 Metro Drive, Suite 429
Minneapolis, MN 55420
(612) 854–2844

Mississippi
Martha Carole White
Executive Director
Mississippi Health Care
  Association
4444 N. State Street
Jackson, MS 39206
(601) 362–2527

Missouri
Earl Carlson, Jr.
Executive Director
Missouri Health Care Association
263 Metro Drive
Jefferson City, MO 65101
(314) 635–9283

Montana
Rose Skoog
Executive Director
Montana Health Care Association
36 S. Last Chance Gulch, Suite A
Helena, MT 59601
(406) 443–2876

Nebraska
Sandra Hockley
Executive Director
Nebraska Health Care Association
3100 O Street, Suite 7
Lincoln, NE 68510
(402) 435–3551

Nevada
Dave Nicholas
Executive Director
Nevada Health Care Association
1150 E. Williams, Suite 203
Carson City, NV 98702
(702) 885–1006

New Hampshire
Jean Claude Sakellarios
Executive Director
New Hampshire Health Care
   Association
130 Silver Street
Manchester, NH 03103
(603) 669–1663

New Jersey
James Cunningham
President
New Jersey Association of Health
   Care Facilities
2131 Route 33
Lexington Square Commons
Trenton, NJ 08690
(609) 890–8700

New Mexico
Jan Wiltgen
Executive Director
New Mexico Health Care
   Association
1020 Eubank NE, Suite B
Albuquerque, NM 87112
(505) 296–0021

New York
James Mullaley
Executive Director
New York State Health Facilities
   Association
290 Ellwood Davis Road
Syracuse, NY 13221–4938
(315) 457–9100

North Carolina
J. Craig Souza
Executive Vice President
North Carolina Health Care
   Association
5109 Bur Oak Circle
Raleigh, NC 27612
(919) 782–3827

North Dakota
Allan B. Engen
Executive Director
North Dakota Health Care
   Association
513 East Bismarck Avenue
Bismarck, ND 58501
(701) 222–0660, or
   222–4867

Ohio
Stephen G. Cochran
Executive Vice President
Ohio Health Care Association
50 Northwoods Boulevard
Worthington, OH 43085
(614) 436–4154

Oklahoma
Jon Hitt
Oklahoma Health Care
   Association
7707 South Memorial Drive
Tulsa, OK 74133
(918) 250–8571

Oregon
Dr. Hartzell J. Cobbs
Executive Director
Oregon Health Care Association
12200 N. Jantzen Avenue,
Suite 380
Portland, OR 97217
(503) 285–9600

Pennsylvania
Robert Benedict
Executive Vice President
Pennsylvania Health Care
Association
1200 Camp Hill ByPass
Camp Hill, PA 17011
(717) 763–7053, ext. 253

Rhode Island
Alfred Santos
Executive Director
Rhode Island Health Care
Association
144 Bignall Street
Warwick, RI 02888
(401) 785–9530

South Carolina
J. Randall Lee
Executive Director
South Carolina Health Care
Association
122 Lady Street, Suite 1118
Columbia, SC 29201
(803) 256–2681

South Dakota
Dennis Callies
Executive Director
South Dakota Health Care
Association
301 S. Garfield, Suite 6
Sioux Falls, SD 57104–3198
(605) 339–2071

Tennessee
Richard T. Sadler
Executive Director
Tennessee Health Care
Association
2809 Foster Avenue
Nashville, TN 37210
(615) 834–6520

Texas
Bob Conkright
Acting President
Texas Health Care Association
P.O. Box 4554
Austin, TX 78765
(512) 458–1257

Utah
Dennis McFall
President
Utah Health Care Association
1255 East 3900 South
Salt Lake City, UT 84124
(801) 268–9622

Vermont
Edwin J. Foss
Executive Director
Vermont Health Care
Association
58 E. State Street
Montpelier, VT 05602
(802) 229–5700

Virginia
Peter Clendenin
Executive Director
Virginia Health Care
Association
2112 W. Laburnum Avenue,
Suite 206
Richmond, VA 23227
(804) 353–9101

Washington
Leonard G. Eddinger, Jr.
Executive Director
Washington State Health Facilities
  Association
410 W. 11th, Suite 201
Olympia, WA 98507
(206) 352–3304

West Virginia
Charles W. Caldwell
Executive Director
West Virginia Health Care
  Association
1115 Quarrier Street
Charleston, WV 25301
(304) 346–4575, or 346–4576

Wisconsin
George F. MacKenzie
Executive Director
Wisconsin Association of Nursing
  Homes
14 S. Carroll Street,
  Suite 200
Madison, WI 53703–3376
(608) 257–0125

Wyoming
Dan J. Lex
Executive Director
Wyoming Health Care Association
809 Silver Sage Avenue
Cheyenne, WY 82003
(307) 635–2175

Index

About the Author

MICHAEL T. LEVY, M.D., is the founder and director of the Geriatric Consultation Center in New York and the Director of Geriatrics at the Staten Island University Hospital. He was trained at Washington University School of Medicine, Albert Einstein College of Medicine, by Anna Freud at The Hampstead Clinic in London, and at The New York Psychoanalytic Institute.

He lives in New York City with his wife, a son who is a New York State wrestling champion, and a daughter who has mastered the art of self-defense.